RACISM, GENDER IDENTITIES AND YOUNG CHILDREN

RACISM, GENDER IDENTITIES AND YOUNG CHILDREN

Social relations in a multi-ethnic, inner-city primary school

PAUL CONNOLLY

London and New York

First published 1998
by Routledge
11 New Fetter Lane, London, EC4P 4EE

Simultaneously published in the USA and Canada
by Routledge
29 West 35th Street, New York, NY 10001

© 1998 Paul Connolly

Typeset in Garamond by Routledge
Printed and bound in Great Britain by Page Bros (Norwich) Ltd

British Library Cataloguing in Publication Data
A catalogue record for this book is available from the British Library

Libarary of Congress Cataloguing in Publication Data
A catalogue record for this book has been requested

ISBN 0–415–18319–7

Dedicated to the memory of my father, Roy Connolly, whom I dearly miss.

CONTENTS

KEY TO TRANSCRIPTS

/   Indicates interruption in speech
[. . .]   Extracts edited out of transcript
. . .   A natural pause in the conversation
[*Italic text*] Descriptive text added to clarify the nature of the discussion

ACKNOWLEDGEMENTS

This work would not have been possible without the practical help, support and encouragement of a number of people. First and foremost, I am indebted to the staff, children, parents and governors of 'East Avenue Primary School'. In many ways they are the 'stars' of this book. They let me intrude into their lives for the best part of two years. They gave of their time and trust and offered me support, encouragement and friendship, for which I am extremely grateful. Unfortunately, the need to use pseudonyms for the school and all those in it to maintain anonymity means that I cannot thank them all personally by name.

The book started life as a PhD thesis, and as such I would like to thank Cecile Wright, whose work first inspired me and who as my supervisor gave me unending help and advice during the first year. From the start of my second year, Sallie Westwood took over as my supervisor. This book has benefited enormously from her invaluable support and encouragement.

I would also like to place on record my thanks to Barry Troyna. While he was not officially involved in my doctoral work he was relentless in the encouragement, advice and support that he gave me. While he would have hated me using the term, he 'empowered' me. He gave me confidence and helped me to feel secure in my work and position within academia. Sadly, Barry died during the time I was writing this book. While I will miss him greatly I feel privileged to have known him and will always cherish the friendship we had, however brief.

I am also very grateful to Keith Faulks, Morwenna Griffiths, Mehreen Mirza, Sarah Neal and Andrew Pollard, who all took the time to read various chapters and offer me invaluable comments. I would particularly like to thank David Gillborn for looking over the whole of the manuscript at very short notice. It goes without saying that any remaining faults and deficiencies are entirely my own.

Finally, there are two people in particular whom I dearly love and wish to mention here. The first is my mum, Brenda Connolly, whom I am extremely proud of and who, over the years, has had the patience of a saint! The second is my partner, Karen Winter, whose love, support and encouragement have enabled me to do all of this. She has always believed in me. She has not only given me emotional encouragement and support through the various 'crises' during my time working on the book, but has also offered me invaluable comments on earlier drafts. Of course, none of this would have been possible without the love and grace of the Lord Jesus Christ, to whom I owe everything.

1

INTRODUCTION

Daniel: You've got a Paki girlfriend!
Stephen: You go out with Neelam! [*South Asian girl*]
Daniel: And so do you! [. . .] You go out with all the Pakis! I go out with all the Whites! [*laughs*]
Stephen: You go out with all of the Pakis! Because I, do I look like a Paki though? You do! You go the mosque, mate, where all the Pakis go!

Nicky: Emma goes out with James and Michael [*both Black boys*] . . . I hate Black boys!
PC: [. . .]Why do you hate Black boys, Nicky?
Kylie: Because they're always around us, ain't they, Nicky?
Nicky: Yeah! . . . What, kissing?
Kylie: [*laughs*] No, chasing!

PC: Where's Jordan today?
Stephen: He's waiting at his girlfriend's house.
PC: Is he? Whose?
Paul: Yeah, waiting for her.
Stephen: And when she comes in, he's hiding, right, and when she comes in he's going to grab her and take her upstairs and then she's going to start screaming and he's going to kiss her . . . and sex her!
PC: And sex her? And why's she going to be screaming?
Stephen: Because she hates it!

The use of racist insults, the introduction of sexually violent images and the argumentative nature of some of the above conversations are all testament to the central importance that Nicky, Stephen and the others gave to the maintenance and development of their gender identities. However, these were not teenagers on the brink of adulthood exploring their sexuality, but young children. The maximum age of those quoted above was 6. This fact may well be surprising considering that these themes of racism, sexuality and gender

1

identities are not traditionally associated with children as young as this. And yet, as we will see in the chapters to follow, for these young children their experiences of schooling and their emerging social identities cannot be understood without recognising the importance they gave to the exploration, negotiation and development of these racialised and gendered discourses in their day-to-day lives.

It is for this reason that this book provides a detailed exploration of young children's social worlds through an in-depth study of 5- and 6-year-old children in an English multi-ethnic, inner-city primary school and its surrounding community. The book is particularly concerned with understanding the complex ways in which racism intervenes in young children's lives and comes to shape their gender identities. As will be seen, while these processes are clearly evident among the young children's peer-group cultures, they only can be fully understood by tracing their origins to the social organisation of the school and the local community.

YOUNG CHILDREN AND SOCIAL RESEARCH: 'SEEN BUT NEVER HEARD'

We should not be too surprised about our general ignorance of these aspects of young children's lives considering the nature of social research in this area. Within the sociology of education, for instance, we find a distinct lack of attention paid to young children's own experiences and concerns. When their behaviour, culture and social identities are not ignored altogether, they tend to be studied in a very restrictive way simply in relation to how they present demands upon their teacher.[1] Moreover, the few studies that have actually focused on primary school children's cultures have tended either to avoid the younger age ranges altogether or to rely solely on observation when studying them.[2] To understand this lack of interest in directly engaging young children and ascertaining their own perspectives it is useful to quote from King's (1978) work, which is now widely recognised as a classic study of infant classes in three English schools:

> How is it possible to understand the subjective meanings of very small children? . . . If teachers are unused to reflecting on their own actions young children seem to be almost incapable of doing so. However, it was possible to observe children's behaviour in the classroom and to listen to their talk (and sometimes to talk with them), and to judge to what extent their behaviour and their talk were related to the actions of their teacher. It was also possible to infer something of a small child's subjectivity by his or her emotional response to a situation. I assumed that a 6-year-old who

cried was probably upset and one who laughed was happy, assumptions not always justified in relation to adults.

(King 1978: 8)

It was clear from King's research that the young children in his study were there to be seen but not heard. There was little point, as he makes quite clear above, in actually talking to or meaningfully engaging with these children. Traditional socialisation and developmental models of childhood tell us that children as young as these are socially and cognitively incompetent; they do not have the basic skills or ability to think through meaningfully, critically reflect upon and adapt their own behaviour. The strategy adopted by King was therefore purposely to avoid direct social contact with the young children. In relation to his own work this meant, among other things, always standing up to avoid eye contact, showing no immediate interest in what the children were doing and, where possible, hiding away in the Wendy House to conduct observations.

What we find, therefore, is a set of assumptions about young children that tend to foreclose any meaningful study of their social worlds in and of themselves. While there are few other studies in the sociology of education that are so explicit about their perceptions of young children, it is tempting to believe that these assumptions still pervade the research in this area some two decades on from King's work. How else can we explain a distinct lack of substantive research investigating the subjective experiences of young children? Why, of all the work that has been done on young children, is there an overwhelming tendency to avoid in-depth interviews and simply to use observations?

RESEARCHING RACISM IN YOUNG CHILDREN'S LIVES

It is precisely this tendency to ignore the subjective experiences and concerns of young children that pervades the more specific studies of racism in their lives. Up until the mid-1980s, very little work sought to engage young children in any meaningful way. An assumption appeared to predominate that there was little point in attempting to encourage young children to reflect upon and articulate their beliefs in relation to 'race'. Rather, as we have seen in relation to other work, it was believed that much more could be learned by simply observing these children and assessing how they react to particular situations. This led to the development of a plethora of psychological studies that commonly clustered around two main methods: attitudinal tests and sociometric analyses. The former commonly offered a child the choice of a Black or White doll and then drew conclusions as to the nature of their racial attitudes from the particular doll that they chose. The latter

3

usually asked a number of young children each to nominate their three best friends and then drew conclusions as to their level of racial preference from the ethnic background of the children chosen.[3] What emerges from these studies is the silence that has tended to surround young children. Very little attention has been given to the voices of the children themselves, and to allowing them the space to articulate their own experiences and concerns.

Sadly, even in the more recent ethnographic work, with its essentially qualitative and open focus using detailed observations and interviews with young children in their 'natural' settings, the same basic picture emerges. While this work has offered some very important insights into the nature of racism among primary school children, it has often tended to avoid young children altogether and/or simply ignore their subjective experiences and concerns.[4] This is particularly evident in one of the more recent in-depth studies of racism and young children conducted by Holmes (1995). This study is particularly ironic given that she adopted a qualitative, ethnographic methodology with the express desire of entering into and understanding young children's social worlds. However, while she spent much time talking to young children, she rarely appeared to listen to them (see Connolly 1997a). Consider the following example, where she was talking to Terri, a young Black girl:

Terri: Some White people are mean. Because some White people some-times, because some White people don't like Black people and they're mean. The other day I was walking to school. I saw this little White girl and I said 'Hi' and then she said 'Hi' and I thought she liked me and she did 'cause she played with me. One day, I was playing with this White girl and her mommy said I couldn't play with her no more. She was mean.

Inv.: Are all White people mean?

Terri: Not all, only some. You're never mean, Robyn. You always play with us.

(Holmes 1995: 60)

According to Holmes, this conversation provided evidence of 'young children's inabilities to engage in deductive thinking'. As she went on to argue, 'rather, these children concentrated on particular individuals and events when forming conceptions about groups of people' (p. 60). And yet, as can clearly be seen from the above, Terri was very careful not to generalise from her experience with that one girl, even – ironically – against the encouragement of Holmes herself. Sadly, the constraining influence of traditional models of child development and socialisation appears to live on.

Moreover, this general approach to the study of young children has a number of wider repercussions. In particular it has led researchers to develop an all too simple and restricted understanding of the nature of racism in the children's lives. If we take the psychological tests described above, then it is clear that the fixation with statistical aggregates and the desire to quantify and measure the levels of racial prejudice among young children have effectively ruled out any understanding of the contradictory and fluid nature of racism and its context-specific nature. Rather, racism has simply been regarded as a static set of beliefs that can be identified and measured among young children. Moreover, this is an understanding which assumes that once a child has internalised these attitudes they will uniformly act upon them, regardless of context. If a child chooses a White doll over a Black one in a laboratory test, for instance, then the assumption is that this indicates they are racially prejudiced and will always wish to avoid and exclude other minority ethnic children.

Even the more recent ethnographic work, in ignoring the particular perspectives and experiences of young children, has been limited in the appreciation it can offer of the complexities of racism in their lives. And yet, as illustrated by the quotes at the beginning of this chapter, as soon as we begin directly to engage young children and offer them the space to articulate their own concerns, then we can be left in little doubt of how competently and with what complexity the children are able to appropriate, rework and reproduce racist discourses in relation to a variety of situations and contexts.

It is this recognition of the social competency of young children and the active and diverse ways in which they make use of discourses on 'race' which forms the basis of this book. In focusing on racism, and in particular the significance of 'race' in the development of young children's gender identities, I wish to move decisively beyond the confines of traditional socialisation and developmental models of childhood to foreground the subjective worlds of the children themselves. The study provides one of the first substantial pieces of work to place young children's perceptions and experiences at the heart of its analysis. Through the use of a large number of interviews with the children and data gathered from detailed observations, the study offers a more in-depth account of how racism intervenes in their social worlds and the active role they play in managing, adapting and reproducing discourses on 'race' within this. More specifically, it draws attention to the ways in which racism represents one of many particular contexts within which young children actively come to develop a sense of their own gender identities and to think about others.

THE PRESENT STUDY

> When you cannot measure it, when you cannot express it in numbers, your knowledge is of a meagre and unsatisfactory kind.
>
> (Lord Kelvin, quoted in Sayer 1992: 175)

There remains a distinct tendency to judge social research by how far one can generalise from the results and develop universal laws of social behaviour and interaction. This kind of 'scientism', as Sayer (1992) argues, has become so pervasive in the social sciences that it still provides the yardstick against which all research, whether quantitative or qualitative in focus, tends to be judged. This is certainly the case in relation to ethnographic work such as my own, with its focus on observation and in-depth interviews, where it is often argued that while the data may be intrinsically interesting they remain simply anecdotal and do not have a wider application. What is the point of doing such an in-depth study of a small number of children in one school if you cannot generalise from it?

It is because of this basic misconception that I want to spend a little time here outlining exactly what this present study is trying to do. The basic starting-point is the recognition that, like tools in a workshop, different research methods perform different functions. To understand the nature of each tool and to judge the effectiveness of its results we therefore need to be clear about its function. It would, for instance, be silly to criticise a hammer for being unable to saw wood. So it is for research methods. If, for instance, we want to develop an overall picture of human interaction, to identify regularities of behaviour and to generalise about particular aspects of society, then quantitative methods are the most appropriate. The data so gathered can be rightly judged on how far it has met these demands. However, while such methods can illuminate interesting correlations between particular social factors they cannot explain the precise nature of the relationship between them. Quantitative data, for example, may therefore show that a statistically significant correlation exists between ethnicity and examination pass rates in education, but it would be wrong to assume that the data can offer any understanding of how and why this is the case. Considering the complexity of society and the countless number of factors that can potentially affect a student's learning, we cannot, therefore, arrive at a general explanation that can account for each and every student's examination performance. To begin to uncover the causal mechanisms, reasons and meanings behind a particular student's behaviour we need to focus in and ask essentially qualitative questions. What is it about the student's experiences of schooling that leads her or him to do less well in examinations than their peers? What particular forms of social organisation, relationships and processes exist within the school that can help explain these experiences?

In this sense, in focusing on concrete social processes and the intentions and experiences of particular people, qualitative methods can help us understand *causality* i.e. what causes a person to behave in a certain way. In essence, this is the function of qualitative methods. Studies which employ such techniques should therefore be judged on the extent to which they can use the data gathered to explain particular forms of social behaviour and interaction. As much as it would be wrong to criticise quantitative data for not helping to pinpoint causality, so it would be equally wrong to criticise qualitative methods for their inability to generalise. Each method can contribute only a certain amount to our understanding of any particular social phenomenon, and it is in the synthesis of the results gained from various techniques that, slowly and surely, we can begin to develop the wider picture (Sayer 1992).

The present study, in using qualitative methods, is therefore attempting to understand the nature of racism in young children's lives and the particular ways in which it comes to influence their gender identities. Moreover, it is concerned with identifying the particular social processes and practices that lie behind the production and reproduction of racist discourses among the children. As we will see, they are social processes that can only be fully understood by tracing back their origins from the immediate focus on the young children's peer-group relations to the broader organisation of the school and the wider events and processes that take place within the local community. In identifying such processes, therefore, I am trying to explain why particular children draw upon racism to develop their gender identities in specific ways. I am not making any attempt to generalise. This is an important point. It would be wrong for me to claim that the data presented here is representative of all schools or that the particular identities outlined for South Asian girls, for instance, are representative of all South Asian girls in the school. Nor am I claiming that the particular social processes identified are the most prominent or pervasive.

My basic method, as will become clear throughout the following chapters, is to draw attention to particular social processes that appear within the young children's peer-group relations, to explain their origins by reference to wider social processes within and beyond the school, and to understand and explain why particular young children are drawn into these processes while others are able largely to avoid them. The aim is therefore to contribute to our understanding of the complex range of racialised social processes that can exist and potentially influence and shape young children's gender identities. For teachers and all those who work with or who have an interest in young children, this book will increase the theoretical resources open to them to appropriate and use to make sense of a particular child's behaviour. However, the explanations offered below cannot simply be applied directly to any child in any context. Rather, it is the responsibility of every reader to ascertain to what extent, if any, the particular processes outlined in this book are apparent in relation to the young children they know. While it is hoped that the following chapters will offer an important aid in understanding particular aspects of the way in which racism impacts upon young children's gender identities, they make no claims, as already stated, to be exhaustive or comprehensive in their coverage.[5]

The primary focus of the present study is a group of 5- and 6-year-old children in three reception/Year 1 infant classes in an inner-city, multi-ethnic school. I spent a year and a half at East Avenue Primary School[6] (between January 1992 and June 1993) attending for three days a week, on average, following the classes around the school and observing and inter-viewing the children. During the course of this time I compiled over three thousand pages of notes taken from observations; read numerous files and documents compiled by the school, including letters to parents, internal school reports and minutes of staff meetings; and conducted 81 interviews with school staff, parents, governors and community representatives and professionals, and 73 group interviews with young children from the three sample classes. The interviews with the children were held in a separate room in the school and generally involved three children. Usually, a child was picked from the class and asked to nominate two others whom they wished to come with them. Over the course of the year each child was inter-viewed at least twice, and more commonly three times. The interviews were largely unstructured, with the children being given the space to articulate their own experiences and concerns (see also Bhatti 1995). My role was simply one of facilitator, in that I would ask very general questions concerning what they did in the playground that day or what they liked to do at home. This would usually be enough for the children to develop their own lines of enquiry and discussions among themselves. My interventions following that were largely confined to encouraging the children to elabo-rate on what they had just said.

This combination of largely unstructured interviews with observations and other secondary source material enabled me to build up a detailed picture of particular aspects of the young children's own experiences and to identify and explore the significance of racism within it. In listening to the voices of the children themselves and foregrounding their own experiences, it was a methodology able to draw attention to the complexities of racism and the contradictory social processes that underlay its influence on the development of the children's gender identities (see Connolly 1996c and also Mac an Ghaill 1989).

THE STRUCTURE OF THE BOOK

While the particular social worlds of the young children and their peer-group relations are explored in detail in the second half of the book (Chapters 6 to 9), the first half is concerned with setting out the broader contexts relating to the school and local community that will enable us to understand the particular cultural forms developed and reproduced by the children themselves. To begin with, Chapter 2 sets out the overall theoretical framework developed for the present study, which provides the underlying structure for the rest of the book. Chapters 3 and 4 provide the broader context for understanding relations within the school. Chapter 3 examines the ways in which 'race' has come to influence and shape national political discourses. Within this, particular attention is given to the development of contemporary debates on the inner city and on education. Chapter 4 introduces the reader to the Manor Park estate, where the school is located, and explores how these broader discourses on 'race' and the inner city have come to influence the nature of social relations there. It details the experiences of the men and women living on the estate and how these have come to shape their gender identities. The chapter also explores the particular ways in which racism is manifest on the estate and experienced by minority ethnic residents. In Chapter 5, we move on to looking at East Avenue Primary School and exploring the way that these broader discourses on 'race' and the inner city reproduced on the estate have come to be taken up and reworked by teachers within the school. Within this, the chapter will be concerned to draw out the way that these teacher discourses come to influence and shape the basic ethos of the school and the nature of its organisation, social relations and disciplinary modes.

Chapters 6 to 9 are concerned with exploring the impact of these discourses on 'race', as found within the school and the local estate, on the social worlds of the young children at East Avenue. Within this, the chapters are particularly concerned with examining the experiences of Black[7] and South Asian[8] young children and how they come to develop their sense of identity partly through the contexts provided by racism.[9] Chapters 6 and 7 are specifically concerned with the construction of masculine identities among Black and South Asian boys respectively, while Chapters 8 and 9 are concerned with setting out how feminine identities are negotiated and reproduced by Black and South Asian girls respectively. Each of these chapters attempts to show the essentially open, diverse, contradictory and fluid nature of racialised relations and gender identities. The aim is to draw attention to the social competency of these children, and their active role in negotiating their identities through drawing upon discourses on 'race', class, gender and age to be found both within the school and beyond, in the domestic environment and the local community.

Finally, the concluding chapter will draw out some of the more salient theoretical and methodological themes underlying the book, and will assess their implications both in relation to future research and for those working with young children.

2

RACISM, CULTURE AND IDENTITY: TOWARDS A THEORY OF PRACTICE

Since the late 1980s, there has developed an intense debate around, and growing critique of, traditional definitions of racism. In particular, a body of work has emerged which is extremely critical of the view that racism can be understood simply as a fixed and static set of beliefs, uniformly adhered to by certain groups (usually White people) and universally applied to others (Black and South Asian people). What this work has shown is that racism is inherently contradictory; that the beliefs associated with it change over time and from one context to the next in any given period; that the subjects of racist ideas and practices also change over time; and that their experience of racism at any one period is likely to depend upon the context in which they find themselves.[1]

When trying to understand and explain racism, then, we cannot take anything for granted. We cannot assume that racism will always be associated with beliefs about racial inferiority; that it will always be signified by skin colour; that it will be only White people who can be racist; or that racism will always be the most significant factor in the experience of minority ethnic groups. Since the 1960s, for example, we have seen discourses on 'race' shift, at least partially, from talk of Black and South Asian people being biologically inferior to talk of them being culturally different (Barker 1981; Gordon and Klug 1986). More generally, we have seen that racism has been directed at people not only because of their skin colour but also because of their nationality, in the case of the Irish, or their religion, in the case of Muslims or Jewish people (Cohen 1988, 1992; Miles 1989). In addition, there has been a growing body of literature that has argued for the need to understand how minority ethnic people's lives are not influenced simply by 'race', but also by class, gender, sexuality, ethnicity and disability (Anthias and Yuval-Davis 1992; Rattansi 1994).

It is the aim of this chapter to build upon this work and develop a theoretical framework that can help us to appreciate the complex and contradictory ways in which racism enters the social worlds of the young children focused on in this study. It needs to be stressed that what follows is inevitably a rather theoretical discussion, simply setting out the main elements of the framework that provides the basis of the chapters to follow. While this chapter will use a number of examples from the present study to help to clarify and explain the main concepts to be introduced, it really needs to be read in conjunction with the chapters that follow. These chapters, in their actual use of these various concepts, will do much work in clarifying the theoretical framework. The reader may well find it useful to return to this chapter for a second time, therefore, after reading the remainder of the book.

RACISM, POWER AND DISCOURSE

In developing our understanding of racism, we need to start by recognising its complexity. Racism is more than just a set of beliefs used to justify one individual or group's discriminatory actions against another. Viewing racism in this way tends to imply that it is somehow external to the individual or group and is simply something that can be used or ignored by them. In contrast, I want to argue that racism, rather than being something external to the individual, is something that they come to internalise. In essence, it provides the conceptual framework which not only guides the way people think about themselves and others but also, in turn, comes to influence and shape their actions and behaviour. It can, therefore, be said to have a *formative* power in the way it can literally 'form' and shape individual and collective identities. This particular understanding of power is one that has been developed most notably by the French philosopher, Michel Foucault, in his notion of 'discourse'. What I want to do here is to outline what is meant by the term 'discourse' and how it can be used to develop our understanding of the formative power of racism.

At one level we can understand particular discourses as representing the social construction of language and knowledge, organising the ways in which we think about the world and what we come to regard as appropriate, valid and true. Discourses on 'race' are no exception to this. For centuries, the academic world has tried to delineate and classify the human population in a similar way to botanists' classification of all herbs and plants. Linnaeus's classification of all living phenomena in 1735 provided the over-arching logic within which later writers attempted to classify and understand the human population. Most notable among these writers was the French anatomist, Cuvier, who argued in a series of highly influential lectures in 1805 that there were three major 'races' within the human population: 'White', 'Yellow' and 'Black'. Moreover, he suggested that these 'races' could be hierarchically ordered in relation to inherent intellectual and physical abilities (Husband 1987: 13–14). It was no coincidence that this type of 'race'-thinking developed on the coat-tails of slavery. To split the human population up into discrete 'races', and to claim that certain 'races', most

11

notably the Africans, were biologically inferior and 'animal-like' in their intuitions and behaviour, provided an important justifying ideology for their enslavement and inhumane treatment. Moreover, this type of classificatory discourse was slightly refashioned and developed in the decades to follow in an attempt to justify the rising prominence of colonialism, whereby countries including England, France and Spain increasingly invaded, conquered and controlled others. According to the influential writer Joseph Arthur, Comte de Gobineau, writing in the mid-nineteenth century, the notion of 'race' helped to explain why certain nations had declined and fallen. As he wrote:

> the people [of particular 'fallen' nations] has no longer the same intrinsic value as it had before, because it has no longer the same blood in its veins, continual adulterations having gradually affected the quality of that blood. In other words, though the nation bears the name given by its founders, the name no longer connotes the same race.
>
> (quoted in Miles 1993: 64)

Conveniently, this perceived genetic degeneration of particular nations, within the growing scientific logic created by Darwin's 'survival of the fittest', provided all the justification that was required to invade, control and dominate other countries.

Such discourses on 'race' have, therefore, progressively come to provide the overall 'logic' within which we think about and attempt to understand each other within the social world. While this neat division of the human population into distinct 'races', with biologically fixed and quite different intellectual traits and abilities, has been proven time and again to be scientifically bogus (see Miles 1982: Ch. 2), we continue to be influenced and shaped by this discursive logic. We still talk about '*race* relations', for instance, and identify people as 'Black', 'South Asian' and 'White'. While the crude biological language of Cuvier and Gobineau may have subsided (in mainstream political and cultural circles at least), there still remains the popular belief that these different 'communities' have a natural desire to want to 'stick together' and be with people of 'their own kind'. For instance, the former British Conservative government minister, Norman Tebbit, spoke in 1991 of how the minority ethnic communities in Britain had still not developed a positive identification with and sense of belonging to the British nation. He argued that this could be seen by applying the 'Cricket Test': who does someone cheer for when they watch an international cricket match? For Tebbit, it was clear that many of the minority ethnic communities still supported Pakistan, India and/or the West Indies against England, and this was evidence of their deep, almost natural, instinct to identify with people of 'their own kind'.

These discourses on 'race', therefore, while they may evolve, develop and change, continue to exert a powerful effect on the way we think about the social world. Moreover, once the logic of separating the human population into distinct groupings or 'races' has taken hold, then it is inevitable that people will begin to view themselves in opposition to others and construct and maintain stereotypes about 'us' and 'them'. Popular stereotypes that continue to command popularity, as we will see in the chapters to follow, include Black people being seen as volatile, aggressive and physical, while South Asians are regarded as obedient and hard-working but also culturally 'strange' and different.

More important, however, such discourses also have real material consequences. For example, the more that Black people are portrayed by negative stereotypes such as being volatile, aggressive and untrustworthy, the more likely it is that employers will actively choose not to employ them. Similarly, the more that South Asian families are seen as culturally different, the more likely it is that other people will not want them to live next door. As a consequence, certain minority ethnic groups will therefore be more likely to be unemployed or to find work only in certain occupations; they may also be forced to confine their choice of home to certain areas, for fear of racial harassment and intimidation. All of these processes, in turn, simply act to confirm people's racist beliefs and stereotypes. The fact that certain minority ethnic groups are significantly under-represented in particular high-status jobs and over-represented in low-status, labour-intensive and menial work serves to confirm the view that they are 'naturally' suited for certain jobs. Similarly, the fact that minority ethnic communities are seen to 'live together' in certain neighbourhoods is also regarded as confirmation of their 'natural tendency' to want to 'stick together'.

Similarly in education, these discourses on 'race' also have real material effects on the schooling of Black and South Asian children. As will be seen in the chapters to follow, the popular discourse that Black boys are volatile and aggressive creates a tendency for some of them to be labelled in this way and therefore more likely to be chastised and disciplined by teachers and other school staff, even for things that they have not done. This can act to alienate some Black boys from school, and therefore impinge upon their overall educational performance. A self-fulfilling prophecy appears to come into operation at this point, where certain Black boys do not do well at school and even begin to resist what they feel to be unfair treatment on behalf of the teachers, only then to be labelled as being 'less able' educationally and more likely to present 'behavioural problems' (see Connolly 1995a).

We have seen so far how particular discourses have an inherently formative power in fundamentally shaping our beliefs and knowledge and the way we come to think about and understand the social world. Moreover, it has been argued that such discourses also influence the way we interact with one another and therefore significantly shape, among other things, our education, where we live and the type of work we can engage in. Discourses such as those on 'race' are therefore not simply about language and ideas, but are equally about much wider social processes and practices. However, the formative power of discourses does not stop there. If discourses tend to define knowledge and beliefs and also, as a consequence, how the social world is ordered and organised, then it is inevitable that discourses will reach into the very hearts of individuals and come to influence and shape their sense of identity. As Foucault has argued:

> in thinking of the mechanisms of power, I am thinking . . . of its capillary form of existence, the point where power reaches into the very grain of individuals, touches their bodies and inserts itself into their actions and attitudes, their discourses, learning processes and everyday lives.
>
> (Foucault 1980: 39)

To illustrate this, I will draw upon an example to be discussed in more detail in Chapters 6 and 8 in relation to Black boys and girls respectively. As will be shown, a significant element of the racialised discourses relating to these children is the construction of them as being physical and good at sport, which in turn provides a tendency for teachers to channel some of the Black boys and girls into sport. This also occurs partly in response to their greater likelihood of being disciplined in school and the belief on the part of some teachers that encouraging them in sport will also help to give them a 'positive' experience of school and thus reduce their growing sense of alienation. The point I wish to stress here is that, because of this tendency to encourage these children to play sport, a number of them inevitably develop skills in this area. Moreover, because of being encouraged to play for the school teams, some of them also develop a reputation among their peers for being 'good' at sport. All of this helps to increase the status of these particular children among their fellow pupils, which then acts to increase their interest and commitment to sport. The final result is that these particular children develop a sense of identity which is, in part, premised on their interest and ability in sport.

The above example provides one (albeit simple) illustration of the way in which discourses on 'race' inevitably come to inform the very sense of self that individuals adopt. Of course, for Black boys and girls these discourses on 'race' are not just constructed around sport but also on notions of Black sexuality and, as touched upon earlier, their assumed intellectual abilities and temperament. All of these differing discourses on 'race' combine in complex ways to influence and shape particular children's identities. It is this deeply formative nature of racist discourses and their complex and multi-faceted nature that will become quite evident throughout the chapters to follow. One of the main aims will be to highlight the precise ways in which discourses on 'race' are manifest within the school and the wider community, and how these discourses, in turn, come to influence and shape Black and South Asian children's very sense of identity.

Of course, there is not just one dominant discourse, but many which come to overlap, articulate with and contradict each other (Laclau and Mouffe 1985). A South Asian girl, for example, is the subject of a number of discourses, including those on 'race', religion, gender, age and class. Each tends to influence her social environment and sense of identity. In this sense she will have a number of competing subjective identities – girl, child, South Asian and working class – each of which will gain greater or lesser prominence depending upon the specific context. When she is talking to a teacher, for instance, it may be her identity as a child that is foregrounded and which informs how the teacher decides to relate to her. However, when she is on her own in the playground, it may be her South Asian identity which is most prominent in the eyes of other children, who may then decide to call her names and taunt her. Then again, within a small group of female friends, it may be her identity as a girl that is most prominent, as they talk about dolls, jewellery and boyfriends, for example.

Moreover, these discourses, whether on 'race', gender or age, do not remain essentially discrete and intact but, through their articulation with one another, will change and become transformed (Laclau and Mouffe 1985). For example, discourses on 'race' will articulate with discourses on gender, so that the particular beliefs and assumptions about Black girls and boys will differ. As will be seen in Chapters 6 and 8, for example, discourses on femininity help to downplay the emphasis on the volatile and aggressive nature of Black girls, while those on masculinity act to over-emphasise these characteristics for Black boys. Thus, in general, we can note two processes at work. First, the salience of these discourses on 'race' will vary at any specific time depending upon the child's particular context. Second, the precise nature of these racialised discourses is not constant, but will also vary over time as they are transformed by their articulation with other discourses on gender, sexuality, age and class.

In examining the schooling experiences and identities of Black and South Asian children in the chapters to follow, therefore, it will be shown how discourses on 'race' do not uniformly impact upon the children's lives, but are much more likely to do so in particular contexts and situations. Moreover, these discourses on 'race' will be shown to be far from uniform and static; rather, it will be seen how their specific nature depends upon the precise way in which they relate to and articulate with other discourses. In this sense, the overall lesson to be learnt is that racism cannot be fully understood without taking into account the particular social contexts in which it manifests itself, nor can it be understood in isolation from issues of gender, sexuality, age and class.

In summary, racism can be seen as a particular discourse which influences and shapes our knowledge of the social world and the way in which we think about one another. These discourses on 'race', while continually changing and evolving over time, all tend to construct difference within the human population and act to fashion and reinforce notions of 'us' and 'them'. It is clear from the above discussion, however, that such discourses are not just restricted to the realm of ideas but have real material effects. Discourses on 'race' can therefore be seen as also ordering and shaping the social world and creating and reinforcing economic, political and cultural divisions. As has been argued, a complex dialectical relationship then exists between ideas and practices, in which the way we think about the social world inevitably informs our actions within it, while at the same time the organisation of the social world itself also contributes to the way we think about it. This is equally so for discourses on 'race', where our beliefs about racial and ethnic differences do not just contribute to real social divisions, but where these divisions in turn provide the backdrop against which we come to develop and modify our beliefs about 'race'.

The importance of viewing racism as a discourse in this way relates to the fact that it can help us come to terms with its essentially *formative* power. It is particularly relevant for a study such as this one, which is interested in how young children come to develop and sustain a sense of identity. The use of the concept of discourse in this instance draws attention to racism's 'capillary form of existence', as referred to above. In other words, it highlights the way that discourses on 'race' not only tend to influence and shape our knowledge of the social world and the actual way it is ordered, but also exert an influence on the very subjective identities of individuals – on their behaviour and how they develop their sense of self. This essentially formative nature of racism will be a theme that runs throughout the chapters to follow.

Unfortunately, however, we cannot leave it there. One of the problems with this overall theoretical framework as it stands is that it seems to ignore the actions of individuals themselves, and their own abilities to act upon and shape their particular environments. In other words, it is as if discourses have developed a life of their own, where individuals are left with no option other than to be passively constructed and shaped by various discourses working on them (see Best and Kellner 1991). But individuals are not just cultural dopes with no ability to think or act for themselves – they do have the opportunity, within certain constraints, to make choices and respond to particular situations in a variety of different ways. While it is important to hold on to the formative and diffuse nature of discourses on 'race', it is also important to develop this overall theoretical framework to allow an appreciation of the active role that individuals themselves play in the construction of their lives and wider social environment. Discourses, therefore, are not independent living entities, but ultimately rely upon the actions and thoughts of individuals for their existence. As Layder (1994) has argued, discourses only find expression in and through human activity.

We are therefore left with the need to adapt this broader theoretical framework, provided by the concept of discourse, to address what has become the age-old sociological problem: attempting to reconcile an acceptance that individuals' lives are constrained while also holding on to the fact that they do have freedom, at least to a certain extent, to think and act for themselves. In other words, if we are fully to understand how young children develop their sense of identity then we have to avoid the belief that they simply, almost robotically, copy and reflect what they are taught, while simultaneously avoiding the opposite idea that they are thus free to think and act in any way they want. It is in the attempt to strike this balance that I want, in the final part of this chapter, to make use of the work of Pierre Bourdieu.

PIERRE BOURDIEU'S 'THEORY OF PRACTICE'

In essence, Bourdieu's concepts of 'habitus', 'field' and 'capital', to be discussed below, provide the actual conceptual tools with which we can study young children's social worlds and the development of their identities in practice. They provide the principal means of understanding exactly how discourses on 'race' come to influence and shape a child's sense of self. As Reay (1995) has argued, however, there are certain problems and inconsistencies within Bourdieu's account of these three concepts and his use of them in practice.[2] There is also a need to develop parts of his work to make it more applicable to the study of racism and young children's gender identities.[3] What follows is therefore not a straightforward exposition of Bourdieu's work; rather, it represents how I have adapted it for use in the present study. In a similar vein to Reay (1996), my approach to Bourdieu's work has been 'a process of adaptation rather than adoption'. The particular ways in which the version which follows differs from that of Bourdieu's account are discussed in more detail elsewhere (see Connolly 1997b).

Habitus

The concept of habitus was developed by Bourdieu precisely in recognition of the fact that while individuals are free to think and act in ways that they choose, their thoughts and actions are also constrained to a significant extent. In essence, he defines the habitus in terms of the way we have developed and internalised ways of approaching, thinking about and acting upon our social world. Over time we come successively to learn from and incorporate the lessons of our lived experiences, which then help to guide our future actions and behaviour and dispose us to thinking in a certain way. As our experience comes to be consolidated and reinforced, the habitus becomes more durable and internalised as we *habitualise* the way we think and behave.

Let us consider an example of a child being brought up in a violent home. That child may, for instance, be a regular witness to her mother being physically and verbally assaulted by her father. Those parents may also tend simply to slap and shout at their child rather than sit down with her and explain why they believe her behaviour is wrong. In such a scenario, violence forms the horizons of that child's experience. It becomes a normalised part of her life and, progressively, becomes accepted as a legitimate way of interacting with and responding to others. In other words, she 'knows no different', as her practical experience of life within the family has not taught her that there are other, equally valid, non-violent ways to behave. Violence, then, can be said to form part of that child's habitus. She has come to internalise her experience of violent behaviour so that it now actually tends to guide her future behaviour and predispose her to think and react in certain ways.

It is accepted that this is a rather simplistic example but it does illustrate how the habitus works. In essence, the habitus acts unconsciously to organise our social experiences and encourage us to think and behave in certain ways.[4] It also illustrates how Bourdieu has used the habitus to address the way in which individuals are active in the choices they make, but also how those choices are inevitably constrained in significant ways. The child in the above example is still actively in control of her life and is not *forced* to behave in specific ways. We can never, for instance, predict with confidence how that child will respond to being shouted at, or praised, or laughed at. However, the choices that she does make do not come from an endless range of possibilities but are limited to 'what she knows'. In this sense, we all tend to try and make sense of particular events by reference to our past experiences of similar occasions. This particular child will be no exception. When someone shouts at her, for example, she may tend to interpret this within the context of her own past experiences, where being shouted at was often a precursor to being slapped. In this sense, if she believes that the person shouting at her on this occasion is bound to progress to hitting her, she may well choose to retreat from that situation quickly in order to avoid the anticipated physical attack, or she may respond with violence as an alternative, more proactive way of defending herself. Either way, while she is free to choose how to respond, her choice of response is constrained by how her past experience has predisposed her to interpret that situation. Other alternative responses, such as sitting down and actively engaging the other person in a debate, are much less likely to be chosen by her, as they are not part of her lived experience. Choosing to debate with the person who is shouting would involve that child redefining them as someone who is 'safe' and willing to respond in debate, something which has not been her experience of similar events in the past.

Having outlined the main characteristics of the habitus, we can now see how discourses come to influence an individual's habitus, and thus how discourses have that formative power to shape an individual's very sense of identity. In essence, the habitus develops through our experience of the social world which is, in turn, organised and influenced through the effects of particular discourses. Thus, discourses on 'race', as discussed earlier, tend to influence and shape the way in which the social world is organised and divided in relation to notions of racial and ethnic differences. Our experience of that division will inevitably come to be normalised and internalised in the way we then think about and interact with others.

This way in which discourses on 'race' come to influence social relations, and then in turn the habitus of individuals involved in those relations, can be illustrated with reference to some of the South Asian boys in the present study. As will be argued in Chapter 7, particular discourses on 'race' operate in relation to these boys to represent them as being effeminate, quiet and non-physical. These broader discursive beliefs inevitably come to influence and shape peer-group interactions. This was found in the playground, for instance, where other boys would tend to exclude South Asian boys from playing football and from 'fighting games' and other such social activities. As will be argued, this is partly as a result of these boys not believing that South Asian boys are sufficiently strong and agile to engage in these activities successfully. It is also due in part to the belief, held among other boys, that to be seen playing with 'effeminate' South Asian boys will have the consequence of undermining their own status and reputation. While some South Asian boys do actively struggle to resist these exclusionary processes and are to a certain extent successful in this, a number of others choose not to risk the potential harassment and abuse that comes with trying to get involved in these wider social activities. Rather, they develop their own games, which tend to take place in the more 'defensible' and less public spaces on the peripheries of the playground and involve more fantasy play around monsters, Superman and other cartoon characters.

For these boys, then, the effect of these particular discourses on 'race' has been to exclude them from games of football and play fighting which, in turn, denies them the ability to gain physical skills and competence in this area to the same extent as their peers. Rather, they come, over time, to develop a habitus which relies less on these particular skills and more on the abilities to fantasise and role-play. In this sense, as in the previous example, it can be seen how these discourses on 'race' come to intervene in these children's lives and help to inform and shape their developing sense of identity. In the last analysis, a self-fulfilling prophecy can be seen to be in operation, as it is an identity which, because it is not built upon competence at sport and being 'hard', tends to reinforce the other boys' racialised perceptions of these South Asian boys as being effeminate. As before, these South Asian boys are not passive in the way they come to internalise these forms of

19

interests and behaviour – that is, their habitus – but are quite active in this process. As will be seen in Chapter 7, some boys do choose to resist these discursive processes, albeit at significant physical and emotional cost, while others actively avoid them and choose to carve out their own alternative social space. Either way, the particular forms of habitus they eventually come to 'inhabit' can be seen as a balance between the product of choice and activity on behalf of the child and the broader constraints and controls that are in operation.

Capital

However, to understand fully how individuals develop their particular forms of habitus, we need to consider the notions of capital and field. In essence, capital can be understood as a range of scarce goods and resources which lie at the heart of social relations. The struggles over such resources provide the main dynamic through which social stratification and change can be understood. Bourdieu conceived of four basic types of capital: *economic capital* in the loosely Marxist sense; *cultural capital* which consists primarily of what is perceived to be legitimate knowledge and behaviour; *social capital* which relates to resources gained via relationships and/or connections with significant others; and *symbolic capital* which basically translates as the prestige and honour associated with the acquisition of one or more of the other forms of capital once it has been perceived and recognised as legitimate by others (Bourdieu 1987: 3–4).

Acquisition of one or more of these types of capital enables individuals to gain power and status within society. For instance, having economic capital (i.e. money, land, factories, etc.) allows individuals to invest the money they have and/or develop a particular business, which in turn will provide them with income and wealth, and therefore power. Similarly, acquiring cultural capital (knowledge of the 'arts' and classical literature, for example) can be used to gain respect and status, and thus help to ensure that an individual can exert more influence and therefore acquire more power. Also, the fact that a person may have a close relationship with a managing director of a large multi-national corporation or with a government minister (i.e. having social capital) will often result in their status increasing in the eyes of others, and with it their general influence. As Bourdieu outlined in his early work on education, these four types are deeply inter-related and partly transposable (see Bourdieu and Passeron 1977). Economic capital enables a person to send their children to private schools and so learn and appropriate certain valued forms of cultural capital. This cultural capital makes it possible to develop valued relationships with others in high-status positions (social capital) and acquire certain positions within society that are associated with particular aspects of symbolic capital, and so on.

However, and as opposed to Bourdieu's account, these forms of capital do not simply relate to social class but can also relate to issues of 'race' and gender. It is clearly the case that White skin, for instance, can represent symbolic capital in certain contexts. Some teachers may be influenced (whether directly or indirectly) by a set of racist beliefs which encourages them to think of White children as being more intelligent and well behaved than Black children. In this sense, having White skin represents a form of symbolic capital which brings with it better treatment and more educational opportunities. The same could be true in relation to gender, where boys as a whole may be seen as more able at certain activities (such as computing, science and mathematics) and are therefore encouraged more in this area. In this case, gender (and in particular being a male) represents a form of symbolic capital which is positively rewarded.

To take another example, we will see in Chapters 6 and 7 that, within the context of male peer-group relations, certain forms of cultural capital become valued and struggled over among the boys. Thus, the ability to be good at football, to be competent at kick-boxing and/or to have knowledge about such things as computer games, the latest action movies and/or 'cusses' and sex are all valued among these groups of boys. Those who acquire one or more of these forms of cultural capital therefore gain status, influence and ultimately power among their male peers. Of course, the opposite is true among female peer-group relations, as will be seen in Chapters 8 and 9. Here, the dominant forms of capital revolve around traditionally 'feminine' characteristics, such as knowledge of and ability to use make-up, having jewellery and fashionable clothes, having a boyfriend and/or being able competently to role-play the positions of wife and mother in games. Those girls who are able to gain one or more of these forms of capital will therefore gain status and prestige among their female friends.

Finally, it is important to note two points from all of this. First, these dominant forms of capital are, in essence, defined and developed through various discourses. Discourses on gender, for example, progressively define and organise the social world into male and female, and then set out the characteristics associated with each. These characteristics relating to notions of masculinity and femininity then provide the basis of the dominant forms of capital that boys and girls strive for. It is clear, however, that there is not just one form of masculinity or femininity, but that these vary in their nature through their articulation with discourses on class, 'race' and sexuality. For example, the dominant forms of masculinity found within the school and surrounding neighbourhood in this study have been forged through the influence of particular discourses on class whereby the boys have little hope of securing decent full-time work; there is therefore a tendency for them to develop their sense of masculinity through street culture and physicality rather than through their particular occupation.

Moreover, as highlighted earlier, discourses do not have a life of their own but rely on the actions of individuals for their continued existence. This is particularly true in relation to the actions of individuals who continue to value particular forms of capital and strive to gain and secure them. In doing so they reinforce the importance of these specific forms of capital and thus help to reproduce the discourses that underlie them. If all boys suddenly decided not to value and aspire to masculine forms of capital, then the underlying discourses on gender that help to sustain these would simply cease to be. It always needs to be remembered, therefore, that this complex dialectical relationship exists between individuals and discourses, with each tending to influence and depend upon the other.

Second, it is through an individual's ongoing struggle to acquire and maintain specific forms of capital that they come to develop their habitus. As, for instance, boys learn how to be 'street-wise' and physical, they slowly develop a certain predisposition to their thoughts, actions and general behaviour. Adopting particular 'masculine' postures, talking in certain ways and displaying the physical skills associated with football or kick-boxing, therefore, eventually become almost instinctual for some boys. In other words, 'being masculine' becomes a *habitualised* part of their everyday lives and provides the sub-conscious organising principle by which they think about and act upon their social worlds. As we will see in the chapters to follow, this is precisely the means by which discourses come to inform and shape an individual's very sense of self. In this particular case, discourses on gender provide the underlying mechanism by which they think in terms of masculinity and femininity. This in turn comes to shape the specific forms of capital over which boys and girls compete, and it is in this ongoing act of striving to acquire and maintain masculine and feminine forms of capital that these discourses on gender begin to influence the very way in which boys and girls come to see themselves and behave.

Field

So far we have examined the concepts of habitus and capital. The habitus represents the way in which we tend to learn from and internalise our past experience of the social world so that it provides an almost subconscious predisposition to thinking and acting in a certain way. As argued above, the most significant way in which the habitus develops is through the continual struggles to acquire and secure particular forms of capital. However, one of the problems we are still left with is the fact that there are different forms of capital – many of which tend to contradict one another. In other words, particular forms of capital will be highly valued in certain contexts and yet be completely devalued in others. The forms of cultural capital associated with femininity, for example, may well be valued among a group of girls but will be decisively devalued among many groups of boys. Similarly, dominant forms of masculine capital may be valued within boys' peer-group cultures but will be devalued among girls' peer-group relations and, equally, within the wider context of the classroom. In this latter situation, for example, being street-wise and aggressive may confer status on a boy among his peers but will signal 'trouble' to a teacher, who may well adopt a punitive stance to this type of behaviour.

There is a need, therefore, to distinguish analytically between these differing contexts and to develop a way of understanding when and where certain forms of capital either become prominent and valued or decline in their significance and actually become devalued. This is where Bourdieu's notion of field comes in and helps to complete the picture. A field can be best understood as a 'field of forces' (Mahar *et al.* 1990: 8), the social arena where struggles take place over specific forms of capital. A field is defined primarily, therefore, in terms of the particular forms of capital present and secondarily through the surrounding relations, developed as people struggle to acquire and/or maintain that capital. The boundaries of any particular field, in terms of what is at stake and who is drawn into its domain, are not fixed but inherently contested by those within the field. It stands to reason, therefore, that there are as many fields as there are forms of capital (i.e. masculine and feminine capital, educational capital, political capital, and so on – see below). Any specific field, so identified and defined through empirical research, can be located within and/or across a number of levels of the social formation and may be quite inclusive or exclusive in terms of its size and reach.

The chapters to follow, for example, are organised around a number of different fields. There is the field of national politics (Chapter 3) where the dominant forms of political capital revolve around the ability to define and influence the national political agenda. It is within this field that we will see how discourses on 'race', at a national level, have been so influential in constructing and reinforcing notions of difference and associating the 'inner city' and the perceived decline in educational standards with issues of 'race' and the presence of minority ethnic communities. There is also the field associated with the local housing estate on which the school is located (Chapters 3 and 4). Here we will examine how particular forms of masculinity and femininity have developed in response to high levels of long-term unemployment and poverty. As we will see, the broader discourses on 'race' found within the field of national politics have in part been taken up, reworked and used by those living on the estate to help make sense of their own experiences. We can also talk of the school as a particular field (Chapter 5) where the dominant forms of cultural capital are expressed in relation to notions of the 'ideal pupil'. Again, we can see how discourses on 'race' and gender within the fields of national politics and as articulated on the estate come to influence teachers' perceptions of the children and how well they meet the requirements of the 'ideal pupil'. As will be amply demonstrated, these perceptions tend to have very real consequences for how the children develop educationally and how they come to see themselves more generally. Finally, we can talk of the fields of male and female peer-group relations, where particular forms of masculinity (Chapters 6 and 7) and femininity (Chapters 8 and 9) provide the dominant forms of capital.

There are three points worth drawing out and stressing in relation to this understanding of field. First, in being able to identify particular fields at various levels of the social formation (from the national level to the neighbourhood and the school and particular peer-group relations) we are able to contextualise children's peer-group relations in a much more comprehensive and meaningful way. Because of the lack of consideration of this wider perspective, there has been a tendency in some ethnographic research on schools to assume that children's attitudes and behaviour simply begin and end with their peer-group interactions. And yet, as the following chapters will attempt to demonstrate, we simply cannot understand the nature of racism in children's lives without this wider context (see also Troyna and Hatcher 1992).

Second, as the habitus is formed in relation to struggles over particular forms of capital, then it stands to reason that each individual will have as many forms of habitus as there are fields they are involved in. In this sense, as discussed earlier, a South Asian girl will have a number of identities or forms of habitus, the salience of each depending upon the particular context (i.e. field) in which she finds herself. Within a field constituted by a small and intimate grouping of girls, her identity as a girl may become primary as the group competes over and strives for feminine forms of capital. However, within the classroom, her identity as a pupil may be the most salient, as the teacher comes to address her in a certain way. Within the field constituted by the local neighbourhood, however, with the particular discourses on 'race' dominant at that level, it may be her identity as a South Asian that becomes most prominent, as she is subject to harassment and abuse. Of course, in reality, these different identities found within each particular field come to influence and shape one another, so that the distinctions made in the above example are far more complex than that. Thus, within the classroom, for instance, the fact that a child is a girl and South Asian will often act to influence the precise way in which a teacher comes to view her as approximating to their notion of an 'ideal pupil'. Similarly, within the field of feminine peer-group relations, the fact that a girl is South Asian will also act to construct her as the 'Other' in the eyes of her female peers and thus make it more difficult for her to gain and hold on to the dominant forms of feminine capital. That said, this understanding of field does provide a most useful way into appreciating and understanding the complex, contradictory and multiple nature of young children's identities – what is often referred to as their 'de-centred selves' (see also Gillborn 1995: Ch. 2).

Finally, it needs to be stressed that each field does not simply represent a network of social relations but can often be seen to be expressed in and through time and space.[5] An example of this in relation to education is apparent in the organisation of any school. Here the school, as a site within the field of education, has developed a whole set of teacher–student relations around dominant forms of educational capital. These relations, which express the pedagogical authority of the teacher, are reflected in the spatial and temporal organisation of the classroom and the school day, and help to reinforce and reproduce that authority (see Giddens 1985). The spatial organisation of children's desks, for example, so that they all face the teacher's desk, is a clear statement about the importance and authority of the teacher and the expected submissiveness of the children. What we see from this is that it is not just a one-way relationship, where specific social relationships develop and then form a particular field; the field itself, in its spatial and temporal construction, also helps to influence and reinforce the nature of those social relations. This will become quite apparent in the following two chapters, in exploring the spatial development of the local housing estate and its effects on the formation of the residents' masculine and feminine identities.

CONCLUSIONS

What has been offered above is a theoretical framework which will enable the study of racism in young children's lives. A summary description of the four main concepts underlying this framework – those of discourse, habitus, capital and field – can be found in Table 2.1. This is intended to provide an overall reference and guide for readers to use while reading through the chapters to follow.

The underlying focus has been upon racism as discourse in recognition of the fact that racism is not just about ideas and structures, but also about the way in which it reaches into the very selves of individuals to influence and shape their subjective identities. It is this essentially formative power of racism that will form the basic focus of the chapters to follow. As will be seen, discourses on 'race' play a significant role in informing the specific ways in which young children come to construct their understanding of themselves as masculine and feminine.

However, in order to operationalise this notion of discourse – to translate it into a practical set of analytical tools to study young children – the chapter has made use of an adapted understanding of Bourdieu's three inter-related concepts of habitus, capital and field. As has been explained, the habitus provides the principal means by which discourses 'enter into' the lives and identities of individuals. It represents the way in which a person's past experience and understanding of their social world has created a learnt, almost subconscious predisposition to think and act in certain ways. The particular way in which discourses do this is through the individual's continuing attempts to acquire and maintain dominant forms of social,

Table 2.1 Glossary of theoretical concepts

Discourses	Underpin our knowledge of and the way we think about the social world.
	Influence and shape the way the social world is structured and organised.
	Shape individual's subjective identities.
Capital	Different types (economic, cultural, symbolic and social) and forms (masculine, feminine, political and educational) of capital.
	Constructed by and representative of dominant discourses.
Habitus	Represents the way that our past experiences of the social world have become internalised and tend to guide and predispose us to thinking and acting in certain ways.
	Developed through ongoing struggles to acquire and maintain various forms of capital.
Field	Defined in relation to particular forms of capital with each specific form of capital having its own field.
	Consists of all those social relations that develop around struggles over specific forms of capital.
	There are numerous fields corresponding to the variety of forms of capital.
	An individual has a number of different 'habituses' each of which becomes more or less significant as they move from one field to another.

cultural, economic and/or symbolic capital. Such forms of capital are underpinned by particular discourses which have progressively come to define and order our knowledge and understanding of the social world. The strategies that individuals use in order to gain and hold on to particular forms of capital are those which eventually become internalised and underpin the development of their habitus. It is through this process that discourses come to insert themselves into the very hearts and identities of individuals.

However, as has also been shown, an individual's identity is not uniform and fixed but fluid, contradictory and multiple. The idea of there being a number of interconnecting fields, each with particular forms of capital at their centre and with individuals constantly moving from one to another, helps us to understand the complexities associated with a particular person's multiple forms of habitus. In essence, what is significant in relation to their identity at any particular time will depend upon the specific social context – the field – within which they are located.

In summary, young children's social worlds are complex and multifaceted. Any theoretical framework that hopes to do sufficient justice to this will also, inevitably, reflect it. As stated at the beginning of this chapter, it is through the actual engagement with and use of these concepts of discourse, habitus, field and capital that an understanding of the relationship between them and their usefulness will become much clearer and more apparent. In this sense, the discussion above may also be worth returning to once the following chapters have been read. It is to the present study and the actual application of these concepts that the book now turns.

3

THE RACIALISATION OF NATIONAL POLITICAL DISCOURSES

It may seem strange that we begin an analysis of young children's peer-group relations with a chapter on national politics. However, young children do not live and play together in a vacuum. Their experiences within the domestic environment, within their local community and within the school more generally, all come to influence and shape how they think about 'race', gender and sexuality. Moreover, events within the local community and the school (to be discussed in the following two chapters) do not themselves take place in a vacuum but develop within the shadow of national political change. If we are to understand more fully the influence of discourses on 'race' within young children's peer-group relations, we need to trace those discourses back through the school and local community to their expression at a national political level.

This chapter will therefore begin this contextual process by examining how discourses on 'race' enter into and are reproduced within the field of national politics. The chapter will begin by outlining the nature of this field and its dominant forms of capital. As will then be demonstrated, even national politics do not take place in a vacuum but are themselves significantly affected by changes within the economic field. The chapter will show that it is here, in a reaction to the dramatic economic crisis of the late 1960s and 1970s, that discourses on 'race' have taken on a pivotal role in the changing nature of national political discourses. Finally, in setting the scene for the following two chapters, the discussion will conclude with an analysis of how these national political discourses have come to influence and shape particular debates concerning the inner city and schooling. As will be seen, discourses on 'race' are integral to all of these levels.

THE FIELD OF NATIONAL POLITICS

For the purposes of this study I want to argue that we can view politics as a field in its own right, defined in terms of the specific forms of political capital and the sets of relations and institutions that have been developed around it. Political capital in this sense can be understood as those forms of cultural, social and symbolic capital that, once acquired, enable individuals and/or groups to gain legitimate control over the state and its institutions. What counts as the state and which institutions come under its control – that is, the boundaries of the political field – are not fixed but are continually shifting and are contested by those within the field. The complex nature of the state dictates that there are numerous specific sites within the political field, including those found at the local, regional, national, European and international level. In this chapter I am primarily interested in the specific site of national politics, and the particular form and nature of the discourses on 'race' that are produced and reproduced by successive national governments at this level.

In its most basic form, the acquisition of political capital can be understood as the ability of certain groups or individuals successfully to portray their own sectional interests as being those of the specific community or electorate to which they are accountable. At the national level, this involves governments being able to 'nationalise themselves': that is, to construct a perception of the nation, of the 'ordinary people', whose interests they claim to represent. To do this successfully requires the ability to incorporate and rework significant aspects of people's lived, commonsense experiences into a broader, more coherent political philosophy that claims to be in the interests of the nation (Gramsci 1971). It is only when people find that a particular political philosophy resonates with and is able to make sense of their own experiences that they are willing to subscribe to it and give it popular support. The field of national politics does not, therefore, simply determine relations within particular local fields such as the school or local community, but also comes to be influenced and shaped by them. It is this interdependent nature of the relationship between national politics and particular localities that, as we will see, is so important in understanding the centrality of 'race' within political discourses.

It is within this context that we can begin to appreciate the importance of changes in the economic field in influencing the field of national politics. The economic booms and recessions that take place at a national and/or international level are bound to influence the policies and arguments adopted at the national political level. However, these economic changes are also experienced, often very personally, by those at the local level. Any national political policy or discourse that develops must therefore not only correspond with the demands of national and international capital, but must also resonate with the experiences of local people. It is for this reason that we need to spend a little time developing the context set by the dramatic economic changes of the last few decades. These changes will then provide the setting for understanding the particular ways in which national political discourses have developed.

The economic crisis of the 1970s

For the two post-war decades to the end of the 1960s, there was in Britain what Gamble (1985: 6) refers to as 'the longest and most rapid period of continuous expansion world capitalism had ever enjoyed'. The promise of full employment and increasing affluence, together with the development and growth of the welfare state, provided the foundations upon which the social democratic consensus was reached. It was essentially a period dependent upon the 'long boom' to underwrite and secure the legitimacy of successive governments, a legitimacy gained through the feeling that the nation, in the words of Prime Minister Harold Macmillan, had 'never had it so good'. However, the onslaught of the global economic recession within the economic field had the effect of fundamentally undermining this hegemonic consensus that had emerged within the field of politics (Currie 1983; Chitty 1989). It was a global recession experienced that much more acutely by Britain because of its largely outmoded industrial infrastructure and relatively low levels of technological advancement. As a result, many established industries collapsed and/or became obsolete in the light of foreign competition. A fundamental restructuring of the economic field at all levels of the social formation inevitably followed, in an attempt to regain profitability. This was a time when Britain saw the introduction of new technologies, the decline of large traditional manufacturing industries and an increase in the service sector. Moreover, the composition and nature of the remaining workforce was also undergoing fundamental change, with a significant rise in female employment and part-time and casual work (Urry 1989; Overbeek 1990).

All these changes were evident as much in the city of Workingham as elsewhere.[1] Workingham was a city whose manufacturing industries were spatially concentrated in and around its central areas. Throughout the 1950s and 1960s, Workingham enjoyed unemployment levels consistently below the national average. However, the mid-1970s marked the beginning of a period that witnessed a dramatic decline in these established industries. Many suffered considerably under the weight of cheap far-eastern imports and the introduction of new machinery and materials. Large factories in the inner urban areas, previously underscoring local community life, were closed down and stood as empty and decaying monuments to times past. As a consequence, the proportion of those employed in manufacturing industries declined to less than half of what it was in the 1950s. The devastating nature of this decline is most starkly evident in the fact that unemployment in Workingham rose fourfold in the nineteen months between June 1974 and January 1976.

A process of industrial decentralisation had already begun in the decade prior to the recession, as large firms moved to the outskirts of the city to expand because of the lack of space in the inner urban areas. However, during the late 1980s and 1990s, this process markedly increased, with many of the remaining manufacturing firms – now generally smaller in size and significantly less labour-intensive – relocating to the business parks and industrial developments on the outer rings of the city. The rise of the service sector in areas such as insurance, banking and finance and public administration was proportionately slightly higher in Workingham than nationally, and by 1989 it had gained just under a 60 per cent share of the total employed population. However, this expansion was never enough to counteract the decline in manufacturing. This was especially the case in the inner urban areas, which benefited relatively little from the rise in the service sector because of a similar tendency for it to locate in the outer rings of the city and to be characterised, generally, by part-time, female and temporary work.

Thatcherism and the (re-)racialisation of the nation

These fundamental economic shifts at the national and local level inevitably had profound consequences for the field of politics. Most fundamentally, they drew attention to the inherent contradictions of the social democratic consensus and ultimately brought about its demise. The Labour government of 1974–9 was no longer able to carry on its levels of public expenditure. Rather, it was forced to adopt the monetarist economic strategy of reducing inflation and drastically curbing public expenditure so as to remove the 'institutional barriers to economic restructuring' thought to be causing domestic firms to relocate abroad and detracting transnational investment (Jones 1989: 36). It was at this point that the post-war social democratic consensus was irreparably ruptured. As Hall (1983: 32) contends, 'as the recession bit more deeply, so the management of the crisis required Labour to discipline, limit and police the very classes it claimed to represent . . . through the mediation of the state'. The existing political philosophy based upon consensus was therefore no longer applicable, and the consensus politics that had until this point underscored successive Labour and Conservative governments had therefore lost its popular support.

It was here, with the need to refashion the dominant national political discourse in order to regain popular support, that we saw the emergence of the New Right in the guise of the newly elected Conservative government of 1979, headed by Margaret Thatcher. The popularity of Thatcherism lay in its ability successfully to 'nationalise itself' and combine the ensuing nationalistic discourse with a strong commitment to monetarism. The collectivism that characterised the post-war nation therefore gave way to a Thatcherite discourse on the nation that stressed economic individualism and self-reliance. It was the undermining of these characteristics, according to this discourse, that lay behind the nation's decline. In this sense the Thatcherite discourse was as much concerned with the political and moral as the

31

economic. As Parekh (1986) has identified, a whole host of economic, moral and political factors were therefore evoked and reworked within this discourse concerning the 'national disease' and prescriptions for its recovery. They were themes designed specifically to reorganise people's experiences and commonsense understandings of the dramatic slide into recession. It was the burden of the public sector and its stifling of the entrepreneurial spirit that was cited at the economic level, while morally it was the growing dependency on the state and the loss of the individual virtues of self-help and thrift. This was all drawn together at the political level, where the decline of 'our' nation and its fighting spirit was to be explained by 'our' peculiarly English reserve which had resulted in a confused patriotism and lack of a sense of collective unity and nationhood.

At the heart of this emergent discourse, therefore, was a revitalised sense of nationhood. In many respects it was the political failure to preserve and maintain a strong sense of national spirit that lay at the heart of the economic and moral aspects of the decline. As Barker (1981:17) explains: 'if it were not for feelings of belonging, of sharing traditions, customs, beliefs, language – in a word, culture – there could be no society. We could not live together and co-operate.' This was the point where a reworked notion of 'race' was central to the political capital of successive Thatcher governments. For it was argued that the increasingly multi-ethnic nature of Britain had had the consequence of undermining the very heart of its national identity and had drained its spirit. Moreover, post-war immigration had not simply rendered the British nation impotent, but had created a time-bomb; an inevitable situation where, in the not too-distant future, violence and conflict would result as the 'British (i.e. White) people' reasserted them-selves and their sense of identity. This was the message at the heart of the then government minister Enoch Powell's infamous 'rivers of blood' speeches in the late 1960s. For Powell, the problem at the heart of Britain's immigration policies was the granting of nationality on the 'right of soil [rather than] the right of blood' (Powell 1988: 41). What this had created was an 'alien wedge' of minority ethnic communities in Britain's inner cities, who could never assimilate or develop the inherent feelings of 'Britishness' natural to the indigenous – White – population and who, instead, would forever harbour yearnings for their 'own' countries. For Powell, the deep, almost biological, desire to 'live with your own kind' – felt by White people just as much as by anyone else – would inevitably result in racial conflict and the flowing of 'rivers of blood' through Britain's inner cities.[2] This was to be a theme central to the emerging Thatcherite discourse in 1978 where, in a television interview leading up to the general election, Margaret Thatcher spoke of the ordinary people of Britain and how they were 'really rather afraid that this country might be swamped by people with a different culture' (quoted in Barker 1981:15).

Because of Britain's particular colonial and imperialist heritage, it was therefore not surprising that it would be 'race' that came to form one of the central organising principles in the refashioning of an active and revitalised notion of the nation (Gilroy 1987; Goulbourne 1993). In many ways it could be argued that 'race' had become part of the national political habitus. Britain's historical legacy and its colonial experience as a nation have progressively acted to provide a certain predisposition for national politicians to continue to develop a racialised construct of the nation in their struggles over political capital.

RACIALISING LOCAL PROBLEMS AND CONCERNS

So far we have seen how contemporary national political discourses have come to respond to the economic crisis by developing a renewed sense of nationhood. Within this, we have seen how 'race' plays a pivotal role, not only in helping to define the host (i.e. White) national identity, but also in scapegoating the 'Others' (i.e. Black and South Asian people) for the nation's decline. However, these national political discourses are successful only to the extent that they can help to make sense of and explain particular social concerns. In this, as stated earlier, they need to draw upon and rework 'ordinary' people's experiences. This was certainly the case in relation to both the inner-city problem and the crisis in education.

The inner-city problem

As we have already noted, many of those living in inner-city areas have experienced dramatic change in the wake of the economic recession. They have witnessed an unprecedented rise in unemployment, a decline of traditional industries, the breakdown of long-standing working-class communities through slum clearance, a rise in crime and a general sense of isolation and lack of community spirit. The general discourses on 'race' and national decline therefore needed to address these experiences directly for them to maintain their popularity.

It was within this context that, as Hall *et al.* (1978) so successfully argue, the moral panics over mugging gained such prominence from the late 1960s onwards. The phenomenon of the mugger provided the medium through which individuals were encouraged to make sense of the inner-city problem. Through intense political and media concern, the mugger came to epitomise all that was wrong with the inner city. He was invariably Black and not 'of' the community. His menacing appearance on local streets, therefore, came to represent the decline of the local community. Moreover, his youth represented change and the fact that he was also unemployed, lazy and driven by greed were all reminders of the changing nature of the times and the loss of the traditional communal spirit. So popular was the moral panic around mugging that, before long, it was no longer necessary to refer explicitly to 'race' to ensure that mugging was synonymous with Black male youth.

Moreover, the parallel moral panics over fears of being 'swamped', initiated by Enoch Powell in the late 1960s, were also central in encouraging people to make sense of their experiences in relation to 'race'. It was therefore the increasing presence of 'hordes' of minority ethnic people, with different languages and cultures, that provided the main threat to the traditional community spirit.

According to these national political discourses, the problems that were increasingly associated with the inner city – unemployment, bad housing, crime and violence – were not caused by economic factors or national government policies, but were to be explained by the arrival of Black and South Asian people. Just as we found with the phenomenon of the mugger, it was not long before 'race' did not need to be explicitly evoked for the inner-city problem to be understood as essentially racial. This is certainly borne out by the development of the government's first inner-city policies in 1968. It is no coincidence that the announcement of the urban aid initiatives by Prime Minister Harold Wilson directly followed the political aftermath of Enoch Powell's 'rivers of blood' speeches (Sills *et al.* 1988; Lawless 1989). Moreover, the plethora of governmental policies directed at the inner city since then, and especially in the wake of the urban disorders of 1980–1 and 1985, have all helped to construct the inner-city problem as essentially racial. As we will see in the following chapter, this racialisation of the inner-city problem provides the immediate context within which local people on the Manor Park estate attempt to make sense of their experiences.

The crisis in education

Education provided another key site within which these national political discourses attempted to explain away the economic recession and lock into 'ordinary' people's experiences and concerns. They were discourses that first gained political expression in a Green Paper produced by the Labour government in 1977. At the heart of the Paper was the belief that it was the failings of the education system that were responsible for Britain's decline. As the Paper argued, it therefore tended to agree with the general feeling that:

> the educational system is out of touch with the fundamental need for Britain to survive economically in a highly competitive world through the efficiency of its industry and commerce. . . . There is a wide gap between the world of education and the world of work. Boys and girls are not sufficiently aware of the importance of industry to our society, and they are not taught much about it. . . .

The country's economic well-being depends on its own efforts, and its standard of living is directly related to its ability to sell goods and services overseas. . . . We depend upon industry to create wealth without which our social services, our education and arts cannot flourish

(quoted in Jones 1983: 71)

The theoretical seeds for this discourse, however, were sown by the *Black Papers*, the first of which was published almost a decade earlier.[3] As Ball (1990) summarises, these papers contained three common themes that provided the basis for the attack upon comprehensive education and its philosophical underpinnings of progressivism and egalitarianism. The first related to the alleged decline in academic standards, particularly in numeracy and literacy. While there was no evidence in support of these claims (Wright 1983), they provided the basis for a strong campaign against progressive education and for a return to a more traditional subject-centred and academically streamed educational system. The second highlighted the recurrent theme of a decline in discipline and the need for a return to more traditional, hierarchically structured forms of schooling.

However, it was the third theme – the growing prominence in British schools of 'politically motivated teachers' – that was by far the most serious of the three and which was believed to lie behind the decline in educational standards and discipline. These teachers were getting 'our' children at a young age, indoctrinating them and undermining the central values that underpin our society. As such they were threatening our very sense of nationhood (see Cox and Scruton 1984; Scruton *et al.* 1985). By the second half of the 1970s, these themes had been taken up by the media and significantly enhanced through a series of moral panics (Chitty 1989; Troyna and Carrington 1990).

As with the general discourses on 'race' and the inner city discussed earlier, the success and popularity of these particular discourses on education need to be understood primarily in their ability to resonate effectively with working-class people's general feelings of dissatisfaction with and alienation from their children's schools. Their experiences of powerlessness in their relations with particular teachers and schools were ideally situated to be taken up and reworked into a discourse that cited an educational self-serving and all-powerful elite as the main problem (Flew 1987; Hillgate Group 1986, 1987). It formed part of a wider set of New Right discourses on the welfare state, seeking to highlight the way that, in the absence of any market mechanisms, it had generally become infested with self-interest and as a result had transformed itself into being producer- rather than consumer-led (Harris and Seldon 1979).

This, then, provided the basic background against which the 'Great Debate' surrounding the nature and development of post-war education was initiated by the Prime Minister, James Callaghan, in his speech at Ruskin College, Oxford, in 1976 and which lay behind the resultant Green Paper quoted earlier. Moreover, with the continual evocation of the nation's interests it is not surprising that these discourses came to be progressively racialised. By the mid-1980s, therefore, they were increasingly being refracted through the political assaults on multicultural and anti-racist education. Through a number of highly publicised moral panics, anti-racist education came to symbolise all that was wrong with education:[4] it represented a serious dilution of the traditional curriculum; it encouraged children to question some of the basic values underpinning society while also seriously undermining their sense of national identity; and it was led by groups of fanatical, politically extreme anti-racists (Palmer 1986).

It was within this context of discourses on traditional subjects and discipline, increasingly refracted through debates on anti-racism, that the Educational Reform Act 1988 was conceived and passed through Parliament (see Troyna and Carrington 1990; Tomlinson and Craft 1995). The central tenets of the Act, including the National Curriculum, Standardised Assessment Tests (SATs), Local Management of Schools (LMS) and parental choice provided the vehicles with which the New Right claimed to reintroduce educational standards and discipline into Britain's schools, removing education once and for all from the hands of politically motivated producers (local government officials and teachers) and giving it back to the consumers (parents). For the 'ordinary' people, therefore, it successfully fed upon their feelings of powerlessness with the promise of giving them back control of schools.

For teachers, it represented a significant ideological shift and redefinition of what counts as a 'good' teacher. At the national political level, teachers were being encouraged to jettison the ideas and pedagogical philosophies that had come to dominate and shape primary teaching and practice for almost two decades. Here the stress was on a return to traditional, more didactic teaching methods and away from the progressivism advocated by the Plowden Report (1967). This was reinforced by the more recent demand for a return to commonsense approaches to teaching, when, in June 1993, the then Secretary of State for Education, John Patten, called for a 'Mums Army' to be enrolled in primary schools to teach young children the '3Rs' of reading, writing and arithmetic.

Alongside this emphasis on traditional approaches to discipline and teaching, primary teachers were also being encouraged to focus on the 'basics' of grammar, spelling and tables. Implicit within this, and certainly something that has been reinforced by the National Curriculum, is a significant ideological shift away from multiculturalism coupled with an overt hostility to anti-racist education (Gordon 1988; Hardy and Vieler-Porter 1992).

These, then, are the basic themes that have come to shape the national political agenda over recent years in relation to education. As will be seen in Chapter 5, they form the backdrop against which teachers at East Avenue attempt to negotiate their own professional roles within the school.

John Major's 'Back to basics'

So far we have looked at the development of national political discourses and their impact upon debates surrounding particular areas of social concern. Underpinning many of these, as we have seen, are discourses on 'race'. In practice, however, these particular concerns are not discussed in isolation, but are often woven together within the context of a more general concern with the state of the nation. This can be illustrated by the following quote, taken from Prime Minister John Major's 'Back to basics' speech at the Conservative Party conference in October 1993, which coincided with the end of the fieldwork. While it ultimately backfired on John Major, it did so not because it no longer made sense to and resonated with people's experiences; for many it was because he and his government had been championing these problems for the previous fourteen years while achieving nothing – problems with crime, the inner cities, education and housing, it was felt, were still increasing. Nevertheless, the following quote quite clearly summarises and represents some of the core themes developed through national political discourse since the mid-1970s, and helps to provide the over-riding context for the following chapters.

> Let me tell you what I believe. For two generations too many people have been belittling the things that made this country. We have allowed things to happen that we should never have tolerated. We have listened too often and too long to people whose ideas are light years away from common sense.
>
> [...]
>
> In housing in the fifties in Britain and the sixties, we pulled down the terraces – destroyed whole communities and replaced them with tower blocks and we built walkways that became rat-runs for muggers. That was the fashionable opinion. But it was wrong.
>
> In our schools we did away with traditional subjects – grammar, spelling, tables, and the old ways of teaching them. Some said the family was out of date and that it was better to rely on the council and social workers than family and friends. I passionately believe that was wrong. Others told us that every criminal needed treatment, not punishment. Criminal behaviour was society's fault, not the individual's. Fashionable, but wrong, very wrong [. . .]. It is time to return to core values, time to get back to basics, to self-discipline and respect for the law, to consideration for others, to

accepting responsibility for yourself – and not shuffling it off on other people and the state.

(*Guardian*, 9 October 1993: 6)

Of course, how people come to read and interpret speeches like this depends upon the particular contexts in which they find themselves. However, for those living and/or working in inner-city areas, their experiences can often encourage them to read many if not all of these themes through the lens of 'race'. In signifying the 'ordinary people' whose sentiments the Prime Minister represents, for instance, the speech conjures up the mythical notion of Britishness as a homogenous (and therefore White) grouping. That these 'ordinary people' were being terrorised by inner-city (read 'Black') muggers and were more generally victims of crime only helps to sediment this racialised view. References to discourses on education and the need to return to traditional subjects and ways of teaching can also act to evoke images of the failure of progressive and *multicultural* education.

The point I want to stress from this is that 'race', as it has become part of the political habitus, does not always need to be explicitly signified to be evoked (see Troyna 1993; Gillborn 1995). The racialisation of subjects such as the mugger, the inner city and educational decline through earlier discourses have helped to sediment and predispose particular people to read and understand current discourses through the medium of 'race' even when it is not specifically referred to (Miles 1989, 1993). How and to what extent particular people evoke racialised discourses in their reading of speeches such as that quoted above depends upon their particular social context and their specific experiences and concerns.

CONCLUSIONS

This chapter has drawn attention to some of the principal factors affecting the nature of discourses found within the field of national politics. As we have seen, it is not only national and international economic change that affects national political discourses, but also changes at the local level. In particular, a complex relationship exists between national political discourses and local fields of relations, where each tends to influence and shape the other. We therefore need to be mindful not to develop a simplistic understanding of national political discourses, seeing them as simply determining what people think. Rather, we need to be aware of how these discourses feed off and essentially rely on the local experiences and concerns of those people.

In essence, what we have seen is that national political discourses, in responding to the dramatic economic changes that have occurred in the late twentieth century, have constructed a racialised understanding of the national interest that tends to scapegoat Black and South Asian people for Britain's decline. Discourses on 'race' have become so imbued in particular debates concerning the inner-city problem and the crisis in education that they no longer need to be explicitly cited for them to be evoked. While we cannot assume that all people will appropriate these discourses on 'race' to make sense of such debates, I want to show, in the next two chapters, that for many people living and working on the Manor Park estate their location within the inner city creates a *tendency* for them to do this.

4

LIVING IN THE INNER CITY:
THE MANOR PARK ESTATE

Reading many ethnographic studies on 'race' and schooling, you could be forgiven for reaching the conclusion that racism simply begins and ends in school-based interaction. With very few exceptions (see Troyna and Hatcher 1992), little work has actually sought to look beyond the school gates to examine how the particular locality plays a pivotal role in influencing and shaping the way that teachers, parents and children come to think in terms of 'race'.[1] For many of these studies, it is as if the general racist ideas and assumptions played out at the national political level are simply assumed to have a direct influence on the individual beliefs and assumptions of those within the school. And yet, as we will see in this chapter, local estates such as Manor Park provide the medium through which these national political discourses are refracted and understood. It is through people's day-to-day experience of living and/or working in Manor Park that they come to appropriate and adapt broader racialised discourses to make sense of that experience. This is equally so for the young children who are the focus of the present study. The development of their understanding of gender relations and of racism on the estate provides the essential source material which they draw upon and rework in negotiating their relationships with other children in the school.

This chapter, therefore, is concerned with providing the context set by the Manor Park estate. It will begin by exploring the historical development of the estate and the importance of national political discourses on 'race' and the inner city, as outlined in the previous chapter, in structuring its present form. The chapter will then go on to examine how life on the Manor Park estate is experienced by the women and men living there. In particular, the chapter will focus on how particular aspects of their feminine and masculine habitus have been developed in relation to their experiences of the estate. This will provide the context for the concluding section, which draws attention to the particular expressions of racism within the estate and how they are experienced by the Black and South Asian people living there.

THE RACIALISATION OF PLACE: THE MANOR PARK ESTATE

The Manor Park estate can be seen as a specific site within the broader field of economic relations. It represents a relatively homogeneous fraction of the working class, primarily defined in terms of their specific relation to economic capital – the majority being either economically inactive or unemployed, and living in council accommodation. As such, the estate in terms of its spatial location and the nature of its built environment has arguably come to represent, and be expressive of, this position. In this section I am primarily concerned with simply mapping out the origins and development of the estate, and the influence of national political discourses on 'race' and the inner city within this.

Living on an island

> Everything's very high, isn't it, high-rise flats, the great big high horrible building on the outside. In those days this was a White area, the head who was here then used to say it was an island of White people living in these flats surrounded by an Asian and West Indian area [. . .] that was her description and it was right. There were mainly White children, White people in these flats, and that's how it's changed over the past years. They're now letting flats out to all types of people.

This was one long-standing teacher's description of the estate and how it has changed since it was built on an area slum-cleared in the late 1950s. The reference to high-rise flats and to the estate's decline following Black and South Asian immigration tends to symbolise Manor Park as an inner-city area. In order to understand these themes more fully, it is important that we trace the origins of these discourses back through the historical development of the city of Workingham and of the Manor Park estate within this.

The central and inner areas of Workingham, since its relatively late industrial development at the turn of the century, have been spatially dominated by closely packed basic terraced housing and industrial premises. However, during the post-war period, increasing numbers of the overwhelmingly White working-class population have been moving from these inner areas and relocating in the new council estates developed on the outskirts of the city. These estates were built in two phases during the inter- and early post-war eras. Their purpose was to meet the housing demands created by programmes of slum clearance relating to the deteriorating terraced housing of the inner urban areas. By the end of the 1950s, there were four principal council estates built to the south and west of the city.

41

During the second phase of slum clearance in the early 1950s, a shift in priorities began to emerge within Workingham City Council, away from simple wholesale relocation of neighbourhoods and towards the renovation and reconstruction of existing areas. In 1957, it was agreed to rebuild the Manor Park area to the east of the city and, over the next ten years, Manor Park became the first estate to be built on a slum-cleared area. However, not long after, the 1974 Housing Act and its influential 'Renewal Strategies' circular played a significant role in encouraging the strategy of gradually renewing existing stock rather than its wholesale clearance. Because of this, Manor Park was one of only a few areas totally rebuilt within the inner urban area. Furthermore, the later construction of dual carriageways and ring roads around the city centre acted to separate the estate from its immediate environment by four major roads, and for these reasons the estate developed a distinct identity for itself. Directly across one of the roads from the estate was the city centre, while in the other directions there remained sprawling neighbourhoods of traditional terraced housing.

The estate was visually dominated by three large high-rise tower blocks, with the rest of the area being made up of rows of maisonettes which were free-standing but organised loosely into larger squares. Alongside each of the four roads at the extremities of the estate were the four-storey-high lines of the backs of the maisonettes. These added to the spatial and temporal construction of Manor Park as a separate and new estate. At the time of its construction, Manor Park was regarded by many as a popular estate, with its own small shopping and neighbourhood centres located at the foot of the high-rise towers. As another long-standing teacher recalled: 'I would like to have lived here when I first worked here. [. . .] It was lovely, clean, you know.' Its 'newness' and convenient location next to the city centre ensured that Manor Park remained a popular estate throughout the 1960s and 1970s, when relatively large numbers of Black and South Asian immigrants were moving to particular parts of Britain. Workingham was particularly affected by the migration of Kenyan Asians during the early 1970s.

It is important to remember that the overwhelmingly White population's experiences of the arrival of Black and South Asian people in Workingham during this time were understood against the backdrop of both the popular racial discourses of Enoch Powell, as outlined in the previous chapter, and the legitimisation and institutionalisation of these through immigration controls (Solomos 1993). This construction of Black and South Asian people as 'alien' and 'a problem' within Workingham was precipitated by the arrival of the Kenyan Asians, whose anticipated migration to Britain had provided the immediate context within which Powell's 'rivers of blood' speech was given and the emergency 1968 Commonwealth Immigrants Act was rushed through Parliament. The debates that ensued through the local media, principally over panics about being 'swamped', provided an important background against which Black and South Asian settlement took place in Workingham.

Because of the rules governing the council-house waiting list and the designation of Black and South Asian migrants as 'low priority', many migrants were forced to seek accommodation in the private rented sector and/or to club together to buy cheap housing (Karn 1983). Not surprisingly, therefore, the majority of Black and South Asian settlement took place to the east of the city centre, in the areas dominated by the stock of cheap, poor-quality terraced housing that had survived slum clearance. As early as 1965, the proportion of minority ethnic people living in the three wards surrounding Manor Park had reached 65 per cent of the total population. By the mid-1970s, therefore, the 'island' of Manor Park had been created, with the new self-contained White council estate surrounded by old poor-quality terraced housing, the majority of whose residents were South Asian and Black. For some, the contrasting nature of the two built environments came to symbolise the different racial make-up of the areas, while the spatial location of the 'island estate' was experienced and understood against the backdrop of popular national concerns, refracted through local debates, over being 'swamped'.

Manor Park estate as a contemporary 'inner-city problem'

The 1991 Census revealed that the ward in which the Manor Park estate is situated was one of the most deprived areas in the country. Successive waves of demographic and industrial de-urbanisation, together with a dramatic rise in unemployment and increasingly concentrated minority ethnic population, have had their effect on Workingham's inner urban areas. What had been a prime popular flagship estate in the 1960s had been reduced to symbolising an 'inner-city problem'. According to the 1991 Census, unemployment had more than doubled on the estate during the previous ten years and had reached an overall figure that was more than three times the national average. However, just over half of all residents on the estate were classed as 'economically inactive' representing, as will be seen shortly, a higher than average proportion of elderly people, young single parents and children on the estate. As regards ethnic origin, there had been a gradual increase in the proportion of Black and South Asian people living on the estate to just under a quarter of the local population by 1991. Within this, about a third were Black and two-thirds South Asian.

These demographic changes over the decade, especially in relation to the increase of 'economically inactive' households, tends to corroborate a view widely held among those interviewed on Manor Park, that it had increasingly become a 'dumping ground' for 'problem families'. As one of the teachers commented:

When I first came here, the type of families that you had on the estate were very different to what you've got now, and I think what they did was try to, like, put all the problem people together and I think that's causing more of a problem. A lot more single parents and families that just didn't seem to fit in anywhere else, and they've sort of lumped them all together, and instead of helping them integrate or helping them, you know, get sorted out, I think problems have come out of their problems, you know, they're all just together and all in the same boat.

This general shift in housing policy could be witnessed most starkly by the changing nature of the age distribution. Over the decade, the number of children on the estate aged between 0 and 4 had risen from 197 in 1981 to 538 in 1991, while the number of those aged between 20 and 24 had almost doubled from 229 to 409 over the same period, just under two-thirds being women. During this same period, the proportions of those in the age groups of 35 and over have all significantly decreased, especially in the pre-retirement age groups.

These statistics tend to suggest a tendency for single-parent households and young people generally to be housed on the estate. The proportion of households with dependent children had risen from 27.1 to 40.4 per cent of all households on the estate between 1981 and 1991, while within this the percentage of single parents had risen from 30.8 to 57.4 per cent of all dependent households. At the time of the fieldwork, this figure was over four times the national average. The overwhelming majority of these single-parent households were headed by women and dominated by younger children – just over half of all single parents had one or more children who were all aged under five, while just over two-thirds (68.5 per cent) had at least one child under five.

The reinforcement and sedimentation of the 'inner-city problem'

Through this apparent trend in the city council's housing policy, Manor Park had come to represent an increasingly homogeneous group within the field of economic relations: one whose characteristics had become synonymous with the inner-city problem. The majority on the estate were economically inactive, over-represented at the extremes of the age ranges, included a growing number of Black and South Asian people and contained a remarkably high proportion of single-parent families. Associated with these trends, as we shall see later, the estate developed a distinct reputation for one of the highest levels of violent crime and domestic violence compared to the county as a whole. Not surprisingly, therefore, this was a housing policy that ultimately became self-fulfilling. The more the estate gained a reputation as an inner-city 'sink' estate, the more it not only became undesirable among the more articulate council tenants, who refused to live there, but also provided the place where 'difficult' or 'problem' households could be rehoused by the council without much complaint from other residents. It is here that we can begin to see the particular discursive processes and practices that tend to reproduce the discourses on the inner city associated with Manor Park.

This discursive construction of Manor Park as an inner-city problem is also arguably compounded by the dominance of its built environment, with high-rise tower blocks and maisonettes – both increasingly coming to symbolise the breakdown of traditional working-class communities and the decline of the inner city, as discussed earlier. However, its built environment is also always changing – coming to be expressive of, while also crucially influencing, social and demographic trends (Keith and Pile 1993). In terms of Manor Park and its social construction as an inner-city problem, it can be argued that a number of discourses played out within the field of national politics have also tended to influence the specific nature and contemporary development of the estate as a specific site within the field of economics. In particular, it is those discourses on the inner city more generally – which, as pointed out in the previous chapter, fuse the more specific themes of racial violence, crime and poverty – that have been influential in the construction of Manor Park's spatial identity. As we saw, they are discourses manifest most clearly within the plethora of urban programmes initiated by successive national governments since 1968. They are programmes derived in part from central government's response to the economic crisis which, as discussed earlier in relation to Workingham, had created the concentration of large numbers of minority ethnic people in small areas characterised by poor housing, high unemployment, bad health and general poverty. It has been argued that, in the context of a fiscal crisis and the need drastically to cut public expenditure, inner-city governmental programmes were developed as low-cost schemes, targeted at small, geographically distinct areas. This helped to increase the legitimacy of the government, which was seen to be doing something 'for the nation' while actually spending very little in overall terms (Sills et al. 1988).

For many local authorities under increasing financial pressure, the resources made available through these initiatives and programmes were viewed as an important, albeit small, source of funding (Sills et al. 1988; Lawless 1989). However, the 'pepper pot' nature of this funding, in making relatively large amounts of funds available for a few small scattered areas, has led many local authorities to bid for the funding through identifying certain areas within their localities as distinctly deprived inner-city neighbourhoods. This, in turn, provides the context within which certain areas tend to be publicly and symbolically designated as inner-city problems within the local popular consciousness. The consequences of these discursive processes can be illustrated quite clearly by an item that appeared in the *Workingham Evening News* during the present fieldwork. It was in response to a report by Workinghamshire Health Authority, aimed at highlighting the need for a more resourced and improved health centre to be built on the estate. The headline read: 'Sad picture of life on an inner-city estate', with the sub-heading: 'Report reveals disturbing saga of crime and illness'. In relation to this, it can be argued that, in making its case for the need to build such a centre in the same way as the city council would make its case for central government urban programme funding, the Health Authority had unwittingly helped to reinforce the symbolic identity of Manor Park as an inner-city problem.

For Manor Park, more generally, such central government programmes have impacted most directly on the estate in a number of ways in recent years, the most significant of which has been the funding gained to improve the external appearance and security of Manor Park, following a bid by Workingham City Council for a grant of £17 million from the Department of the Environment's Estates Action programme. While this project has arguably had little impact upon the general social and economic problems facing Workingham as a whole, it did undoubtedly have important consequences for the Manor Park estate.

The building work resulting from the Estates Action project was nearing completion during the fieldwork. There were principally two aspects to the work. On the one hand, there was what has been described as a process of 'enveloping', where the external features of the maisonettes, such as roofs, doors and garden walls, were renovated and replaced. On the other hand, in relation to the attempt to make the estate more secure, alleyways were blocked off, new security doors were constructed and railings were erected. As described earlier, most maisonettes were built in rows and organised in squares. The outcome of the building work was to block off all the alleyways running underneath and between the maisonettes, effectively linking the single buildings and creating much larger square blocks with a large communal courtyard in the middle. Ground-floor maisonettes were given their own small private gardens, while the first-floor maisonettes were able to share the central courtyard with other families on the block. Climbing frames and other facilities such as benches were provided in these areas. There was only one entrance to each courtyard, and the doors serving these, together with doors leading into each wing of the block, were replaced by large, reinforced security doors with intercoms.

Externally, a number of railings were erected alongside surviving pathways. One main path ran through the centre of the estate from one side to the other. Black iron railings, eighteen feet high, ran along either side of the pathway, making it impossible to enter or leave the pathway other than at either end. Other railings helped to secure the private gardens of ground-floor tenants in maisonettes. Approaching the estate from the city centre, one could now see a ten-foot-high iron railing running the full length of the road and punctuated occasionally by paths leading to a strong security door at the base of a maisonette block. Immediately behind the railings stood the maisonettes, also running the whole length of the road and creating an impression of a perimeter wall containing the estate.

For many, the overall impression left by this work has been, in the words of one teacher at East Avenue, one of 'foreboding, I mean I think that's the word, it looks like Colditz, you look like, as though you're fenced in, penned in'. The majority of the parents interviewed on the estate agreed that, while it made them feel more secure, it made Manor Park look like 'a prison'. As one of the parents said: 'It is a good thing, yes, it is more secure now [. . .] but it's bad really, it looks like we're living in a jail, you know, rather than a house [. . .] because they've built up everything all around so it looks like a jail', while another parent commented on how 'these big massive railings are horrible, it looks like a prison. [. . .] It looks horrible. It really does. I hate it.' Added to this was the difficulty that many residents now faced in travelling around the estate. As one parent explained: 'There's no short cuts at all now on any path [. . .] which means you've got to walk all the way around and it's like there's no freedom at all now.' It could be argued that one of the consequences of this building work has been the tendency to create a certain image of the Manor Park estate that speaks of crime. From the outside, the perimeter railings are reminiscent of a prison, while inside the estate, as will be discussed in more detail below, many of the residents have had their movement significantly restricted and have become increasingly isolated from one another.

GENDER IDENTITIES ON THE MANOR PARK ESTATE

So far we have explored how the historical development and contemporary nature of the Manor Park estate has been constituted against the backdrop of national political discourses on 'race' and the inner city. This provides the context within which we can now look at how life is experienced by those living on the estate. As has become apparent from some of the interviews with the parents living on the estate, it can be argued that while Manor Park remains a site within the broader economic field it has also, for some, become a field in its own right. As we will see below, the inability of many of these women and men to find work and to live up to the dominant forms of capital found within the economic field has encouraged some to develop alternative forms of capital to struggle over and aspire to. In looking at particular aspects of the dominant forms of femininity and masculinity developed on the estate, I want to show how these forms of capital have also come to be expressed through the gender identities of the women and men living there.

47

It needs to be understood, however, that what is to follow does not claim to be a representative account of life on the estate or a comprehensive depiction of the many diverse elements of the masculine and feminine identities found there. Far from it. In many ways the following has been written in retrospect – with the needs and concerns of the later chapters in mind. In this sense, my primary concern has been to identify those particular discursive elements and practices, found among some of the residents of the estate, which most help us understand some of the dominant forms of capital associated with the young children's peer-group relations. These will be drawn out and highlighted at the end of this chapter.

Strategies of survival and the masculine habitus on the estate

Over half of all males living on Manor Park were under 30 years of age. This is largely accounted for by the high proportion of those aged under 5 and those aged between 20 and 29. For many of these young men, the negotiation and development of their masculine identities was conducted against the backdrop of high levels of unemployment (Mac an Ghaill 1994; Skelton 1996, 1997). Over two-thirds of those between the ages of 20 and 29 were without work. Moreover, with the on-going de-urbanisation of industry and the replacement of full-time occupations with part-time or temporary jobs increasingly favouring women, for the majority of these men there was no realistic hope of ever finding permanent full-time work.

Within this context, it became apparent that some of these young men have come to re-evaluate their position within the broader economic field and question the value and appropriateness of its dominant forms of capital. Rather, what was found on Manor Park was the emergence of alternative forms of masculinity, which recognised the futility of aspiring to full-time permanent work and instead emphasised the ability to seek out alternative ways of making a living, of survival (Westwood 1990). For a small minority of men, these ways most commonly centred around petty street crime such as robbery and theft, burglary, drugs and 'pimping'. The ability to 'handle yourself' on the street and thus to be street-wise tended to form an important aspect of their cultural capital. This ability to handle yourself while successfully negotiating the complex sets of relations that emerged around activities like theft, drugs and pimping inevitably involved the threat and possible use of violence. Furthermore, not only did the spatial and economic location of Manor Park encourage the adoption of these strategies of survival for some young men but also, because of its characteristically transient and isolated population, the estate itself provided the context where many of these crimes, and the violence that accompanied them, were played out. This latter factor tends to be supported by the official police statistics, which suggest that Manor Park at the time of the fieldwork had one of the highest rates of violent crimes, robbery and burglary within the city. The total number of crimes of these types recorded for the small area of Manor Park during this time was greater than that for all the rest of the inner city of Workingham.

Of course, there are many problems in reading too much into criminal statistics. It could be argued, for instance, that crime on Manor Park may well be similar to many other areas. The higher rates of recorded crime may simply be due to its reputation for being a 'bad' area, which may then encourage higher levels of policing in that area, leading inevitably to a greater number of arrests. Moreover, it could be argued that the more police patrol the estate, the more likely it is for people to feel confident in reporting crimes to them.

In many ways these debates concerning the 'true' level of crime on the estate are largely irrelevant for the present study. Whatever the reality of life on the Manor Park estate, for many of its residents it has become interpreted and experienced as one interwoven with violence and crime. While it may well be only a small minority of young men engaged in such acts on the estate, these events, when periodically witnessed, can have the effect of simply reinforcing this perception. One of the parents, for instance, believed that the violence had got progressively worse on the estate over the last few years. As she said:

> I think it's going to the dogs, it's getting worse. I mean, they're trying to build it up to make it nicer, but it's not working. They need to fix the inside first and get the community thing sorted out because at the moment you've got robberies over here, people sticking people with knives over there. You've got a pub over here full of crack-heads and drugs, and, I mean, that's by the sports centre, that's by the shopping precinct – kids have got to go out there! I mean, you get a break-in or somebody mugs you – in the afternoon!

What is interesting from the above quote is the reference made to children and how perceptions of violence of this type can form part of the context within which they grow up. This, together with the specific notoriety of the pub for being 'rough', was something commented upon by another parent:

> It's a bad estate for kids. There's a lot of drugs on this estate going about. There's prostitutes standing right at the top of the road on the corners. So it is bad for children to see that an' all. But my kids are in bed anyway, so they don't see things like that, but what I'm saying is that it is bad. The other night there was a lot of people arguing, a lot of people coming out of the pubs fighting outside and that.

What we see developing in relation to the Manor Park estate, therefore, is a particular folklore that dwells upon and foregrounds its allegedly violent nature. It is a folklore reproduced not only by those living on the estate but also, and more significantly, by those working there, including social workers, teachers and the police. As regards the police, for instance, one parent felt that when the area police cars were called in their response had often been characterised by the use of excessive force:

> I've seen people, I mean one person, can't have been any bigger than me, and there was a van, a car, dogs, you know, and they were really . . . and I think it was because there were that many that he felt the need to fight back and the situation started getting worse. And I think if it were one-to-one things might not have got so bad. That was outside my house.

It could be argued that this perception of the criminal and violent nature of Manor Park has possibly become part of the police's own collective habitus, where it can tend to influence the way in which they respond to incidents on the estate. Without further data it is difficult to draw any firm conclusions. However, in drawing upon other studies on policing inner-city areas (Keith 1993), it could tentatively be suggested that the above parent's experience could be understood in relation to the possible existence of a circular self-fulfilling process, where the more the police use excessive force, the more local people will become disaffected with them and resist, and hence the more the police will feel the need to increase the level of their responses. Again, while particular confrontations with the police may be sporadic and infrequent, for those witness to them such confrontations can tend to consolidate further the experience and perception of the Manor Park estate as one punctuated by violence.

It needs to be stressed again that these are not being held up as particularly representative incidents of crime and violence. Indeed, the majority of men on the estate rarely involved themselves in the types of violence set out above. Rather, I want to suggest that, for some, these incidents tend to form part of the folklore of the estate, which feeds into the way many people living and working there come to organise their experiences. It is therefore the 'fear of crime' that is important for some of the residents. Alongside the built environment and its rather impersonal prison-like atmosphere, it provides one of the contexts within which some of the young men on the estate are left to negotiate their own forms of habitus. Moreover, for some of the young boys constituting the focus of the present study, this perception of violence also has a tendency to influence the emergence of their own sense of identity. Whether or not these men and boys are engaged in violence themselves, it can be argued that they have learnt that they still need to present an image that they 'can handle themselves' in order to survive in an estate they have come to associate with violence. As such, the related notions of being street-wise and physical have tended, for some of the men, to become embodied, through their habitus, in the way they come to hold themselves, walk and talk (Bourdieu 1984; Westwood 1990). As will be seen in Chapters 6 and 7, this is as true for some of the young boys at East Avenue as it is for the men.

Single parenthood and the construction of a feminine habitus

For some of the single parents of Manor Park, the forms of femininity that they come to value are equally bound up with, and constructed through, their experience of life on the estate. One particular aspect of that experience for some of the mothers interviewed was that of isolation. In part it was an isolation that related to the predominance of discourses on Manor Park as a violent estate. As one parent explained:

> I don't like to walk through the estate on my own [now] because [. . .] a lady I had a discussion with, she got mugged across the road from where she lived the other week and she was unconscious and mugged. Another lady was beaten up and mugged around the corner.

This quote alludes to the way in which discourses on violence in Manor Park are reproduced through the retelling of certain events, events that as we saw in the previous section cumulatively form part of the folklore of the estate. Ironically, for these particular women, the erection of iron railings as part of the project to make the estate 'safer' has made this fear more acute. Because of the railings, there are a number of paths on the estate where a person cannot get on or off them except at the beginning and end. As one of the parents explained: 'There's no way out so you're stuck, if someone attacks you that's it, there's no way out [. . .] there's already been an attempted rape on this path.'

Talking to these women, it appeared that this sense of isolation tended to be compounded by the lack of appropriate social organisations and projects on the estate that they could turn to. While there were a number of projects on the estate, including an after-school playgroup for 5- to 11-year-olds, a neighbourhood centre and a tenants' association, it appeared that these acted, in a variety of ways, to discourage the development of extended social networks. The tenants' association, for example, was generally spoken of quite highly by the parents in terms of the help and support it has offered them when dealing with the city council over housing problems. Its singular focus, however, and the way it was used only to sort out particular housing problems, meant that it did not offer an appropriate place for parents to

51

meet and develop social networks. Similarly, the playgroup, run by a project worker, was popular with many parents who made use of it as a valuable – and one of the only – resources on offer for their children. However, as with the school, it was a place where parents simply dropped off and picked up their children, and as such provided little opportunity for extended social interaction. Some social interaction did occur at the playgroup among a small number of parents who ran it before the arrival of a new full-time project worker, but this appeared to be very exclusive. As the project worker explained:

> Under the previous management there was a perception that it was a closed organisation, acting largely in its own interests and the vision of those people. [. . .] It wasn't seen as a place where parents and children off the estate were particularly welcome and it was seen as unsafe [. . .] and that's really common in community groups – quite often the community comes together, a caucus is formed and the rest of the community is left out.

Since the change in management, there has been a concerted effort to raise the profile of the playgroup through the production of newsletters and the promotion of its activities. The impact of these changes, however, has still to be seen and ascertained. In talking with some of the parents, it appeared that this type of social caucus, synonymous with the playgroup, tended also to be characteristic of the neighbourhood centre. Thus, while it offered a number of activities including keep-fit classes and mother and toddler groups, it too was regarded by many as unwelcoming and failing to promote its activities. For some of the parents this was compounded by the cost of the activities at the neighbourhood centre, which tended further to discourage involvement. The nature of the financial problems faced by these mothers is illustrated in the following quote, taken from an interview with two single mothers. In the sacrifices Jean alludes to in ensuring that her son is able to go trampolining, the following also tentatively suggests possible ways that femininity, through motherhood, was constructed by these parents:

Cathy: Even the keep-fit classes, I mean, I used to go but [. . .] I'm just finding it too expensive. I mean, unless you've got a discount card it's one pound eighty, even then it's a pound with your discount card. It's on twice a week so that's two pound a week. I can't even afford that.

Jean: And trampolining's the same. It's in the middle of the week, it's on a Wednesday, and it's one pound five. Now I have to really stop myself from spending that money before it come to a Wednesday,

and if you're running out of bread and that it's hard to stop yourself spending the money.

For a significant proportion of the single mothers interviewed, other than
having one or two immediate friends, their experience of Manor Park was
one of isolation. Ironically, it could possibly be precisely the fact that people
were literally 'living on top of each other' in a confined space that added to
this isolation. Arguably, it was the fear of the 'public gaze', of other people
knowing your business and of gossip that, for some single parents, provided
the impetus for avoiding others. This is illustrated in the following conversation with one parent, who spoke of how she had suffered from depression
since she had separated from her partner:

Reshma: I had that depression for three years and I didn't recognise Preena
            [*her daughter*], for three months she was away from me, so you
            could imagine what type of life I led – total isolated.
PC: [. . .] You say you were isolated, did you not know many people
            on the estate?
Reshma: I did know many people, it's like I said again, erm, people like a
            bit of gossip, everybody does. You just got to walk down the street
            and they'll say: 'That's Reshma over there!' and they'll say: 'Oh,
            it's her who kicked her fella out, it's her doing this, it's her doing
            that!' It's getting unbearable. It's come to a stage where I've had
            enough.

This sense of isolation was possibly compounded by the built environment of the estate. Not only were there people literally living on top of one
another, but also the effect of the building work, in creating large courtyards
of previously separate maisonettes, had arguably helped to focus people's
attentions on to one another. While for some (longer-standing) parents this
had created pockets of 'community spirit' based around the 'blocks', for
many others it appeared to have enhanced their sense of isolation under the
constant gaze of others. As one parent explained, the amalgamation of
maisonettes into larger blocks: 'makes it a lot easier to see who's in and
who's out 'cos there's only one way in and out of your courtyard so everyone's
going to know when you go out [. . .] and when you come back'.

For some women, this feeling of being under the public gaze tended to be
exacerbated by their general experiences of dealing with the city council and
the sense of public humiliation that this can bring. It appeared to be an
experience mediated through their lack of cultural capital when dealing
with council officials, and the sense of powerlessness and inferiority that this
engenders. These themes are illustrated most graphically in the following
interview with two of the parents. Here, Jean is talking about her experience
of visiting the council's rent office on the estate:

Jean: The woman on reception is really nasty, isn't she? [...] She won't let you see them unless she's convinced and she tells you to tell her, in front of everybody, and if it's something personal you don't want to stand there and tell everybody what your business is. Well, you feel like a dog when you go down there, you're treated like shit really.

Cathy: Well, the whole estate's like this, I mean the maintenance depot's like that. I mean when the kids' dad walked out on me I didn't really want to tell the whole estate, but I had to go down when I wanted them to change my locks and that, and I had a big complaint that because I had to tell everyone and when I went to the estate office I had to tell everyone and it's not the sort of thing you want to discuss in front of everyone – the fact that, you know, the kids' dad's just walked out on you, you know, and it's not a thing that you want to discuss.

[...]

Jean: How can there be morale on the estate when you're treated like dirt?

All of these factors, then, appeared to encourage an experience of isolation for some of the women on the estate and to limit their ability to develop social networks through which they could gain help and support. This has arguably been compounded by the fact that many of those who have been rehoused on Manor Park have been separated from their family and friends, who still live on the satellite council estates. Other than one or two immediate friends, therefore, the social world for some of the women interviewed tended to be centred around their children. Lack of money and the restrictions that two or more very young children bring tend seriously to inhibit the mobility of a significant number of the parents in this study. Other than one playground opposite the school and next to the building where the playgroup is located, the only green areas where the parents could take their children were the courtyards on to which all maisonettes in the block faced.

For some, their maisonettes therefore represented the only social space they could retreat to and avoid the public gaze. With young children, however, this offered itself as a highly pressurised and stress-inducing environment. One parent, quoted earlier, talked of the depression she experienced for three years as a result of her housing situation. Another parent, quoted below, graphically illustrates the stress and anxiety she has experienced living alone with her children in a top-floor maisonette:

I'm trying to get the council to move me. Me doctor's wrote quite a number of letters about the stress it's caused me, with me son being hyperactive and living in an upstairs house, having nowhere to play. [...] Because of their age-groups I don't let them out on their own, I don't like them roaming around the estate on their own, they go out when I take them so it means when they're not at school, or I can't take them anywhere, they spend a lot of the time indoors.

This focus on the children and the home provides the context within which some of the women came to construct and value a specific form of femininity. Ironically it was one centred around the traditional patriarchal emphasis on domestic competence. The ability to rear your children successfully and to look after your home formed a significant aspect of the cultural capital striven for among these particular women. This is illustrated in the following quote from one parent who, in complaining about the work-sites created by the Estates Action building work and the trouble she faced trying to keep her children and house clean, highlights the sense of importance she gave to these things. As the conversation develops, it also draws attention to how success at parenting and the ability to control your children was used as a specific form of cultural capital with which to question the abilities of other mothers:

Cathy: And just at the minute the workmen are treating it as if it's just a building site – they forget people live here and we've put in claims for compensation for carpet and that, but, I mean, they've, like, dumped all that red sand and that, and of course kids head straight for it and it's not covered or anything, and she's [her daugher] ruined, like, two pairs of shorts just this weekend because once it gets in that's it, you can't get it out. It's just completely ruined clothes and everything else, and, I mean, the mud's just getting everywhere.

Jean: They don't secure the, they don't secure the/

Cathy: /Depot – I've seen kids in there a couple of times 'cos they've been trying to hot-wire the dumper trucks basically. [*laughs*]

Jean: They did one at the back of Connaught Close recently/

Cathy: /And driving it all around/

Jean: /Nearly smashed an old man's window with the dumper truck, and in the end they wedged it in between the black gates and ran off because they couldn't get it back out.

Cathy: Some of the parents, some of the kids are out, ten o'clock at night. There's two, I mean, they're only about eight, nine, and he runs around with a key round his neck, literally, so you know he's been left on his own to go in and out and, I mean, it was him, you say owt to him and it's just a mouthful of abuse.

It was, then, the practical difficulties and stresses that inevitably arise from raising young children in an environment like Manor Park that provided one possible context within which notions of femininity could be constructed more centrally around themes of motherhood and the practicalities of child-rearing. The ability to control your children, to make financial sacrifices for them and generally to keep your children and home clean and tidy were important aspects of the cultural capital of femininity for some of the women. However, as we have seen from some of the quotes above, these traditional patriarchal expectations can be extremely damaging to many of the women, leading to high levels of stress and depression. And it is arguable that the ability to be successful in this way was valued so highly precisely because these are almost impossible expectations within such an economic and social environment.

It is within this context, and the day-to-day demands that motherhood places on the body, that children became one particular focus through which some of the women express their femininity. For these particular women, therefore, the stylistic presentation of their children took on an important symbolic role in affirming their own mothering competence and feminine tastes and styles relating to men and women. A number of young children at the school, mostly Black and White but including some South Asian children, had their ears pierced, wore silver-plated necklaces or bracelets and/or were dressed in clothes such as short skirts, designer jeans, jackets and trainers, more associated with youths and young men/women than 5- and 6-year-old children. In some ways it could be argued that these children became representations of their mothers' own tastes and aspirations. It was a process also possibly representative of the conceptions of childhood held by some on the estate and what was perceived as the social and economic necessity that draws the transition into adulthood that much closer. These young mothers' lived experiences tended to encourage a world-view or habitus which spoke of the need to grow up quickly and to be street-wise by the time you have left school at 16. Rather than their children being seen as dressed inappropriately and reflecting the mother's own immaturity (which is overwhelmingly how the teachers saw it), it was offered by these particular women as an expression of their cultural competence and success at single parenthood, that could not only provide such stylish clothes but also illustrated how well their children were maturing.

It needs to be stressed again that this is necessarily a partial and incomplete account of these women's lives. My primary interest in interviewing parents was to deepen my understanding of their children's experiences of living on the estate. As such, the women who were interviewed here were never really given the space to express their more general desires and hopes. The above accounts should not be read, therefore, as implying that domestic competence is the only or even the main aspiration held by these women. Indeed, the emphasis they gave to their children's welfare could have been partly a reflection of what they felt it appropriate to say in my presence – a man they would obviously have connected with the school. Unfortunately, these were themes that I was unable to explore in any greater detail; it was not until the fieldwork had finished that I began to think about how the specific fashions valued by many of the children at East Avenue could be partly related to this particular aspect of their domestic environment. While the above account helps us, at least in part, to understand how fashion has become part of the cultural capital for some of the children, especially the girls, it needs to be remembered that the account also tends to falsely present the women in a rather flat, one-dimensional way, as being almost exclusively preoccupied with their homes and children.

RACISM AND SOCIAL RELATIONS ON MANOR PARK

What I have done so far is to sketch out, in a very broad way, specific aspects of masculine and feminine cultural forms as they have been constructed within the particular spatial and social context of the Manor Park estate. Of course, such cultural forms are also inherently racialised, especially within the context of a place like Manor Park which provides the site where a whole host of discourses on 'race', crime and the inner city are played out. In this last section, I want to explore the ways in which the discourses on 'race' introduced in the previous chapter come to inform and structure life on the Manor Park estate. In this sense I want to draw attention to the ways in which the experiences of the men and women living on the estate, as outlined above, come to be refracted and understood through the lens of 'race'. In doing this, the following sections will highlight the way in which the expression of racism on the estate is inherently gendered.

Living in fear: the South Asian population

The general sense of the decline of the community, experienced by many people on the estate in terms of both the underlying fear of violence and a sense of isolation, has partly come to be refracted through discourses on 'race'. As mentioned in the previous chapter, the arrival of many of the minority ethnic communities now resident in Workingham took place against the background of a range of discourses that spoke of the breakdown of the community, and specifically of inner-city areas, in relation to Black and South Asian immigration. The island mentality shared by some of those on the estate, as outlined earlier, ensured that such debates concerning the 'swamping' of Britain's inner cities were particularly acute for some of the residents of Manor Park. Moreover, the increasing numbers of Black and – especially – South Asian people moving on to the estate in recent years have tended to fuel these discourses. There was a tendency for South Asian people, particularly, to be discursively constituted as the living symbols of these changes. For some residents, their culturally and linguistically distinct presence came to symbolise the decline and break-up of the traditional community, and provided the medium through which the growing sense of isolation came to be understood. The fact that South Asian mothers were seen to stand together in the playground when waiting to collect their children, talking to each other in their own language, helped to consolidate and represent the isolation experienced by other parents. Moreover, the number of South Asian shops that appeared in the surrounding neighbourhoods, coupled with the dramatic rise in unemployment experienced by those living on Manor Park, provided the basis from which popular racist discourses could be invoked to blame 'the Pakis' for pinching 'our' jobs [*sic*].

It is against this background that we can come, at least in part, to understand the position of South Asian people living on the estate and their experiences of racism. Most of the South Asian parents interviewed talked of living in a continual state of fear on the estate, rendering many of its public spaces effectively 'out of bounds' for them. One mother told in an interview of how she had been attacked in a phone box quite recently. As her interpreter explained:

> About a few weeks back she was phoning to her mother-in-law from the telephone box. Whilst she was on the telephone, talking, about three boys aged 14, 15 years old just opened the phone box and said bad things, you know, used very foul language like 'fuck off!', a couple of bad words, and she just left the telephone and she just ran as soon as she could get out of it because she's abused all the time. They pick on [South Asian] women and victimise them.

Many of these South Asian women and their children also had experiences of being abused in the local playground, opposite the school. One mother told of how 10- and 11-year-old children 'throw stones and things when you take children to the park. Especially on [. . .] evenings and a Sunday. They'll say things, you know, shouting and throwing at you.' Another mother told of how one child from the school had come up and spat on her the previous day as she sat in the park. As she explained, he had done that 'because my little girl was on a slide and he didn't like that – to see us playing'.

Some South Asian women found themselves liable to experience racial abuse even when they were simply walking through the estate. The following incident, as explained through an interpreter, not only illustrates this but also alludes to the involvement of children from the school in these racist incidents. This is a theme that I will return to shortly:

> Some of these children are children from our schools – they're very young – 5, 6, 7. They'll sort of imitate, they'll act and they'll call bad names, you know, they'll shout it out, they'll follow her when

she going, when she going anywhere. And they've learnt a few words as well, some of the children, in Gujerati as well. They've sort of, some of these children have attended the Gujerati classes with Mr Chohan [*section 11 teacher at the school*] so they've learnt a few words, you see, good and bad. And mum's ever so frightened to, for any of these to go out, you see, how can you go out of your home with things like this – whenever you go out you're in fear all of the time.

A number of the South Asian parents also talked about how they have experienced racist abuse at home. One woman, who worked nights, talked of how she had been victimised by her neighbours just the night before, and how she is fearful of leaving her house alone at night:

Like last night, I go to work at ten past nine. I was coming from the stairs and two lads, they were next-door neighbour, and they are a bit like that, they went downstairs, I knew it must be them – I saw them going down, and they must have left a box of matches, something lit inside the matches – a cigarette end – I came down a few steps and the box of matches all of a sudden went 'fume' like, you see [. . .] they probably left it there on the stairs and, er, I don't speak to them, I don't even talk to them. I just say hello and that's it. Because I know I work nights and if something's going to happen it's bound to happen in the night, you see, when I'm not there.

Another South Asian mother told of how some of her neighbours had been victimising her and, as she explained, were: 'nicking milk bottles, nicking my door mats every time I bought them. Putting shit through my door, er, pissing at my doorstep, all sorts of stuff.' I asked her whether it was just her neighbours and she replied:

Reshma: No, quite a few kids as well beating Preena [*her daughter*] up every time she went downstairs to play. Quite a few. I couldn't see who they were 'cos when they hit her she'd come up to tell me but by the time I'd got downstairs they'd be gone. She used to come up with bruises and all sorts of things.

PC: So what would they do?

Reshma: Hit her and all sorts of thing. Yeah, bricks, you know, stones, push her over, she'd come home with cut knees and everything. Everybody thought at school that I was beating her up every day. I wasn't, you know. The council wouldn't believe me, the school wouldn't believe me, so where does it leave you? You're lumbered with it at the end of the day, ain't it? You like it or you lump it.

Life on Manor Park for a significant proportion of the South Asian residents was therefore often experienced as one of fear and racist abuse. This provides an example of the way in which national discourses on 'race', reproduced within the field of politics, have come to be taken up, reworked and reproduced on the Manor Park estate. What is also important to stress, however, is the central involvement of some of the children in these racist incidents – often children from East Avenue Primary School. It therefore tends to illustrate the way that these broader discourses can at times encourage adults to make sense of their experiences in certain ways, and also how this discursive framework relating to the South Asian 'Other' can be adopted and reproduced by the children themselves. It forms an important backdrop, as will be seen in the following chapters, for understanding how these discourses are appropriated and reworked again within the young children's peer-group relations, to help some of them make sense of their particular concerns and experiences.

The criminalised 'Other': Black people on the estate

For some of the Black people living on the estate, theirs was an experience of racism that was very different from that outlined in relation to South Asian people. At one level, as was also found by Back (1993) in his study of Black and White youth, the widespread and insidious nature of racist abuse between some of the Black and White men was overcome through the development of a variation of what Cohen (1988) referred to as a 'nationalism of the neighbourhood' (see also Westwood 1990). Here, racist abuse and violence were transcended through the development of friendship networks between these Black and White young men, based around an exclusive restructuring of the experience of life on the estate. This was possibly aided by the cultural capital of Black cultural forms generally, and especially the dominant discourses around Black masculinity that tended to construct an image of Black men as physical, athletic and sexual. On an estate like Manor Park, which tended to be experienced by some through the discourses on violence outlined earlier, this discursive construction of the Black man as quintessentially masculine provided him with a certain degree of symbolic capital among his male peers.

However, it was this very construction of Black men as quintessentially masculine that possibly also drew out the insecurities of some young White men, who arguably found that their own sense of masculinity was threatened by their presence (Mac an Ghaill 1994; Sewell 1995, 1997). It was possibly for this reason that a number of Black men had been attacked at night by groups of White men as they walked through the estate. As one of the Black women explained:

I mean, it's just like, you know, like, after eight o'clock at night you don't usually come out, you know, you get your 'Black this an' that'. You know Simon's mum [*Black child at school*], her husband got chased by some guys, just walking along minding his own business. If they catch you they beat you up, take your money, take your jewellery, whatever, they take your clothes an' all.

It could be argued that this sense of threat tended to be compounded for some of these White men by the thought of Black men being in a relationship with White women. This could possibly explain the harassment experienced by the following White woman, who had a Black child. As she explained:

I did have a few problems a few months ago where there was somebody, I couldn't find out who it was, as you go, when you walk up the stairs the blocks have got railings all along and they were sticking, stringing chewing gum all along the railings and covering my spy-hole with it. They did it when I was in the house [. . .] obviously the kids running up the stairs and holding on to the railings have got it all over their hands, clothes and [. . .] it was definitely done on purpose and the way it was strung along, all the way along the railing and down some of the bars so, it was definitely done on purpose.

What emerges from this is the gendered aspect of racism on Manor Park and the way that specific discourses on 'race' can be developed through some men's particular forms of masculine habitus. Moreover, it could be argued that the more general discourses on Black criminality have come to be reworked and reproduced on the estate, where the specific site of Manor Park and the levels of violence and crime that have come to be associated with it have, in turn, been reconstructed and understood for some through the presence of Black people. As we saw in the previous chapter, in some ways Black people have come to represent the folk-devils who are perceived to be behind the decline in law and order, the undermining of respect for one another and the general decline in community spirit (Hall *et al.* 1978; Gilroy 1982, 1987). This is illustrated in the following quote, taken from an interview with the police officer responsible for community policing on Manor Park. While drug dealing on the estate has been engaged in by White and Black men alike, we can see the way that the officer firmly comes to define this as a Black problem. Notice, too, the evocation of broader racist themes as she talks of how they like 'hanging around [. . .] in the sun':

Drugs, drug dealing, a big problem [. . .] It's mainly your 18 to 25 [year-old] West Indian male on Munster Road, quite blatantly. I say, they're not dealing blatantly, what they're doing is they're hanging around the streets, sitting round the streets in the sun, pulling up in cars. They're not committing any offences that I can actually deal with them for. I know that they're setting up drug deals. I'm quite aware that if I had a camera or some other way of doing observations, unobserved on the Munster Road, I'd no doubt see little packages changing hands, er, that sort of thing. When it comes down to me just walking through, they commit no offences. It's no offence any more. I mean, we haven't got these 'suss' laws any more, or loitering with intent laws any more, that we can move people on, so the shopkeepers can whinge as much as they want but there's nothing I can do.

This construction by some of the police of all Black people as criminals had the effect of further inhibiting their ability to walk through the estate, especially at night. As one Black woman explained when asked about the police:

If you're Black, you're a druggie, ain't ya? [. . .] That's just how they [*the police*] are. Or, if you're out late, you're a prostitute – you can't be visiting somebody and go home at midnight unless you're with someone. [. . .] 'Cos if I'm baby-sitting for Marcia I run from Marcia's house to my house, it's only round the corner but I run. Because I'll get stopped by, you'll get cars pulling up, you know, crawling next to ya, or, if you're walking on the other side of the road, then they'll cross the road, so you'll cross over and they cross over – so I just run! [. . .] It's just the fear that you're going to get stopped.

For some living and/or working on Manor Park, the presence of Black people on the estate therefore came, within specific contexts, to represent a threat – whether a threat to their personal safety, to the community spirit as a whole or (especially if they are male) to their own conception of themselves. It is in this respect that the general problems experienced by residents on the estate can, at times, be reinterpreted and refracted through the lens of 'race'. One mother talked of how an elderly man living in the maisonette below her was being continually disturbed by children. While he would challenge them whenever he could, he would particularly pick out her own younger Black children, who were not involved, and direct his anger against them as they passed his flat. As she explained:

There's, erm, there's an elderly gentleman, White, who lives in the same block as me and he's downstairs by the door you use to come in and out of the block. And if the kids run downstairs before me and run out the block he'll stick his head out the door and tell them to 'fuck off, you little Black bastards!' and things like that, so the police are prosecuting him at the moment for it. [. . .] It's mainly racist remarks when they run by his window as they're coming into the block [. . .] it just seems to be with the little kids.

CONCLUSIONS

We have seen in this chapter how national political discourses on 'race' and the inner city have not only come to influence and shape social relations on the Manor Park estate but have also had an impact upon the identities of the women and men living there. Within this, I have made it clear that this is not meant to be a representative or comprehensive account of life on the estate. Rather, I have written the chapter largely in retrospect, with a number of themes and concerns in mind that will emerge in the following chapters. It is therefore with regard to these that this chapter should ultimately be understood. In this sense I have drawn attention to four basic elements of direct relevance to the chapters to follow. First, I have highlighted the existence of discourses on violence, their predominance within the folklore of the estate and the way that these provide the backdrop against which some boys and men tend to develop their masculine identities. Second, the chapter has highlighted the sense of isolation experienced by many single mothers on the estate and the way they have come to express their sense of femininity through the stylistic presentation of their children. Third, I have drawn attention to the tendency for South Asian people to be constructed as the 'Other' and scapegoated for communal decline through persistent acts of racial abuse; and finally, the chapter has highlighted the tendency for Black people on the estate to be constituted as a 'threat', principally to law and order but also, in relation to some White men, to their sense of masculine identity. As will now be seen in the following chapters, these are all themes that re-emerge, albeit in differing forms, in the context of the school and the young children's peer-group relations.

5

TEACHER DISCOURSES AND EAST AVENUE PRIMARY SCHOOL

It would be wrong to assume that the national political discourses on education outlined previously are uncritically taken up and implemented by each and every school in a uniform way. Any particular school is located within a complex web of competing demands. East Avenue Primary School is no exception to this. As we have seen in the previous chapter, it is located in what has become perceived as a 'rough' inner-city area. Moreover, it is an area that is ethnically diverse and experiencing significant levels of racist incidents. The children at East Avenue, and for that matter their parents, are therefore felt to have specific needs and present particular demands upon the school. Any national debates and policies on education will therefore need to be read and reinterpreted through these local concerns. How the teaching staff at East Avenue respond to the national attacks on progressivism and on multicultural/anti-racist education can thus only be understood through an appreciation of their experiences of working at the school and the particular demands this places on them.

And yet, few ethnographic studies of schools have sought to understand how particular locales play such a pivotal role in influencing and shaping the way schools interpret and implement national educational policies. As we will see with East Avenue, however, the particular ethos of the school and the specific pedagogical priorities that have been identified cannot be understood without this local context. In particular, following a brief description of the school, the chapter will look at how the Manor Park estate provides one important context within which the two principal pedagogical roles – of teaching and discipline – have come to be negotiated by many of the teachers at the school. The chapter will then explore how multiculturalism is addressed within the school, before finally offering a brief overview of the three infant teachers whose classes form the basic focus of the following four chapters.

As with the previous chapters, this chapter has largely been written with the later chapters in mind. It draws attention only to those features of the school which help to contextualise the young children's peer-group relations. It should therefore not be read as a representative nor comprehensive account of the experiences, strategies and styles of teachers at East Avenue. These have been more than adequately covered elsewhere, and will be tangentially referred to only as and when appropriate (see Woods 1990).

EAST AVENUE PRIMARY SCHOOL

East Avenue is a relatively large primary school, housing three nursery classes and twelve infant (Years 1 and 2) and junior (Years 3 to 6) classes. There were 407 children on roll at the beginning of the autumn term 1992, with 132 of these representing either full- or part-time nursery places. Overall, of the children on roll at the beginning of this term, almost half were White, with approximately a quarter being Black and South Asian respectively. Of those who were South Asian, the vast majority were Gujerati-speaking. As regards their religion, around two-thirds of these were Hindu and the remaining third were Muslim. Only two children in the school during this time were Sikhs.

In relation to the school staff, the majority of the teachers and classroom support staff were White. The only minority ethnic staff were Mr Chohan, the full-time co-ordinator of Section 11 staff at the school, Mrs Kotecha, a full-time nursery teacher, and Mrs Mistry, the school's part-time home/school liaison officer. In addition to Mr Redmond, the headteacher, and Mr Chohan, there were only three other male members of staff. One was an infant teacher while the other two were junior teachers. One of these latter two, Mr Pearson, was also the deputy head.

All pre-school children living on the estate were offered a full-time place in one of the three nursery classes for at least one term immediately before entering the Infants. Most of these children would have also attended the nursery on a part-time basis (either every morning or afternoon per week during term-time) for either one or two terms prior to becoming full time. The three reception/Year 1 classes at East Avenue form the focus of the present research. Table 5.1 sets out the number of children at both the start and end of the 1992/3 academic year by gender and ethnicity. Children would move into one of these classes from the nursery at the beginning of the term following their fifth birthday. Typically, this meant that each of the three classes would have intakes of between two and four children at the start of the spring and summer terms. Children would then spend a minimum of three terms in that class before moving up to one of the two Year 2 classes at the end of the summer term. As a consequence, while some children would enter one of the reception/Year 1 classes at the start of the autumn term and spend three terms there before moving up to one of the Year 2 classes, other children, entering the class at the start of the spring term in January, would spend five terms there before moving up to Year 2. Prior to this particular academic year, there had been four reception/Year 1

Table 5.1 Number of children in the three sample classes by gender and ethnicity

	White		Black		South Asian		Total	
Ms Patterson								
Girls	4	(9)	2	(1)	1	(1)	7	(11)
Boys	6	(7)	2	(3)	4	(3)	12	(13)
Total	10	(16)	4	(4)	5	(4)	19	(24)
Mrs Brogan								
Girls	8	(6)	1	(5)	1	(3)	10	(14)
Boys	6	(6)	3	(2)	1	(3)	10	(11)
Total	14	(12)	4	(7)	2	(6)	20	(25)
Mrs Scott								
Girls	3	(6)	3	(4)	4	(5)	10	(15)
Boys	4	(7)	3	(3)	1	(2)	8	(12)
Total	7	(13)	6	(7)	5	(7)	18	(27)

Note: Numbers on the left of each column relate to the start of the autumn term 1992, those in parentheses relate to the summer term 1993.

classes and two Year 2 classes. However, because of the growing numbers of Year 2 children, Mr Wallace's reception class began the academic year in which the fieldwork took place with a vertically grouped Year 1/Year 2 class. Together with six infant classes, there were also six junior classes – two parallel classes for Years 3 and 4 and two single classes for Years 5 and 6 – indicative of the disproportionately younger population living on the Manor Park estate.

THE SOCIAL ASPECTS OF TEACHING AT EAST AVENUE

As has been argued elsewhere, the teacher's role can be understood to contain two principal functions, teaching and discipline (Pollard 1985; Woods 1990). While these two are integrally related, this division provides a useful way of organising the data in relation to teacher discourses at East Avenue. This and the following section will therefore explore how some of the teachers in the present study have come to negotiate their roles partly within the context provided by the Manor Park estate. In this section I want to focus on the teaching role. As we will see, it appears that the more general discourses on poverty and single parenthood have tended to encourage many of the teachers to increase the social aspects of their teaching.

Teacher discourses and the parental role

To some degree, all schools can be said to adopt some form of social or moral role in relation to their children. For the primary school, and infant classes more specifically, it has been argued that the influence of this is much more pronounced, as teachers not only have a legal responsibility but are also more inclined to adopt the position of 'surrogate mother' in relation to their role in the child's 'primary socialisation' (Berger and Luckmann 1967; Woods 1990). Here, as a number of ethnographic studies of primary schools have suggested, the infant classroom, with its home corner, toys, building and other educational equipment, displays on the wall and carpet area, can be seen as largely reminiscent of the early home environment and the relationship between mother and child (King 1978; Pollard 1985). It could possibly be argued that it is because of this distinctly gendered and feminised environment that women are over-represented as teachers in infant classes.

At East Avenue, however, there appeared to be a tendency for this parental role to be far more pronounced, as many of the teachers came to redefine their teaching role at least in part through their experiences of working on the Manor Park estate (see also Skelton 1997). Here, the dominant discursive themes highlighted in the previous chapters in relation to the inner city and familial and communal decline can be found in the following quote from an interview with one member of staff, whose perceptions of the estate and the parents and children living there was representative of many of the teachers' views:

> When I first came they [the children] were very poor, they all came from very poor families but they had double parents, mothers and fathers, and they had a few standards. I mean, they were rough and ready but the parents did care about them. A lot of them were dirty, were not very clean and not in the beautiful clothes they wear now, but there was a home, they came from a home where they felt that they were loved, and they weren't half as bad as they are now. Gradually the whole estate has changed, so you've got all these single parents and problem families, and the way I look at it is the parents have got all these problems themselves, they haven't got time to cope with the children's problems, in fact I don't think they realise that the children have problems or that they've got to do anything to instil discipline or moral values or any of those things – they don't realise that that is their job.

What is interesting about the above quote is the way in which the present children and parents on the estate were discussed against the backdrop of discourses on the traditional working class. Here, I want to suggest that the estate, through its built environment, has come to symbolise for some the arrival of a 'new' poor, with the rows upon rows of terraced housing, so reminiscent of working-class community spirit and solidarity, giving way to high-rise tower blocks and grey shabby maisonettes that tend to speak of a new, isolated, insular and self-centred population. Through many of the interviews with the teachers at the school, it became apparent that although the vast majority were quite willing to accept and understand the predicament of these young parents, in a significant minority of teacher accounts there was a distinct undercurrent to these discourses, that constructed a more 'undeserving poor' (Mann 1992; Morris 1994).

In this, it is interesting to note how the struggles and commitment of the young mothers, as discussed in the previous chapter, to dress their children in good, fashionable clothes, were reinterpreted by many of these particular teachers as a sign of selfishness and immaturity. As we can see in the quote above, the fact that these young mothers were perceived as being less poor (i.e. they can afford 'beautiful clothes' for their children) made it even less excusable that they allegedly spent little time either socially or educationally with their children. At least the old traditional working class, who were that much poorer and struggling to 'make ends meet', still found time to love and care for their children. This theme in relation to immature and selfish young single mothers is developed by Mrs Woods, head of the nursery department:

> We've got more single parents in the school now, more broken homes. [. . .] These mothers love their babies. When a mother brings her baby into school it's beautifully kept, really loved and taken care of. Once they get past the 2-year-old stage they get more of a nuisance value and they haven't the patience with them, and they get behavioural problems and they don't know how to deal with them. They have very poor parenting skills.

For a significant number of the teachers at East Avenue, their perception of young mothers having very poor parenting skills and little commitment to their children appeared to encourage them to increase the social aspects of their teaching role, in compensation for these 'inadequacies' [sic]. As the following quote, taken from an interview with Mrs Campbell, illustrates, this emerging role was perceived by some of the teachers as becoming 'surrogate parents':

> We're having to give them what the parents aren't giving them – the security, the continuity and, well, just the love and under-standing and listening to the children [. . .] and understanding them and realising their needs. We've got such a short time in the

day that we've got to try and be mother, father, teacher and nurse all in one go.

Moreover, for some of the older female staff, this parental role was often extended to incorporate the young mothers themselves. As Mrs Scott, one of the three reception/Year 1 infant teachers, explained: 'I think it helps me now I'm older because I'm like a granny; I'm the same age as a granny [. . .] and the mums are often only 19 or 20 [. . .] Here you feel like a mother to all of them.'

Accounting for the parental role

It is important to stress that this emphasis made by many of the teachers on the social aspects of their teaching role was intricately bound up with the teachers' material experiences. It was the day-to-day problems they faced in trying to motivate and teach a large number of children while also trying to keep order that arguably provided an important context within which many teachers were constantly forced to renegotiate and make sense of their teaching role. Mrs Sharpe, for instance, spoke of how she had to prioritise her social role at times over her academic one, and made reference to how she regretted the fact that she could no longer always 'send children up' to the Infants able to read. In this sense, it could be argued that the children that leave the nursery and enter the Infants became living testimonies to the teaching competence of the nursery staff. The fact that they were not 'producing' what they felt was an adequate number of children who could read appeared to add that much more immediacy to the need to make sense of and explain that perceived 'failure'.

Moreover, it could be argued that the imposition of the National Curriculum, in drawing attention to and emphasising, much more explicitly than ever before, the attainment targets that children should have reached by the time they leave particular classes, had the effect of exacerbating these concerns for many teachers. In essence it provided an essentially public yard-stick against which their teaching competencies could be measured. It appeared, therefore, that children provided living testimonies to the professional success of a teacher. This can be illustrated with reference to the three infant classes at the heart of the present study. Here, the three teachers felt that they were constantly being judged by both the junior and the nursery staff. To a certain extent this was true. The following comments by Mr Wilson, a junior teacher, were not dissimilar to many of those uttered to me by other junior staff about the infant classes:

I just feel that lower down the school they're mollycoddled a lot more; they're not given over to find stuff for themselves, and if they're given a task everything's presented to them. They sit down, don't have to sharpen their own pencils, their rubber's there, every-thing's given to them. They're not given that degree of, 'OK, I need to do this, what do I need? Where can I find it?'

Conversely, for many of the nursery staff it was felt that the infant classes lacked appropriate discipline, as gauged by the perceived changes in behaviour of their children once they were 'sent up' to the Infants. As Mrs Deakin, a nursery teacher, argued:

We try and enforce when they go out they walk in a line and they hold hands, and when they walk upstairs in single file on the left-hand side, all that sort of thing, and when they get to 5 and they go over there [*i.e. to the Infants in the main building*] it all seems to go to pot!

Arguably, both of these quotes speak as much of the problems and pres-sures felt by these two teachers and their need to reassert their own professional competence as of anything else. However, general order and discipline was something, as will be seen shortly, of which infant teachers were acutely aware. And it was here that some of the infant teachers drew upon the broader discourses on the inner city found within the estate to make sense of their struggles. This can be seen in the following comments, for instance, made by Mrs Scott. They were made following an incident in the sports hall, significantly viewed by a number of other teachers, where a large proportion of her children were excessively noisy and 'ran wild' in the main hall prior to a PE lesson. In attempting to explain their behaviour, she said:

If you take them up to the hall upstairs and it's empty, they – a lot of them – will just run round. [. . .] I think it may be because they're confined at home possibly, in flats, aren't they, confined a lot. Some of them aren't allowed to play out much.

'Free time' and teaching the 3Rs

This emphasis on the social/parental role among the infant teachers appeared to be most commonly expressed in the three sample classes (with the partial exception of Ms Patterson)[1] through the frequent use of significant periods of 'free time'. These were periods during which the children were free to choose an activity, from playing in the home corner to drawing, reading or playing with the construction toys. It was not wholly confined to the infant classes, however. According to many teachers, it provided an important space for the children, not always available at home, where they could learn through play. As one teacher argued:

> A lot of the children come in and you find out parents haven't really talked to them. We've got one child at the moment whose mother just says, 'Right, go on in,' when the child comes home from school, puts the telly on and then she goes, the child says she has a fag in the kitchen, you know, she doesn't play with them. There are children in here who don't have any toys at home [. . .] the only time they get to play is at school.

The teachers' use of free time was not only a valuable and important educational strategy. For some it appeared to be an essential strategy in helping them, at times, to avoid the constant struggle to maintain children's interest in academic matters while also presenting an impression to the outside observer that their children were 'busy' and actively engaged (Sharp and Green 1975). It could be argued that it has become part of some of the teachers' habitus, as it became a taken-for-granted part of their teaching practice.

However, this emphasis on the parental role did not simply lead to a 'low-achievement orientation', as Denscombe (1980, 1985) found in his own work where the low expectations of the children's performance held by the teacher, together with the low academic aspirations of the children themselves, became mutually reinforcing. As discussed earlier, especially at a time when the National Curriculum, with its attainment targets, provided a more public and explicit set of yardsticks by which to judge the competence of individual teachers in relation to their children's progress, there remained an emphasis on academic achievement.

One of the ways in which many teachers tried to balance their parental role and use of free time with that of their more 'traditional' academic responsibilities associated with teaching was in concentrating on the '3Rs' of reading, writing and arithmetic. This was certainly the impression gained by Mr Wallace, a Year 1/2 infant teacher, when he first started teaching at East Avenue. As he explained, he initially found that:

> The children were able to achieve more than I thought in several areas. They were more advanced in areas of written work and reading and some number areas. I think that perhaps the methods of teaching at this school are quite structured and based around the 3Rs, quite tight structure. So perhaps in the formal subjects children were further advanced than I thought and perhaps in other areas the children were less advanced, in terms of their language and their understanding and their listening skills.

It could be argued that this focus on 'the basics' enabled teachers to 'produce' and 'send up' children to the Juniors who were *at least* numerate and literate. Moreover, the frequent use of free time not only maintained an air of 'busyness' in the classroom but enabled some of the teachers to conserve the time and energy that they would otherwise have needed, constantly trying to motivate what was perceived to be the 'difficult' minority of children in relation to formal written work. In turn, this was time that they could use to concentrate on the small number of children who did appear to excel in the class. Within the perceived gaze of teaching colleagues, these children appeared to perform an important role in re-affirming the teacher's competence. In this, many teachers would from time to time send a child to another teacher to show them how good their work was, while also more generally using the presentation of merit stickers at Birthday Assemblies to elaborate upon how well that particular child had done under their supervision.

What is interesting from this is that, while this emphasis on the 'basics' tended to resonate quite closely with the national political discourses outlined in Chapter 3, for many of the teachers it did not appear to be primarily influenced by them. What this shows is the importance of specific localities in providing the medium through which such discourses can often be refracted and reworked. Many of the teachers' arrival at a focus on the '3Rs' was therefore not because of any fundamental disagreement with progressive teaching methods (which, incidentally, they still made frequent use of through their emphasis on free time) but because of the articulation of a number of discourses on the inner city and single parenthood that the teachers had reproduced and embedded within their own experiences.

East Avenue: the family they never had

These discourses, appropriated and reworked by teachers on the inner city and familial decline, also appeared to have found expression through the broader organisation and structures of the school that formed the basic field in which the teachers were located. In this sense it could be argued that the school as an institution came to represent the children's surrogate family. The main weekly assembly, for example, held on Thursday mornings and attended by all children and teachers at the school, including the nurseries, was named 'Family Gathering', while the Friday morning joint infant and nursery assembly, held in the hall on the ground floor, was called 'Birthday Assembly'. Here it appeared as if the school was actively trying to create a 'family' environment and to offer the children the stable, consistent and secure family that they had arguably missed out on. The current structure and distribution of male and female staff at the school tended to add to this traditional family approach. The headteacher, Mr Redmond, led the main Family Gathering assembly. It was here, with the whole school gathered, that he attempted to set the ethos of the school through weekly talks and stories with moral themes. While the general academic themes of hard work, co-operation and consistency were stressed from time to time, the most prominent and recurring theme was that of tolerance, mutual respect and friendship.

Birthday Assemblies were led by the head of the Infants, Mrs Christie, with both infant and nursery children and teachers attending. They were held in the smaller hall on the ground floor and while they were similar to Family Gatherings in that they also contained a moral message and were structured around songs, there were important differences. The first, and most immediate, was that Birthday Assemblies were far more personalised and inclusive of the children. All children were encouraged to take their turn in the 'band' that stood at the front with drums, tambourines and triangles, accompanying the songs. Stickers were given out to two or three children nominated by their teacher from each class for good work or behaviour. Most importantly, every child at the time of their birthday was called to the front, given a present of sweets and sung to by the rest of the assembly. This personal, more intimate atmosphere was aided by the smaller size of the hall.

Through its two principal assemblies, therefore, it could possibly be argued that the school had recreated the traditional family with the father and mother role represented by these two weekly gatherings. In summary, the symbolic role of the 'father', played by the headteacher Mr Redmond, appeared to be expressed most directly through Family Gathering. He, in effect, led the family of East Avenue and was in a more formal and public position to set the values, rules and general ethos expected of his children. In contrast, Birthday Assembly appeared to represent the institutional expression of the 'mother' of the family, Mrs Christie, who catered more directly to the emotional and personal needs of the children. In many ways these assemblies could be interpreted as progressively representing the specific institutional expression of the more general discourses on the inner city and single parenthood that were being reproduced by the teaching staff.

THE MAINTENANCE OF DISCIPLINE AND ORDER AT EAST AVENUE

Orchestrating order in the classroom

From the foregoing discussion, it can be seen how the second main characteristic of the teaching role – that of the maintenance of discipline and control – is largely inseparable from the teaching role (see also Denscombe 1980; Woods 1990). In many ways it can be argued that the two go hand in hand, as good teachers are seen to be able to interest and motivate their children, which then, by default, ensures order. One aspect of the cultural capital associated with a good teacher that we can possibly gain from this, therefore, is the successful organisation of the classroom. This involves, as

Woods (1990: 69) terms it, the 'orchestration' of the class, so that children are kept busy and relatively quiet without the teacher having to resort to shouting. The frequency with which teachers at East Avenue did resort to shouting was perceived among many of their colleagues as indicative of their lack of competence in the classroom and, ultimately, their loss of control. Through interviews with the teachers it was apparent that there was, as a result, a general sense of self-consciousness concerning the frequency with which they resorted to shouting.

Not only was shouting perceived by many as a public admission of failure, but its frequent use was also physically draining and, in the long term, arguably ineffective. The cultural capital required to prevent this appeared therefore to revolve around a teacher's ability to orchestrate her/his classroom socially, spatially and temporally so as to reduce problems of conflict with and between children and thus to maintain order (see Giddens 1985). We have seen one particular example of this in the widespread use of free time. This appeared to significantly reduce the levels of conflict that would possibly otherwise have emerged in attempts to motivate children to concentrate on written work for the whole of the day. Another common strategy evident in the three sample classes appeared to develop within the continued influence of the traditional developmental models of childhood. Here it was generally felt that young children had low attention spans and self-discipline and therefore were in need of constant supervision and a highly ordered, structured environment. At East Avenue, however, given many teachers' perceptions that parents had failed to socialise their children adequately, this arguably tended to give even more prominence to the need for a structured day.

Possibly as a result of this perceived need for structure, the school day was extremely fragmented. Temporally, the classes were very ordered, with the day separated into many segments, each signalling a different activity (see also Pollard 1985; Hartley 1985). In all three infant classes the children were therefore prevented from spending too much time on any one activity. According to some of the teachers, this helped to prevent the children either getting bored or becoming so familiar with that particular environment that they were able to learn and develop strategies of avoidance and (possibly) resistance. The temporal segmentation of the day was also compounded spatially in terms of various activities taking place in different parts of the school.

The gendered nature of order and control

This movement between various spatial locations at particular times of the day involved a notable degree of classroom management for the teachers. Whether it was taking the class to the toilet, to the cloakroom, outside to the playground or generally co-ordinating children within the classroom, various strategies were required to enable the practical management and control of large classes. As Clarricoates (1981) among many others has found, one of the principal ways of organising this was through gender, where many of the daily routines of classroom life, such as those listed above, were organised separately for boys and girls.

At East Avenue, gender would also, at times, influence the allocation of types of work and other activities to particular children in the classroom. Here, as discussed earlier, part of the teachers' cultural capital could be seen in terms of their ability to engage the children and keep them busy. However, in trying to set work on a whole class basis, this required a lot of forward planning. As Mrs Brogan explained:

> The main thing is to have lots of work, be prepared. Children work, they all work at different speeds and a lot of them, you give them something that you hope would take them fifteen, twenty minutes, and they come back after two or three minutes and say they've finished it. Really it's just, have lots of things up your sleeve.

However, this is not always strictly possible, given the numbers of children to control and the pressures that this inevitably brings. Within the often stressful environment of the classroom, with the multitude of demands placed upon the teacher at any one time, the allocation of extra work to particular children can often take place on a rather ad hoc and pragmatic basis. And it is here, through the teacher's habitus, that it appeared that some teachers were more likely to draw upon their own set of taken-for-granted assumptions about gender, and to allocate different work and activities to boys and girls. These assumptions can be illustrated by the following quote, also from Mrs Brogan:

> The boys, they generally seem to be very silly, not all of them but most of them in this class are silly, they don't concentrate so much when they're working. Any sort of written work, I usually get better results from girls, and if I had a table with colourings on it would be the girls that would go and sit at it, not the boys, they go for the Lego.

These assumptions were largely representative of those held by many of the teachers, to varying degrees, of girls being more creative while boys were seen as more competent at number work. At times when teachers are extremely busy, they need to know that the extra work they give to particular children will keep them occupied and, moreover, keep them engaged for a sufficient period of time. And it is here that assumptions about preferences of boys and girls for specific subjects and activities can be influential. At East Avenue, for example, some teachers were found to be inclined to encourage girls to do more 'creative' work, whether that was writing or drawing, while boys were slightly more likely to be encouraged to do more practical work on the computer or play with specific toys.

It is also interesting to note how some of the teachers' perceptions of order and discipline were also gendered. Here, as alluded to by Mrs Brogan in the quote above, boys were often seen as more disruptive and a greater threat to classroom order and stability. This was also evident in the playground, where this perception of boys' greater tendency to present behavioural problems appeared to encourage specific strategies aimed particularly at them. One of the most prominent of these, as will be discussed later and in the following chapters, was football. This tended to be used as a specific form of control for the boys at playtimes, when a number of footballs were given out, all to boys, and was seen by many teachers as a means of both occupying and spatially controlling a significant minority of boys who would otherwise, it was argued, probably be quite disruptive. As Mrs Phillips, one of the ancillaries, remarked, 'It stops them from fighting each other [and] gives them something to concentrate on.' For girls, because of their perceived passivity, there was remarkably less time given specifically to encouraging them to play particular games. However, on a few occasions Mrs Pringle, another ancillary, would be seen to organise skipping games with a large number of girls, usually between fifteen and twenty. This gendering of order and control within the school will be explored further in the following chapters, in terms of its particular effects upon the development of children's identities.

Surveillance, control and the racialisation of discipline

This social, spatial and temporal structuring of the school environment enabled many teachers at East Avenue to adopt the relatively more passive and removed disciplinary role of surveillance. Particular times of the day, together with the specific areas of the school within which the child was located, acted to signify what was considered appropriate behaviour (see also Pollard 1985). Other than in the playground, children were not allowed to get up and walk around at will. Whether it was a school assembly, a PE lesson or an activity in the classroom, there were specific spaces where a child should stand or sit and adopt a particular demeanour. This was in stark contrast to the teacher, however, who was able to move around particular spaces, at any time, with relative freedom (Giddens 1985). Indeed, it was precisely the action of the teacher in walking around the tables in the classroom where the children sat, or hovering around the back and sides of assemblies, that appeared to create a constant sense of surveillance among some of the children.

The ultimate power invested in such an approach appeared to be the way it encouraged a degree of self-regulation among the children. After all, many of the children were, at times, never totally sure whether the teacher's eye was on them or not. The headteacher, who stood at the front of Family Gathering, therefore played an important surveillance role (Foucault 1979). His constant gaze, together with his intermittent naming and, sometimes, public humiliation of specific children who were not paying attention or who were talking, appeared to be enough for most of the others to be constantly aware of his presence and gaze. Similarly in the classroom: with the teacher sitting in a strategic position within the room, it was often enough for her simply to stop talking and momentarily stare at the 'offending' child not only to encourage that child to return to their task at hand, but also to signal the teacher's presence to the other children.

Moreover, many teachers also encouraged the children to adopt a surveillance role. These teachers would be seen regularly encouraging the children to be their 'eyes and ears' and so to increase the effectiveness of their gaze. This is illustrated in the following quote taken from Mrs Christie, who was addressing a Birthday Assembly. She was bringing to a close a long discussion concerning the increasing number of incidents involving children breaking branches and ripping up plants in the playing field. Here, we also see the way that the collective notion of the 'family' at East Avenue was used to signal that these were crimes against 'all of us':

I think we've all got the message; if we're going to have a lovely set of school grounds we have got to look after them. You have got to look after them [. . .] if you see someone doing something ever so silly or awful [. . .] you should go and tell somebody straight away so that we can do something to stop it.

Indeed, the collective sense of 'shame' that this episode appeared to create seemed to have encouraged a number of children eagerly to thrust their hands in the air and offer the names of those involved to the teacher.

It would be wrong to assume from the above discussion, however, that the way in which the school was organised and the strategies of surveillance adopted and encouraged by the teaching staff were wholly successful. One of the main themes to be derived from the following chapters is the agency and creativity of the young children themselves in responding to, subverting and resisting the dominant modes of surveillance and control developed within the school. The children at East Avenue were, in this sense, what Riseborough (1985) referred to as 'critical reality definers' (see also Nias 1984; Woods 1990); their actions were integral in shaping the nature and form of teacher practices.

Teachers were, therefore, often required to intervene directly in terms of the maintenance of order. Obviously it would be impossible for them to address every specific misdemeanour or to discipline each and every child who had been 'naughty'. Instead, as touched upon above, many teachers aimed to reinstate order and control through re-emphasising their 'omni-science' (Wolpe 1988; Woods 1990: 66). It often appeared to be through the strategy of singling out and making public examples of specific individuals that many teachers attempted to remind other children of their gaze. Most typically, this tended to involve one or more of the following: a child being publicly chastised in front of the whole class or assembly; in assemblies being made to stand up where they had been sitting, or sit at the side near a teacher or at the front; in the classroom being moved to a different table, told to stand in the corner or stand outside in the corridor; and in the play-ground being told either to stand next to the wall and 'cool off' or to go and wait outside the staff room.

However, one of the problems with this form of control was its inevitably arbitrary nature. Misbehaviour among children was usually a social activity, involving a number of children at any one time and often encouraging misbehaviour among other separate groups of children. At such times, the teacher was often forced to think quickly and act immediately to reintroduce order. And it was here that it could be argued that the teacher's specific habitus, with its discursively constructed and taken-for-granted assumptions about particular children, tended to be so influential.

It appeared to be at this particular point that the broader discourses on 'race', crime and the inner city that were manifest within Manor Park had a tendency to influence and shape some of the teachers' practices. The difficul-ties faced by these teachers in relation to order and control appeared at times to resonate quite closely with their general perception of the street-wise and hardened male living on the estate. Arguably, these in turn provided the discursive frame through which some teachers' experiences came to be lived and understood. To the extent that these discourses were themselves refracted through the racist stereotypes relating to the perceived trouble-some and violent nature of the Black male in particular, it was not surprising that Black boys in the school tended to be rendered acutely visible at times of crisis. In this, it could be argued that the more the teacher was forced to act spontaneously and thus was denied the opportunity to investigate and discern which child was the main culprit for any particular misdemeanour, then the more these racialised discourses had a tendency to encourage some teachers to focus on Black children in the sea of faces at assembly or in the classroom (see also Wright 1992; Gillborn 1990). This can be illustrated in the following incident in Mrs Scott's classroom. Here, Mrs Scott had just moved Jordan, a Black boy, to another table and repri-manded him for 'messing about'. She was still standing over the children whom Jordan had formerly sat with, and had struck up a conversation with Stephen, another Black boy, about his planned visit to his father in prison:

Mrs Scott: So you might be visiting him tonight?
Stephen: [*nods*]

Mrs Scott:	You're good. I don't think you'll be going to prison. [*louder, some children in the class look up*] You'll have to remember when you're a man not to fight, steal, throw bricks. [*pause*] In fact, even when you're ten.
Daniel (White):	Can you go to prison when you're ten?
Mrs Scott:	Well, not prison, but you can certainly be taken away.
Daniel:	Go to a naughty children's home, eh?
Mrs Scott:	Something like that – a young offenders' centre they call it. That's right, a young offenders' centre. [*She then looks over to Jordan on another table on the far side of the room, busy with his head down, colouring in his picture, and shouts over*] You'll have to remember that over there! [*Most of the children stop what they are doing and look over to Jordan's table*] If you kick and fight when you are over ten you'll have to go to a special school – a young offenders' centre.

This incident was not untypical of the way in which certain Black children, and Black boys in particular, would be singled out for public chastisement more than others.[2] There were many examples gained from observations throughout the school year, where Black boys would be sent to stand outside the classroom, told to stand up or move in assemblies, and be singled out and instructed to stand by the wall or outside the staff room during playtime. While Black boys were not the only ones to be disciplined in this way, they were significantly over-represented within these processes.

What is less typical about the above example, however, is the explicit way in which Mrs Scott drew upon the broader discourses on 'race', crime and the inner city in her relationship with the Black boys. Here, the perception of young Black males as violent criminal rioters, constructed through the articulation of these discourses, was seen by Mrs Scott as the inevitable way that Stephen would develop unless he carried on making a distinct effort not to fight, steal and throw bricks. For Jordan, however, his future life had already been mapped out by Mrs Scott. It could be argued that while most teachers at East Avenue were not observed to make such explicit references in their interactions with Black boys, this does not necessarily mean that such discourses were not influential. In some ways, as discussed in Chapter 3, such racialised discourses do not need to be explicitly referred to for them to be evoked. In the absence of any more direct observational data similar to that above, we can only continue to surmise why it is that Black boys, in particular, are far more likely to be singled out and publicly chastised in comparison to other children. On many of the occasions I observed, their particular behaviour did not appear to be very different from that of their peers; it does not seem unreasonable, therefore, to point to the possible influence of the broader discourses on 'race' found within the estate as one possible explanatory factor.

MANAGING MULTICULTURALISM AT EAST AVENUE

What we have seen so far is the importance of the locality in mediating how many teachers and schools come to interpret and implement national educational policies. The mere presence of discourses at a national level cannot, therefore, simply be assumed to be read in the same way, nor to act uniformly across all regions and localities. This is equally true of national political discourses on multiculturalism and anti-racism. As we saw earlier, at this level multiculturalism and anti-racism have increasingly provided the lens through which the more basic concerns with educational standards and discipline have been organised and expressed. However, as I want to suggest, the particular political concerns and priorities faced by the city of Workingham and the Manor Park estate appear to have significantly undermined the influences of these discourses and, instead, focused the local authority and the school's attention on the importance of a multicultural/anti-racist approach. This was particularly the case for East Avenue where, in contrast to concerns argued by some that the Education Reform Act 1988 would increasingly act to marginalise multiculturalism in schools (see Taylor and Bagley 1995; Troyna 1995), the opposite appears to have been the case. As will be seen, there has been a more concerted interest in developing multicultural/anti-racist policies at the school over the last few years.

Multiculturalism and the Local Education Authority

In order to understand the development of multiculturalism at East Avenue and the particular context within which the new headteacher was appointed, we need to offer a brief outline of the immediate political context provided by the local county council and education authority. Prior to the implementation of the Education Reform Act 1988, East Avenue came under the direct control of Workinghamshire County Council. The principal city served by the county is Workingham, which has a substantial Black and South Asian population as outlined in previous chapters. It is this fact, together with the particular social and economic changes affecting the city, which has come to form the basis around which specific political struggles and various priorities have been set at the local political level. The Labour Party gained control of the county council in the May elections of 1981, at a time of heightened political activity around the issue of 'race'. This activity was set in motion principally by the urban rebellions of that year in Brixton, Manchester and Toxteth, and in Bristol the previous summer. The response by a number of Local Education Authorities (LEAs) serving inner-city areas, including the newly elected ruling Labour group in Workinghamshire, was to adopt multicultural policy statements and, to varying degrees, set in motion a range of policies. It appeared that education, again, seemed to bear the brunt of much wider and more deeply engrained social and economic changes. It was the fact that Black and South Asian children were not adequately 'performing' in schools that, it was argued, led to their greater likelihood of being unemployed, and this in turn created the conditions within which they were likely to turn to rioting. It was arguably the belief that multicultural education would reduce Black and South Asian students' sense of alienation and disaffection from school, and therefore, in the long term, reduce the problems of urban disorder, that was possibly one important factor underlying many LEAs' development of multicultural education strategies.[3] This would appear to be corroborated by the fact that the number of LEAs holding multicultural policy statements rose from just two to over twenty in the year following the urban rebellions of 1980 and 1981 (Bhat *et al.* 1988: 169; Connolly 1992). For some writers, these policy initiatives have been interpreted as therefore representing elements of social control rather than truly progressive and egalitarian measures in their own right (Carby 1982; Troyna 1984a).

This provided one important context within which the ruling Labour group on Workinghamshire County Council set up a sub-committee and later a multicultural education working party, with the remit of preparing a multicultural education policy and strategy for schools in the county. By 1983, an adviser on multicultural education had been appointed and a Centre for Multicultural Education established, with a full-time co-ordinator. By the mid-1980s the Centre had a whole range of INSET courses up and running, fully funded by the LEA, to provide resources for and encourage the setting up of links with individual schools.

The arrival of a new headteacher at East Avenue

While these approaches were not without their limitations, it appears that they did provide an important context against which a new headteacher, Mr Redmond, was appointed to East Avenue in 1989. As discussed in the previous chapter, the Manor Park estate had developed as one of the key sites through which discourses on 'race', crime and the inner city had been played out in the city. The appointment of a new headteacher for East Avenue, especially with the implementation of the Education Reform Act looming and promising to give substantial powers to schools and particularly head-teachers, was therefore an extremely strategic one. Within such discourses, a person who was committed to multiculturalism and 'reaching out' to the local community was obviously believed to be of primary importance to a school like East Avenue, and that was precisely what Mr Redmond had to offer. For the three and a half years that Mr Redmond had been at East Avenue at the time of the fieldwork, he had been primarily responsible for a number of significant changes to the organisational structure and general ethos of the school, especially in relation to the development of a multi-cultural/anti-racist policy. In focusing on this, however, we should not be drawn into understanding these changes simply in relation to the single actions and leadership of the headteacher. While he was a significant 'policy entrepreneur' (Young and Connelly 1981) in relation to the changing nature of East Avenue, he was so largely because of his location within a wider, complex range of discourses that have been discussed and outlined in detail above. Arguably, these have been discourses that have not only made his initial appointment possible but have also acted, as will be seen, to add support to and smooth over the implementation of various social and multi-cultural educational policies in the school (see also Troyna 1984b).

During his time at the school Mr Redmond had been responsible for appointing five new teaching staff, who were similarly young in age and committed, to varying degrees, to a more liberal and/or radical approach to education generally and multiculturalism in particular. As will be seen shortly, this created a small but significant cleavage among the staff: between the old, established traditionalists and the new, younger and more liberal staff who provided the central dynamic through which changes brought in by Mr Redmond were implemented. Indeed, these new staff were referred to by one teacher, in an interview with me, as Mr Redmond's 'nice little niche'. Significantly, all three South Asian teachers in the school were appointed under the headship of Mr Redmond.

It was primarily through the initiatives of Mr Redmond and a small and committed number of new staff that the school developed its multi-cultural/anti-racist approach (see also Gillborn 1995). In this it is interesting to compare the school's existing multicultural statement with the draft statement on anti-racism that Mr Redmond had written for inclusion in the following year's school booklet, where it is evident that the growing emphasis within the school is on racism and bullying, rather than simply hoping to encourage greater awareness of each other's cultural heritage. This is to be compared to the national discourses on education that have not only failed to offer a clear and explicit policy as regards multi-cultural and anti-racist education but have, as we have seen, increasingly been jettisoning any notion of multiculturalism (Troyna and Williams 1986; Troyna and Carrington 1990). At the time the fieldwork was undertaken, however, the school's 'anti-racist' stance was confined largely to the headteacher's talks in Family Gathering over the need to be tolerant of one another and about the unacceptability of racism. Part of the reason Mr Redmond invited me into the school was to gain a more detailed insight into the nature of racism in East Avenue, so that they could build a more comprehensive whole-school approach. In the meantime, the most prominent expressions of the school's developing multicultural approach could be seen in relation to the celebration of Diwali and, more implicit although nevertheless equally important, the use of sports to encourage the positive participation of Black boys in the school. It is to these that the chapter now turns.

School assemblies and Diwali

Within the context set by the multicultural education policy of the LEA and the commitment of Mr Redmond and the newly appointed staff, multi-culturalism had been gaining increasing prominence within the school. In the early stages, however, tensions did emerge between the new and more liberal staff and the more long-standing traditionalists. One of the most prominent points of conflict in recent years at the school revolved around the issue of praying in Birthday Assemblies. While such prayers were addressed only to 'God', Ms Patterson complained that it was still offensive to ask children to close their eyes, bow their heads and put their hands together for prayer. She added that while Jesus was not overtly mentioned, it still gave the strong impression of a Christian service. As the following quote from Mrs Woods illustrates, this was seen by many of the more tradi-tionalist staff as going too far and being expressive of a general shift towards privileging 'the Asians' in the school (see also Bhatti 1995: 71):

> Very often it's perhaps heads and teachers who are more sort of protective towards the Asian children, like putting your hands together in prayers and saying 'Amen'. Now I don't think the Asian parents mind that at all. I've never had one Asian parent come to me saying, 'I don't want my child to be in a Christian assembly, I don't want my child to say Amen, put their hands together.' But it's the White teachers who come in and say that.

This perception that the head was favouring South Asian people was held by a significant number of the more long-standing, traditional teachers. The fact that Mr Redmond had appointed three South Asian members of staff during his time at the school was simply held up as evidence in support of this belief. It is also interesting to note here how the particular discourses on the inner city and inadequate parenting found on the estate can at times be taken up and reworked within these discourses. Here, the White parents were seen by some of these teachers as having no faith. This, as Mrs Woods went on to argue in the same interview, together with the general decline in morality and the shift to criminality on the estate, increased the need for the teaching of the basic Christian doctrine:

> I feel it's the Christian faith that's not being adequately supported. I know we celebrate all the festivals, but this is still a Christian country and a lot of the Asian children, they get their religious instruction out of school, whereas sometimes school is the only

place a child gets religious instruction, and I'm talking not just about the Bible and the stories of the Bible but I'm talking about the Ten Commandments and the way to behave towards each other, those basic things. [. . .] Again, the White children are missing out. In our anxiety to accommodate and provide for the needs of the ethnic children we have neglected the White children, and perhaps we just need to bring it up a little bit to get it in balance.

Beyond these sporadic tensions, however, there was a broad and almost unanimous consensus in favour of multiculturalism. This can possibly be partially understood against the backdrop of the teachers' experiences of working at East Avenue and the problems they faced. For some teachers, their perception of the disruptive behaviour and poor educational abilities of the children appeared to be partially explained in terms of 'race'. As in the inner-city rebellions described earlier, it was felt by some that Black and South Asian children's behaviour and/or poor educational performance could be understood in terms of the school not catering for their needs or making them feel welcome. It is possibly for this reason that even the most traditionalist teachers came to accept a pragmatic sense of multiculturalism.

This arguably provided one of the contexts within which the school came to spend more time, year by year, in its celebration of Diwali. It came to be the flagship of the school's multicultural approach, where a whole Family Gathering was given over to the festival. Over recent years it had become more and more embedded within the school, as individual classes were expected to prepare their specific part of the assembly during the weeks leading up to Diwali. Each class would contribute something, whether a dance, puppet show or a story. During the preceding weeks, the three infant classes would colour pictures relating to the festival and be read stories about it. It was significant that in the Diwali assembly itself a number of the more long-standing traditional members of staff would attend wearing saris. Much of the initiative that lay behind the celebration of Diwali at East Avenue came from Mr Chohan, the co-ordinator of Section 11 teaching at the school. It was also Mr Chohan, together with Mrs Coombs, the other full-time Section 11 teacher at the school, who read most of the Diwali stories in the infant classes.

However, the impact of these multicultural initiatives on the children cannot simply be assumed. The ways in which the young children came to interpret and understand these initiatives will be discussed in the following chapters. Ironically, it appeared that, in the absence of a more comprehensive approach to multiculturalism and anti-racism, such events tended to be interpreted by some of the children as simply reinforcing their existing racialised beliefs.

Football and Black boys

Alongside the celebration of Diwali and the strong discouragement of racist incidents, the other main strand to the school's multicultural approach was through sport, and particularly football (see also Carrington 1983). The present popularity of football at East Avenue can be traced back to the arrival of Mr Redmond and his appointment of Mr Wallace. Before that time, while there was a Year 6 school team, coached by the deputy head, Mr Pearson, football and sports more generally appeared to have been given little priority in the school. The arrival of Mr Redmond and Mr Wallace represented a significant change to this, however. Their shared interest in football with Mr Pearson ensured that this game was progressively given more time and importance within the school (see also Skelton 1997). By the start of the academic year in 1992, there were four football practices per week for the junior children, held on the school playing field after school; three were led by Mr Wallace and one by Mr Redmond. The school had entered two teams into local county school leagues, and Mr Redmond refereed all matches while Mr Pearson continued to be the coach of the first team.

The interest and enthusiasm that these three men had for football at the school was very evident in their prolonged analyses of past matches and discussions of various players and team tactics for future games. This obvious enthusiasm appeared to have an influence on the rest of the school, as will be seen. In particular, it could be argued that this was possibly one of the reasons behind the apparent increase in the popularity of football among boys in the playground over the past few years, remarked upon by a number of teachers and dinner supervisors. During junior morning playtimes and dinnertimes throughout the year, the main part of the playground, or playing field in dry weather, was dominated by older junior boys playing football. The games were highly organised and heavily guarded. These boys represented the 'footballing elite' in the school and were principally composed of those Year 5 and 6 boys who played in the school teams. Other boys could not simply join in but had to be invited. Their spatial dominance, together with the status that was generated surrounding footballing ability, appeared to permeate through to the younger infant boys, many of whom seemed to watch and learn from the older boys.

Not surprisingly, football was a very male affair. Girls were systematically excluded from participating in games during playtimes, and only a small handful of older girls felt able to brave the 'hostile and patronising' attitudes of the boys that they argued they faced when attending football practices after school. Moreover, what was equally striking about the footballing elite was the over-representation of Black children. While about a quarter of the children at East Avenue were Black, when it came to the footballing elite this proportion increased to three-quarters. And it is this fact that possibly suggests that the use of football, and to a lesser extent sport more generally, could be seen as a significant element of the school's multicultural strategy. For the three male teachers involved, it was regarded as a positive way of trying to reach out to and engage a number of older (predominantly Black) boys perceived as already becoming disaffected with the school. As Mr Wallace explained:

> I think it's a very positive thing for a lot of the children [. . .] there's several examples I can think of where there's children who've struggled in various areas of the classroom, maybe their behaviour's been poor and there's been a lot of negative responses because of that — not for anyone's, not anyone's fault in particular, but football's given an avenue for kids to succeed where perhaps they wouldn't be otherwise. And that's true for all athletics I think. [. . .] Some children's behaviour in the school, in general, has improved, perhaps as a by-product of them gaining a bit of responsibility or a bit of credibility at football.

It needs to be remembered in this that the significant over-representation of Black boys within the school teams meant that when the teachers referred to football and 'the footballers' they were predominantly referring to Black boys. For Mr Redmond, football provided one of the only chances these boys had 'for them to have a normal relationship, and a positive relationship, with a teacher'. This perception of the role and function of football was also evident during dinnertimes, when Mr Redmond was observed, on a few occasions, going out and chatting to the boys, and at times playing football with them. In referring to this he commented that:

> It's quite nice for me to get out of the staff room, if you like, and, you know, have a bit of a kick about. Erm, it's not a sort of, you know, one of the lads sort of thing, but it is nice, enjoyable time where we can have a chat about football. Er, maybe seeing me in a bit more of a human light.

It appeared that one of the effects of all of this was the tendency to contribute towards a specifically masculine ethos within the school. It was an ethos that also permeated into more formal contexts, including assemblies, and tended to create a level of resentment among some of the other, mainly female, staff. In relation to assemblies, one reason for this resentment appeared to be the amount of time given over to discussions about football by the headteacher (see also Skelton 1997). Significantly, these often lasted longer than the 'moral' talk given by him. Another possible reason related to the way that some teachers, especially those who were directly responsible for teaching these particular boys, felt it grossly unfair that their perceived bad behaviour, generally manifest in the classroom and playground, was either being ignored or, according to some, being rewarded by the prominence given to them in assemblies. This general feeling can be illustrated in the quote below from an interview with Ms Patterson, who had complained on several occasions to the headteacher. In the following, she was referring to another Family Gathering, which I had missed, and was explaining to me what had happened:

> There was just so much about football, I mean it just went on for ages and ages and ages and it was all about the *Man*-of-the-Match and the Sports*man*ship and how good this sportsmanship was and how wonderful it was and it was like Mr Wallace and Mr Redmond and Mr Pearson having their little joke, and it just went on for too long and it was all male-oriented. The squad stood up – they were all boys. The thing is that these boys who were standing up are the boys that are always in trouble at dinnertime and the ones that mess about in the class, but it's totally overlooked. They represent the school even when they can't behave in school [. . .] there's no consistency at all. These kids shouldn't be representing school if they can't behave in school. [. . .] I told Stuart [*Mr Redmond*] what I felt about the terminology and, erm, basically when they were going to play a match, when he was getting the people together in the car, he said, 'Come on, lads, because we want to find, erm, we want you to all be good sports*persons*,' and laughed at me! Which, I mean, I suppose it is funny and I'm sure it wasn't meant in any nasty way, but if you're going to take that attitude then what's going to change? It's going to carry on being sexist rubbish, isn't it? It's going to carry on being all the lads together, get into our cars, we're going to drive off and slaughter them, you know. It's just crap! And the thing is, it's very competitive: 'We won!' 'We won!' 'We drew!' 'Unfortunately we lost' – it's not the fact that you, that they all, had a good time.

This emphasis on developing a masculine rapport had the consequence, as Ms Patterson alluded to in the above, of allegiances being made at times between the boys and male teachers, sometimes at the expense of female teachers. To take the analogy of the school as a family one stage further, it could be argued that this was symbolic of the general collusive relationships sometimes found between fathers and sons, and the adverse effects of this on mothers and daughters.

VARIETIES OF APPROACHES TO TEACHING AT
EAST AVENUE

In this final section I want to introduce the three infant teachers whose children form the focus of the following chapters. This will provide the
immediate context for understanding the particular influences of the
teachers in the children's peer-group relations. Moreover, in looking at their
approaches to teaching and organising their classrooms, it will also demonstrate the variety of strategies adopted by teachers at East Avenue. In doing
this, however, the main point I want to develop is that, while there are very
significant differences in the outlook of the three teachers, these differences
can be argued to affect only the degree to which the broader discursive
processes and practices outlined above take effect in particular contexts,
rather than more directly contradicting and challenging them *per se*.

Of the three reception/Year 1 infant teachers, Mrs Brogan remained most
closely associated with the particular characteristics and strategies of some of
the teachers outlined earlier. This had been her first and only teaching post
and she had been at the school for eleven years. She developed an approach
through her years of experience at the school which relied quite heavily on a
segmented structure for the day, the strategic use of free time and a more
detached, calm approach to the children. She was rarely heard to shout at her
children compared to the other two teachers and, while her notably 'laid-
back' approach sometimes formed the basis of jokes and occasional teasing
on behalf of her colleagues, it did represent the 'line of least resistance' to
teaching at East Avenue; enabling Mrs Brogan to cope relatively easily with
the demands of teaching from day to day.

In contrast, Mrs Scott was much older, had been at the school for fourteen
years and was keen to retire. Her only reason for remaining at East Avenue
was because of her financial need to support her husband, who had retired
early through disability. A common view among her colleagues, shared by
Mrs Scott herself, was that she had reached her limit and was only mini-
mally coping. As Mr Knox, an experienced supply teacher used regularly by
the school, commented:

> I think she's fading, starting to fade, myself. I think there's too
> much tension, you know, and it's getting to her. She's been losing
> her temper here and there. You've got to be calm and love coming
> in and teaching these kids because if you don't, if you can't put that
> effort in and enjoy what you're doing with these kids, it shows.

Mrs Scott had reached a situation where the more she tried to control her
class, the more she resorted to direct intervention and control, which only
appeared to add further to her general tiredness and fatigue. This, in turn,
tended to exacerbate her perception of being out of control and the need to

control the children even more. In other words, while the institutional support was there for her to distance herself far more from the children, her general levels of stress and anxiety, together with her waning commitment to the job, had impeded her ability to do this successfully. Moreover, it appeared that her tendency to rely heavily on other support staff (section 11 teachers and ancillaries), who would at times take a leading role in particular sessions, tended only to add to the discontinuity experienced by the children and Mrs Scott's own perceptions of being out of control. Her approach was therefore very didactic and controlling. The incident discussed earlier with Jordan and Stephen was quite representative of this style. She would often resort to shouting; continually 'bombard' certain children, to use the word of one ancillary teacher; and would generally organise her class very tightly. The latter fact was illustrated, for instance, by her tendency to use the carpet, throughout the day, to bring the children together between activities more frequently, in comparison with the other two classes.

While Mrs Scott could be said to be the most 'disengaged' of the three teachers, Ms Patterson could, in contrast, be arguably seen as the most 'engaged'. She was much younger and had been a teacher for four years. She was very committed to her work, was the regional representative of the NUT (National Union of Teachers) and keen to incorporate progressive, anti-oppressive practice into her teaching, including, most prominently, anti-racism. Her enthusiasm was most readily noticeable when contrasting her approach with that of Mrs Brogan and Mrs Scott. For example, Mrs Brogan and Mrs Scott would bring their classes together quite frequently, especially towards the end of the day, for a story, a video or singing. This appeared to be as much to give each other a break as anything else. Ms Patterson, in contrast, purposely avoided doing this, arguing that there was no point showing the children a video unless she intended to follow it up with the class. Also, she felt that the children already did enough singing. She used free time to a much lesser extent than the other two teachers, preferring to develop games and activities that the children could continue throughout the day. Hers was therefore a very structured and pedagogically controlled classroom. This approach appeared to irritate Mrs Brogan and Mrs Scott at times, as they perceived it as an indirect criticism of their own approach. The fact that Ms Patterson spent so much time preparing for lessons, and developing new and innovative themes around which to plan her teaching over the term, was seen at times as being typical of a teacher 'fresh out of training school'.

The differences in these three approaches and their effects on the experiences of the children will become more evident through the remaining chapters. However, I would maintain that these differences were ones of degree rather than being qualitative or quantitative. There were still large parts of the timetables of the three classes that were unavoidably shared, including playtimes, school assemblies and other combined lessons such as stories, PE and singing. The three classrooms were also strongly influenced and structured by the imposition of the National Curriculum and the need to reach certain attainment targets with the children.

Overall, while the more controlling and didactic approach of Mrs Scott appeared to lead her to publicly chastise and over-discipline Black children more than Mrs Brogan or Ms Patterson, this process was still evident in their classes, albeit to a lesser degree. Ms Patterson, for example, explained to me one day that she was aware of all the research on Black children and the problems of labelling them, and yet she still found that it was the Black children in her class who were more likely to present behavioural problems. Although Ms Patterson was far less likely than Mrs Scott and Mrs Brogan to publicly chastise her children, when she was compelled to discipline particular children she did appear to discipline Black children more.

Her awareness of racism and her commitment to anti-racist education suggests that there are broader and more complex reasons for her actions and behaviour than simply her own racist beliefs. Some of the Black boys in her class were more likely to be drawn into arguments and fights with their classmates. However, as we will see in the following chapter, this needs to be understood within the broader context of the young children's peer-group relations.

The broader point I would like to tentatively develop from this is, therefore, the need to come to terms with the wider discursive context within which the teachers find themselves. It could be argued that, without appropriate institutional support, individual teachers' actions, however progressive and laudable, can only tend to affect the degree to which these discourses on 'race' – manifest within and beyond the school – are reproduced rather than successfully challenge them to any great extent. In this I want to suggest that we need to move away from the focus on teachers as the sole 'reality definers' of the school, as has often been the case in studies of infant classes. Not only are they, and their actions, located within a whole range of complex and interlocking discursive processes and practices, but the children themselves are very active in their reading and reworking of the teacher's underlying messages. There is a need, therefore, to highlight the subjective worlds of the young children themselves, so as to increase our understanding of how these broader discourses on 'race', manifest nationally, locally and in the school, come to influence and shape these children's social worlds. It is this that will provide the focus of the remaining four chapters.

CONCLUSIONS

This chapter has been concerned with drawing out some of the broader discursive processes and practices, found within the school, that help us to appreciate the particular contexts within which young children come to develop their gender identities. In particular the chapter has drawn attention to the way that the broader discourses on 'race', crime and the inner city, manifest within the field of Manor Park, appear to have influenced and shaped the way that some teachers at East Avenue came to understand their dual roles of teaching and discipline. As regards the former, the chapter has drawn attention to the influences of discourses on single parenthood and familial decline in encouraging many teachers to foreground their own social/parental role in relation to teaching. As regards the latter, the chapter has shown how discourses on 'race' and gender appear to have significantly influenced the nature of discipline within the school and the prominence of Black children, and boys in particularly, within its disciplinary modes. The importance of locality was also highlighted by the way in which the school had progressively increased its commitment to multicultural/anti-racist education, against the far more hostile tide of opinion found within the field of national politics. Multiculturalism, the chapter has shown, was evident in two main aspects: the celebration of Diwali and the encouragement of Black boys into sport. All these factors, together with those discussed in the previous two chapters, provide the main contextual ingredients for understanding the nature and form of the young children's social worlds, and it is to these that the book now turns.

6

FROM BOYS TO MEN? BLACK BOYS IN THE FIELD OF MASCULINE PEER-GROUP RELATIONS

The tendency for relations between teachers and Black[1] male students to be ones characterised by antagonism and conflict has provided a central concern for research on 'race' and education (see, for instance, Wright 1986; Mac an Ghaill 1988; Gillborn 1990; Sewell 1997). Overwhelmingly, the focus has been on older adolescent men and has drawn attention to the way that teachers tend to disproportionately discipline and publicly chastise Black male students in comparison with their peers. Given the weight of such work it is surprising that very little research attention has been paid to the schooling experiences of younger Black boys. The work that has been done (see Wright 1992; Nehaul 1996) tends to support the findings of the previous chapter that the processes leading to the over-disciplining and chastisement of older Black male students appear to be ones that, for some younger Black boys, sadly can be traced right back to the beginnings of their school careers.

However, relations between students and teachers are only one, albeit extremely significant, facet of Black boys' schooling experiences. What has been largely neglected in the literature on Black male students, of whatever age, is the influence of peer-group relations on their experiences of schooling. This is surprising given the fact that children will spend a far greater amount of their school time in direct contact with other children than with their teachers. It is for this reason that this chapter will focus on male peer-group relations among the young children within the school. It will offer an insight into some Black boys' experiences of these relations and, within this, aims to highlight a number of racialised processes that appear to articulate, to varying degrees, in the construction of their sense of identity. After drawing attention to some of these processes, the chapter will explore the differing ways they can shape and influence Black boys' schooling experiences. In using two particular case studies, the chapter will highlight some of the specific contexts in which Black boys appear to be more or less likely to be drawn into these racialised processes.

In relation to this and the following three chapters it is important to reiterate the qualifications made in the introductory chapter. In particular, I want to stress that no claims are made here concerning the generalisability or representative nature of the processes to be outlined below. They are neither held up as generalisable to all schools nor as even representative of all Black boys in this school. Indeed, the use of case studies is precisely an attempt to draw attention to the breadth of the differing experiences of schooling that Black boys can have. Furthermore, even the particular processes identified are not claimed to be the most prominent within the school, only that they exist.

What is being offered here and in the remaining chapters, therefore, is an aid to appreciating some of the processes that could possibly be in operation in other schools and which have the potential to influence and shape the racialised nature of young children's gender identities. At one level it is intended to contribute to the growing body of knowledge that teachers can use to assess their own practice and social relations in the school more generally. However, the extent to which any of the following may be occurring in any particular school can only be ascertained through concrete analysis of specific relations there. These chapters are only meant as a check-list to aid the teacher in identifying some of these processes.

TEACHER DISCOURSES ON BLACK BOYS

Before focusing on the children's peer-group relations, it is important to provide the necessary context created by Black boys' broader experiences of school life. In the previous chapter I drew attention to the tendency for some Black boys to be drawn into the disciplinary modes of the school. It could be argued that one of the more significant consequences of this was the tendency for these Black boys to be seen as troublesome and as presenting behavioural problems. In this section, however, I want to tentatively suggest that these more overt processes were not the only ones that could act to reproduce this perception. In particular I want to draw attention to two far more subtle and, on the part of the teachers concerned, well-meaning processes that can nevertheless tend to add to the perception of some Black boys as troublesome.

The first of these can be found in the more personalised discourses that particular teachers often developed about specific Black boys. Here, in the space available to forge more personal relationships with their children, many teachers appeared to be less likely to draw upon broader racialised discourses on Black boys and, instead, developed an understanding of a particular child's behaviour by recourse to many other individual-specific factors that did not explicitly refer to 'race'. This can be illustrated in relation to Paul, a Black boy in Mrs Scott's class. Here Mrs Scott made no reference to 'race' in her internal school report on his progress but simply referred to what she felt was the problem of him being 'easily led'.

Of course, many children were described as being 'hyperactive', 'excitable', 'over-sensitive' and/or 'easily upset' in this way during the field-work. However, these labels were found to be much more frequently used in school reports and informal conversations among staff in relation to some Black boys in comparison with other children. In this sense we need to examine whether this could have an indirect effect in possibly helping to reproduce the more racialised discourses surrounding these particular boys. In relation to Paul, for instance, his perceived tendency to be 'easily led' existed alongside a more explicit discourse on 'race' also used by Mrs Scott, at times, to explain his behaviour. This is evident in the following conversation I had with Mrs Scott in the playground one day. She was discussing Paul's father who was, at that time, in prison:

> One day I had a to-do with him [Paul] and, because he doesn't even, he tends to be a bit wild; he doesn't listen to what you're saying. [. . .] But I shall imagine Paul's father is a big West Indian man, because Paul is quite big and the mother's blonde, and I can imagine, you know, perhaps have to be in maximum security if he's got a temper or some other thing.

Not only was Paul's misbehaviour located within the context of his violent *Black* father but this was also reinforced by contrasting this 'big West Indian' with the bonny, rosy-cheeked, blonde and therefore *White* mother. This relationship between the more overtly racialised discourses on some Black boys and their tendency to be also characterised in terms such as being 'easily led' and/or 'hyperactive', as highlighted in the case of Paul, can be said to be self-serving. These latter labels, while not referencing 'race' explicitly, do have a tendency to encourage others to focus on that particular child's behaviour. As such they could be argued to increase the likelihood of feeding into the more explicit racialised perceptions of Black boys as 'trou-blesome'. In this sense it is possible that labels such as being 'easily led' can, at times, serve as little more than a euphemism for more explicit discourses on 'race'. These latter discourses can be argued to be already so well estab-lished and understood that they do not require the use of explicit signifiers to be evoked. In this sense it could be argued that once Black boys, more generally, have come to be discursively constructed as disruptive and aggres-sive, then this provides the essential context within which a whole range of other discourses, which do not make explicit reference to 'race', can tend to reproduce that child's racialised identity (Miles 1989, 1993; Troyna 1993).

The second process I want to draw attention to relates to what appeared to be a number of teachers' more proactive and 'constructive' strategies aimed at trying positively to engage Black boys. In this it was commonly thought by many of the teachers that to encourage, praise and involve 'problem' children positively in their lessons and activities would help to engage them in the tasks at hand and thus detract them from what was perceived to be their more 'anti-social' behaviour. This was a strategy that was adopted by teachers for a number of specific children. However, as before, it was a strategy I found used disproportionately for certain Black boys. It can be illustrated in the following incident involving Mr Knox, a supply teacher who was due to take Ms Patterson's class for their weekly PE lesson that morning. These lessons were held over in the sports hall at the neighbourhood centre on the estate. This is a fairly representative example of the type of strategy often used by some teachers positively to engage 'troublesome' children generally and some Black boys in particular. In the following, the children were sitting on the carpet as Mr Knox took the register. While doing so, he was being interrupted intermittently by late arrivals, one of whom was Devan, a Black boy who was also perceived as being a 'problem' child.

Mr Knox: [*Devan and another child enter the room*] Who's just come in? [. . .] We've got, Devan's here now, isn't he? Devan's here. Now Devan, when he's with me [*puts his arm around Devan and turns to rest of class*] Devan is a very, very good boy! Is Kuldeep here? [*looking at register while still holding on to Devan*]

Child: No.

Mr Knox: No Kuldeep? Right. Now, Devan, remember last term when you were with me? Who was a very, very good boy?

Children: [*a number shout out*] Devan!

Mr Knox: Now I bet you he walks beautifully to the sports hall. Devan, come and take these down for me, please. [*hands him registers*] I bet he walks beautifully to the sports hall.

This proactive strategy adopted by Mr Knox and evident in the above also formed the basis of the interaction in the following incident later that morning in the sports hall. Here the children had changed and were stood in a line waiting for the lesson to begin. Mr Knox was talking to Wendy, a member of staff at the sports hall who helped the teachers organise the PE lessons.

Mr Knox: That's very, very good! [*turns to Wendy*] You know this young lady [*putting his arm around one of the girls*] this morning, she's been brilliant.

Wendy: Has she been good?

Mr Knox: Brilliant! Soon as she came in the classroom she sat down, you know, and she's been so quiet/

Wendy: /Well that's super!/

Mr Knox: /And Devan! Every, he's been as good as gold and his manners! And he's held the doors for people without being asked!

Wendy: [*to Devan*] Are you feeling quite well? [*Devan nods*] Yes? Well, gracious me! Right, Devan's going to be the leader today then.

As before, one of the possible consequences of this type of strategy was to inadvertently draw attention to the child's behaviour. In that it was used disproportionately for some Black boys then it could well be argued that it also had the potential of feeding into the more explicitly racialised perception of them being behavioural problems. In this sense it is arguably illustrative of the way that relations do not always have to be overtly antagonistic and disciplinarian for them to reproduce the belief that particular Black boys are 'bad'.

BLACK BOYS AND THE FIELD OF MASCULINE PEER-GROUP RELATIONS

Having touched upon the broader context provided by Black boys' relationships with their teachers, the chapter can now focus more directly on relations among the children. As will be shown, it was within the specific fields provided by the children's peer-group relations that their gender identities appeared to be most immediately forged and reproduced. For many of the Black boys at East Avenue their racialised identities were continually constructed and reconstructed within the field of masculine peer-group relations where boys struggled over the various forms of cultural, social and symbolic capital most associated with masculinity. There appeared to be more traditional expressions of masculine competence, including who could run the fastest, finish a piece of academic work the quickest, play football most competently, and who had the longest pencil! However, there also seemed to be a range of more specific masculine forms that were strongly influenced by broader discourses manifest within popular culture and which came to be appropriated and reworked through many of the boys' experiences of life on the Manor Park estate.

This was an experience, as highlighted in Chapter 4, that was overshadowed by the folklore of violence associated with the estate (see also Kenway and Fitzclarence 1997). For some men and boys it appeared to create a perceived need to present themselves as physical and street-wise. It was an influence that provided the most immediate lens through which some of the boys at East Avenue appeared selectively to read and appropriate popular culture. Computer games, especially those in the genre of *Street Fighter* and *Mortal Combat*, tended to provide one of the contexts within which many of these boys could be seen together regularly rehearsing and perfecting the basic kicks, punches and manoeuvres associated with this form of fighting.

Indeed, such was the popularity of kick-boxing among many boys that, in school assemblies on a number of occasions, the headteacher had to refer to the dangers associated with it and remind children that it was banned.

Alongside such public displays of physical competence, also reinforced principally through football and races, a second significant aspect of many boys' cultural capital appeared to be knowledge, especially *adult* knowledge. As will be seen shortly, to talk about girls and sex, to understand and competently use a broad range of swear words or 'cusses', and to know about the latest movies and popular music, all seemed to be signs of masculine maturity and thus tended to act as significant forms of cultural capital for these boys (see Kehily and Nayak 1997; Dixon 1997). In many ways, along- side competent displays of physicality, the appropriation of such adult ways of knowing formed a significant strand of some boys' presentation of them- selves as street-wise.

Against the backdrop of the broader discourses on 'race' manifest within and beyond the school, some Black boys came to be positioned in quite specific ways within this field of male peer-group relations. Through the discursive processes outlined above and in the previous chapter, it could be argued that they had already come to be constructed as disruptive and phys- ical in the eyes of some children. Their frequent confrontations with teaching staff seemed only to act further to reinforce this perception (see also Ross and Ryan 1990). Moreover, the use of sport, and especially football, to try and engage some of the older Black boys also appeared to help reproduce the discursive themes of Black boys being sporting and athletic. Arguably, these broader discourses therefore acted to construct a perception of many Black boys as hyper-masculine (Weekes *et al.* 1995; Sewell 1995, 1997). This, together with the general celebration of specific Black cultural forms within popular culture, quite possibly had the consequence of investing Black boys with a significant level of symbolic capital within the field of masculine peer-group relations (see also Hewitt 1986; Jones 1988; Back 1996).

This positioning of Black boys within the field of masculine peer-group relations appeared to elicit a number of contradictory responses among some White boys in the school. At one level they appeared to hold a grudging respect for Black boys. Being seen as aggressive, hard and good at sport, Black boys were, after all, perceived as walking symbols of masculinity. However, it was precisely because of this that some of these White boys appeared to be slightly threatened by the presence of particular Black boys. The competent displays of masculinity by these Black boys could arguably be seen to bring into question their own masculine status. It was therefore this sense of threat that provided the context which led some White boys into physically and verbally confronting particular Black boys as a means of reasserting their own identity.

These confrontations were not experienced uniformly by all Black boys, however, but appeared to be heavily reliant on context. In this it could be argued that two main factors – visibility and territory – tended to increase the likelihood that certain Black boys rather than others would be open to verbal and physical abuse from White boys. The first of these – visibility – related to the numbers of Black boys playing together in the playground. In this sense it was the Black boys who more regularly played together as a *group*, i.e. Stephen, Jordan and Paul from Mrs Scott's class and Peter, Devan and Michael, the former two from Ms Patterson's class, who seemed more likely to attract the wrath of some White boys. Here it was arguably their increased 'visibility' as a *group* of Black boys that appeared to add to their likelihood of being attacked by White boys wishing to challenge what they perceived as their 'macho personas' (see also Gillborn 1995: 165). In contrast, there were a few Black boys who appeared largely able to avoid the gaze of these White boys and thus avoid such confrontations. As will be seen later, this was certainly the case for Wesley, the only Black boy in Mrs Brogan's class at the beginning of the school year, who played mostly with a small group of White male friends from his class.

The second main factor seemed to relate to what the White boys perceived as the infringement of their territory by certain Black boys. Territory was a notion defined in a broad and fluid way. At one level it revolved around notions of loyalty towards other boys who were, for example, being picked on. This sense of loyalty was defined not only in terms of more intimate friendship groups formed in the playground, but also in more general terms of membership of the same class and/or year group. As will be highlighted below, the contingent and fluid nature with which lines of inclusion and exclusion were drawn in this way resulted in the formation of a complex and contradictory web of social relations among the children. On another level, these notions of territory seemed to be highly gendered and developed in terms of a sense of ownership of certain girls, again identified in very contingent ways (see also Mac an Ghaill 1994: 87). Against this territorial background, then, the more that White boys perceived Black boys as encroaching on their territory – either through conflict with their friends or classmates or through playing with 'their' girls – the more these White boys appeared inclined to verbally and physically challenge the Black boys.

It is this complex set of discursive processes on 'race' articulated in the construction of the gender identities of some of the Black boys that I now want to highlight and explore in more detail through my first case study of a friendship group of four 5- and 6-year-old boys: Stephen (African/ Caribbean), Jordan (dual heritage), Paul (dual heritage) and Daniel (White) from Mrs Scott's class. In doing this I want to illustrate the way in which their masculine identities were formed against their experience, as a *group* of Black boys, of the complex set of social processes outlined above and in the previous chapters. While Daniel was the only White boy in the group, I want to maintain that his regular association with the other Black boys drew him into some of these racialised processes. I want to stress at this stage, however, that what follows is a case study and is not held up as being in any way representative of all Black boys in East Avenue. In many ways it is an ideal-typical case study of the particular consequences, in relation to their developing sense of identity, for those Black boys who appeared to be most completely drawn into the specific set of racialised discursive processes on Black boys. In this sense their emerging identities were quite distinctive. Neither Peter, Devan nor Wesley, for instance, appropriated and reproduced the particular types of discourses on gender and sexuality that these four boys did. Thus, rather than offering a representative account of Black boys' experiences of schooling, I am primarily interested in drawing our attention to and increasing our understanding of the range of discursive processes that can directly affect certain Black boys (see also Sewell 1997). This first case study can therefore be located towards the end of a broader continuum where the processes can be seen to have greatest effect because of their appearance as a *group* of Black boys. The second case study, involving Wesley, a Black boy who tended to play only with two White boys from his class, provides a corrective to this and is located towards the other end of the continuum, as it draws attention to the contexts within which such processes have least effect.

THE 'BAD' BOYS

Fighting to survive

The four boys, whom I have collectively named the 'Bad Boys',[2] constituted a relatively stable friendship grouping that lasted throughout my fieldwork. They were all in Mrs Scott's class and had been there for two terms prior to the start of the academic year 1992–3, which was the focus of this research. They would be seen regularly sitting together in class and/or playing together in the playground, either as a group of four or in some variation of three or two. The friendship group could be regarded as quite an open and public affair, however, and a number of secondary friendship networks mushroomed out of this basic grouping. Stephen, for instance, was regularly in control of one of the footballs in the playground and had developed relationships with a number of other boys around this. Stephen and Jordan, and Paul and Daniel, also regularly played kiss-chase with their respective 'girlfriends', which also widened out the social networks. The nature of the Bad Boys' friendship group and their resultant identities were therefore as much the consequence of relationships developed with others outside that group as they were the result of relationships forged within the foursome.

This is particularly true in terms of their relationship with other boys, which was one that appeared to be dominated by their experience of a significant level of provocation and bullying. These often physical confrontations arguably formed a staple ingredient of the Bad Boys' playground experiences. In the following quote, taken from an interview with two White boys, Jason and Craig, the significance of territory in relation to such confrontations is highlighted. Here territory had come to be defined around girls and, as can be seen, it was the fact that a group of Black boys were playing with White girls, some of whom were from their class, which lay behind the White boys' apparent sense of threat and consequent assaults on the Bad Boys:

PC:	[. . .] But tell me about before, you know, Daniel and Paul.
Jason:	Ah, yeah!
PC:	From Mrs Scott's – what was all that about?
Jason:	Erm [. . .] Mark, Nicky, me, Craig [*all White*] started it [. . .] we started it but/
Craig:	/and, and, and we made a plan didn't we?
[. . .]	
PC:	You started it [. . .] with Daniel and Paul? Why?
Craig:	It, it started when/
Jason:	/You know John [*White*], John was catching Christine. [*White*]
PC:	Yeah?
Jason:	That's why we just done it.
PC:	John from Mrs Scott's class?
Jason:	Yeah – they got Christine in *our* class.
PC:	Right, and you didn't like that?
Jason:	No!
Craig:	No!
PC:	Why not?
Jason:	[*to Craig*] You saying it not me now – I've said something.
Craig:	No, you, I didn't even do anything/
Jason:	/Yes you did, you said your gang had a plan, did they?
Craig:	The plan was to, erm, get John out the way [. . .] with, er, just me, right, who made the plan up.
[. . .]	
PC:	I don't understand, if you were trying to get John then why were you fighting with Paul and Daniel?
Jason:	But Paul and Daniel are on their side!
PC:	Oh, right! So what were Paul and Daniel doing then?
Jason:	Er, erm/
Craig:	/Chasing after Jason's girlfriend!
Jason:	Oye! Shush!

PC:	Jason's girlfriend? Who's that?
Craig:	Emma! [*White*]
[. . .]	
PC:	Do you not like them chasing after Emma then?
Jason and Craig:	No!
[. . .]	
PC:	So do you think Christine likes to be chased by the boys?
[. . .]	
Jason:	I don't know!
PC:	You don't know? So why did you try and stop John, then, if you don't know whether she liked/
Craig:	/I, I was trying to stop him!

The above extract hints at the complexity of relations as lines of inclusion and exclusion were drawn and redrawn. The initial encounters began when John, a White boy from Mrs Scott's class, started playing kiss-chase with Christine from Jason and Craig's class. Jason and Craig seemed to take exception to this and tried to stop John. This, however, only appeared to drag Paul and Daniel into the conflict; they were seen as being on John's 'side' as they were from his class. It was their involvement in the ensuing conflict and the way in which the fights between them and the two White boys came to predominate and overshadow John's involvement that alludes to a more long-standing conflict between these White boys and the Bad Boys. As highlighted in the extract above, one of the most significant factors underlying this appeared to be Paul and Daniel's involvement with 'their' *White* girlfriends, Emma and Christine (see also Mac an Ghaill 1994; Sewell 1995).

That the underlying motivation behind the ensuing fights seemed to relate to these prior relations, rather than to John *per se*, was also illustrated by the course of events that developed out of these initial encounters. The incidence of verbal and, moreover, physical confrontations between the boys grew in severity and frequency over the following week. John was no longer involved after the initial incident and the groups that were initially formed around notions of classroom loyalty soon became transformed and racialised as more and more boys were drawn into the conflict. At its peak there were between ten and fifteen infant boys involved and separated into two gangs: one all White and drawn together around friendship patterns relating to Craig and Jason; the other primarily Black and drawing upon friends of the Bad Boys.

The fights that ensued were particularly violent, with running battles taking place across the playground where individual boys were being prized away from their allies and kicked and punched to the floor. While there they would at times be kicked in the back and head before their friends had time to regroup and rescue them. The fact that such incidents happened very quickly and intermittently and took place across a wide expanse of space probably lay behind the fact that the teachers and dinner supervisors on duty did not appear to notice the seriousness of what was happening. These essentially violent confrontations, while petering out over the following week, appeared to provide the basis from which resentment between the two groups of boys remained for the rest of the academic year and would be seen to resurface periodically.

From 'boys' to 'men'?

It could be argued that, with incidents such as those outlined above forming a staple part of the Bad Boys' experiences of schooling, they would inevitably come to develop and value, through their habitus, a sense of physicality. Not only did some of the fights mentioned above seem to be expressive of the carefully rehearsed moves found in computer games such as *Street Fighter* and *Mortal Combat* or films in the genre of *Karate Kid*, but so also were the post-discussions and analysis of the events engaged in by the Bad Boys. The following extract is taken from an interview with Paul and Daniel, following one of their fights with the White boys discussed above. The emphasis on successfully getting these boys 'over' and 'down' and the particular actions they mimicked and performed while engaged in these discussions tend to illustrate the importance that Paul and Daniel attached to being successful fighters. In this sense, being physically competent had arguably become part of the boys' cultural capital. However, in conversations with them it was apparent that, while this may have had its roots in the ongoing conflicts with White boys, it had become part of their habitus; something that they learnt to value and strive for in its own right.

PC: You said when they came up to you to start with; you were playing with some girls?
Paul: Yeah, I had some fighting but he [*Daniel*] didn't!
Daniel: Yes I did!
Paul: No you didn't!
Daniel: Jason [*White*] pushed me in a puddle!
Paul: Yeah, what did you do? Nothing!
Daniel: No.
Paul: So you didn't fight, did you? I did! 'Cos I got, erm, one of them over.
Daniel: Yes I did fight! When I was running, I was going to kick them.
Paul: But missed them, didn't you!
Daniel: What?
Paul: Missed them!
Daniel: No I never!
Paul: Well, I got, I got, I had two people over from me.

PC: You had two what, Paul? What did you say – you had two people what?
Paul: Down!
PC: Down?
Paul: Three! – Sean, Craig and Jason [*all White*].
Daniel: Yeah, I, I, you got Sean down by kicking him, didn't ya?
Paul: No! He ran and I got my foot out so he tripped over,
Daniel: Yeah, and then he was going to kick you, weren't he?
Paul: Yeah, but he couldn't – he was running and trying to get me but [*gets up to rehearse the actions – Daniel also gets up*]/
Daniel: /But he missed, didn't he?/
Paul: /I put my foot out and he went over! [. . .] Then I tripped Karl [*White*] over, and I punched James [*White*] down so he was, so he was down.

The above discussion related as much to the context within which the stories were told as it did to the reality of the incidents referred to. Here it needs to be borne in mind that these 6-year-old boys were conducting this argument in front of me, an adult male. In this sense their conversation was an essentially public one and the emphasis on physical competence was arguably as much for my benefit as it was for theirs. As mentioned earlier, it appeared that one of the key aspects of cultural capital struggled over by the boys was *adult* knowledge. The ability competently to discuss previous fights or reel off a whole array of 'cusses' and/or talk about the latest films and music seemed to increase a boy's status within his peer group. Moreover, in my presence the introduction of 'taboo' or 'adult' subjects involving violence, cusses and sexuality also tended to provide a relatively successful strategy for challenging the dominant discourses on childhood manifest within the school (see also Kehily and Nayak 1996). As such, it could be argued that they provided a strategy through which the children could challenge my authority as an adult and surrogate teacher (see also Walkerdine 1981). It is with this in mind that the transcript above and those to follow need to be understood. They were arguably not just representative accounts of the boys' general conversations, but could also well have been expressive of a more immediate struggle, partially between themselves but also, more importantly, between them and me. Whatever the case, it does indicate quite successfully some of the forms of cultural capital most prized by the boys, and as such draws attention to the underlying dynamics of the field of masculine peer-group relations and the construction of racialised identities within this.

Not surprisingly, these interviews became very popular with the children, who appeared to see them as a means of telling, learning and reproducing adult ways of knowing. This emphasis on adult knowledge is illustrated in the following transcript, where I was temporarily absent from the room.

Given the nature of the verbal exchanges, the atmosphere was surprisingly not one of antagonism. Rather, it was one of mild competition reminiscent of a verbal sparring match where these 5- and 6-year old boys competed in terms of the breadth of their knowledge of cusses (see also Kehily and Nayak 1997). While some of the following cusses may well have been originally learnt from their older siblings or elsewhere, it is apparent that they were not simply passively reproduced but were actively appropriating, adapting and reproducing:

Stephen: Come on then, you fuckin' bitch!
Jordan: Come on then!
Stephen: Come on, sit down!
Jordan: Eh! Miss Coombs! [*pointing to photo on wall*]
Stephen: You fucking Sappa!
Paul: Zappa!
Stephen: Sit in you seat! Quick!
Jordan: Oye! There he is!
Paul: Who?
Stephen: You're a fucking bastard!
Jordan: You fuckin' dick-head!
Stephen: You fuckin' dick! Bitch!
Jordan: Bitch! Ass-hole!
Paul: Arse-hole!
Jordan: Ass-hole! Bitch! Dick-head! Fuck off, dick-head! Fuck off, fucker!
Paul: Fucker! Fuckin' bastard bum-bum!
Stephen: Come on then, you fucking bastard! Calling me fucking names!
Jordan: Yeah like/
Paul: /you bastard!
Jordan: Fucker! Dick-head!
Stephen: Lickin' your arse off, pussy-sucker! You White pussy-sucker!
Jordan: You Black/
Paul: /You're blind, you Black/
Jordan: /You Black bastard!
Stephen: You White/
Jordan: Pussy! You smell pussy!
[*inaudible – creole accent. Boys seem to be standing and play-fighting*]
Jordan: Booofff! [*play-hits Stephen*]
Stephen: No, don't – don't fight me! Paul, sit down quick! Quick, Paul! [*banging out beat on table, making bass noise with mouth*]

Knowledge of cusses appeared therefore to be an important aspect of the cultural capital valued by these boys. As such they seemed to be heavily guarded, with accusations often being made of one boy copying the other or using their cusses. In this, Stephen was considered the 'expert'. In one interview he shouted out the following rhyme very quickly, so that only the occasional words were audible to the other boys: 'Hey Pakistani, let me see your fanny, let me smell [*sniff, sniff*] fuckin' hell!' Much of the remainder of the interview was then spent by the other boys trying to guess and repeat the rhyme, with Stephen seemingly sitting back as the 'expert', judging the various contributions and ultimately concluding how they fell short of what he had actually said.

An inescapable aspect of the cusses reproduced above was their highly gendered and sexualised nature. The Bad Boys were certainly not the only boys in the school to structure their identities in relation to girls, but they were relatively unique, among the sample classes of 5- and 6-year old boys, in terms of their level of understanding and the emphasis they placed on sexuality in forging and reproducing their identities. To understand this, we need to remind ourselves of the centrality of girlfriends in the ongoing conflicts with some of their White peers, as described earlier. Here the affirmation of boyfriend/girlfriend relationships appeared to be made through the essentially public games of kiss-chase that took place across the playground. Having a girlfriend seemed to secure a significant level of social capital for boys among their peers, and therefore the essentially public nature of games of kiss-chase meant that much was at stake in terms of developing and maintaining their (heterosexual) status and reputations (see also Hatcher 1995; Epstein 1997a).

This was equally true, as will be seen in the following chapters, for some of the girls as for these boys. Sexual orientation and relations defined through boyfriends and girlfriends thus seemed to provide one important source of identity for these children (see also Mac an Ghaill 1994). In this sense, as Epstein (1997b: 105) rightly argues, 'struggles around sexuality are intimately connected with struggles around gender and that the . . . implicit heterosexism found within schools derives from and feeds macho and misogynist versions of masculinity'. It was this that arguably lay behind the conflicts described earlier between the Bad Boys and some of their White peers, as they publicly struggled over the social capital that was constituted around girlfriends. In this sense it could be argued that girls had become discursively constructed as the symbolic markers of territory that, in the case of the White boys discussed above, had been perceived to have been transgressed by the Bad Boys.

What made such struggles more acute for the Bad Boys was the way in which they, as Black boys, appeared to be more likely to be teased and encouraged into games of kiss-chase by girls than any other group of boys. Tara, for instance, a White girl from Year 2, was observed teasing Stephen and Michael, another Black boy from Year 2, calling them 'big fat baboon bum' and gesturing them to chase her. Nicky and Emma, the two White girls from Mrs Brogan's class at the heart of the conflicts outlined earlier between the Bad Boys and some White boys, were also overheard chanting in earshot of some Black boys: 'We are the champions, we know what to do, get all the Black boys and stick 'em down the loo!' As we will see in more detail in Chapter 8, Black boyfriends, through particular discourses on Black masculinities, had therefore become significant forms of social capital for many girls within the field of feminine peer-group relations.

It is arguably within this broader context that the Bad Boys developed a particularly sexualised and derogatory set of discourses in relation to girls. As we have seen, girlfriends appeared to play a significant role for many boys in relation to the development and maintenance of their masculinity within the field of masculine peer-group relations. Inasmuch as girls were therefore essentially constructed as symbolic markers of territory through the conflicts over girlfriends, then it was inevitable that they came to be both objectified and sexualised by the boys. This process was that much more acute for the Bad Boys, as they were not only more likely to be encouraged into games of kiss-chase by girls but, once involved in these games, were far more likely to be drawn into conflict over these girls. A further example of how the Bad Boys had come to discursively constitute girls as property within the broader masculine struggles over territory can be illustrated in the following interview with Stephen, Paul and Daniel. It followed an argument between Stephen and the other two boys over girlfriends. Paul and Daniel appeared to be annoyed at Stephen and Jordan playing with 'their' girlfriends, Emma and Nicky. These themes emerged again in this transcript. What is particularly interesting here, however, is the distinction Stephen makes between having girlfriends but not girls-as-friends:

PC: So, Stephen, before, remember before break time when Nazia [*South Asian girl in his class*] wanted to look at your work and you wouldn't let her? Why didn't you let her have a look?

Stephen: I hate girls!

PC: You hate girls?

Stephen: Yeah!

[. . .]

Daniel: Why, well, why do you chase girls then, like ours?

Stephen: No, I don't chase you lots of girlfriends!

Daniel: Yes you did!

Stephen: No I don't!

Daniel: Yes you did!

Stephen: No I don't, no I never this morning!

Paul: No, last morning, didn't you?

Stephen: Last morning? What last morning? What last morning? Yesterday – that was yesterday, though – that was yesterday!

Paul: After dinner, that thingy! Yes, you do get a lot of girls!

Stephen: No, I not – no, I don't, Paul!

Daniel: You do!

Paul: Why do you get Nicky and Emma, then?
Stephen: No I don't – I only got 'em yesterday!
Paul: So why did, so why sometimes you chase your girlfriends, so why,
             so you must like girls!
Stephen: [*angry*] So what if I've got a girlfriend? It doesn't mean I like girls,
             does it?
Daniel: Yes it does!
Stephen: [*to* PC] Does it?
PC: Doesn't it?
Stephen: [*more subdued*] No, it don't!

It could be argued from this that the Bad Boys' sense of masculinity has
been partially constructed in opposition to girls. While having a girlfriend
therefore appears to present a boy with a certain amount of social capital, to
be associated with a girl *as a friend* seems dramatically to undermine that
boy's claims to be masculine. Arguably, the only 'legitimate' relationship
boys can have with girls within the field of masculine peer-group relations is
therefore in the way they are objectified and sexualised as girlfriends. It is
here that we found the Bad Boys engaging in 'sex-talk'. As Mac an Ghaill
also found in relation to the adolescent males in his study, these 5- and 6-
year-old boys were also striving to prove their sense of masculinity through
sexual narratives that

> carried the predictable misogynous boasting and exaggeration of
> past heterosexual conquests and male heroic fantasies, in which
> women were represented as passive objects of male sexual urges,
> needs and desires. These male 'fictions' appeared to be crucial
> elements in setting the parameters of the prescriptive and proscrip-
> tive sex/gender boundaries that served to police schoolboys'
> performance by making them act like men.
>
> (Mac an Ghaill 1994: 92)

This can be seen in the following interview with the Bad Boys where girls
had been discursively constructed as passive, inanimate objects to be 'sexed'
as if they were on a conveyer-belt:

PC: Which girls do you like to play with the best?
Paul: Nicky and Emma!
Daniel: And Emma!
Stephen: I like Natasha [*dual heritage*] and Marcia and Samantha. I like, I've
             got fourteen girlfriends!
Paul: Woo-woo!
Stephen: I've got a hundred girlfriends!
Daniel: If you've got one you can't have no more!

Stephen: Yeah!
Daniel: Your girlfriend will tell you off!
Stephen: No!
Daniel: Yeah!
Stephen: No!
Paul: How you going to sex 'em, then?
Stephen: I'll put all of them on top of each other and when I've done one –
put her over there, then when done another one put her over there,
then another one put her over there, then over there, and over
there and over there.
Paul: I've got, I've got a million!
Stephen: I've got four hundred and eighty-two!
[. . .]
PC: Stephen, when you say you've done one, what do you mean when
you say you've done one?
Paul: Sexy baby!
Daniel: He throws it over and then he puts, then he has another one, then
he picks her up, throws her over and has another one.

One of the overwhelming themes arising from these discussions was one
of power and domination (see also Mahoney 1985; Lees 1993; Dixon 1997).
This is most graphically and worryingly illustrated in the following transcript taken from an interview with Stephen, Paul and Daniel. Jordan was
away from school that day and I began by asking them whether they knew
where he was:

PC: Where's Jordan today?
Stephen: He's at home boiling his head off!
Paul: No! Kissing his girlfriend!
PC: Kissing his girlfriend? Who's his girlfriend?
Stephen: He's waiting at his girlfriend's house.
PC: Is he? Whose?
Paul: Yeah, waiting for her.
Stephen: And when she comes in, he's hiding, right, and when she comes in
he's going to grab her and take her upstairs and then she's going to
start screaming and he's going to kiss her . . . and sex her!
PC: And sex her? And why's she going to be screaming?
Stephen: Because she hates it!
PC: Because she hates it?
Stephen: Yeah!
PC: So, if she hates it, why does he do it?
Stephen: I don't know!
Paul: Because he loves her!
Stephen: He'll sing, 'I want to sex you up!'

As before, the context to these discussions was all-important in gaining an understanding of their nature and form. While the content of the above transcripts quite vividly illustrates the ability of children as young as 5 and 6 to cope with and reproduce such sexualised views, it cannot simply be regarded as representative of their perceptions and behaviour. The Bad Boys did not engage in such discussions on a continuous or even frequent basis. The focus of their conversations regularly jumped between computer games, racing, fighting, cartoons, bikes and other toys as well as girls and sex. Moreover, from observations of the boys in the classroom and playground, it appeared that they were more likely to introduce discussions about girls and sex in my direct presence than elsewhere. In attempting to make sense of this, and in the absence of any further evidence, I would suggest that the Bad Boys' greater likelihood of raising these issues in my presence can possibly be understood as part of their struggle to subvert and undermine my authority as an adult. Here it could be argued that the boys were, at least in part, introducing specifically 'adult' and 'taboo' themes precisely to challenge my dominant position. In this sense it could be argued that the boys were therefore not only competing between themselves to develop and maintain their masculine status but were also doing so with me. For the Bad Boys these interviews could therefore be seen as offering a way of partially subverting the dominant discursive positions of adult/child so central to the school by the introduction of adult themes and ways of knowing (Walkerdine 1981; Wolpe 1988). As Kehily and Nayak (1996: 219) also found in their own research, sexuality provides 'a fertile ground for exposing contradictions in power'.

Contested racialised identities

I have already alluded to the significance of 'race' in investing a significant amount of symbolic capital with the Bad Boys. The importance of this form of capital was felt as keenly within the group of boys as by those outside it. On a number of occasions, especially during interviews, the Bad Boys could be observed apparently competing with each other over the 'legitimate' claim to being Black. This was especially so for Paul and Jordan, who were both of dual heritage and whose identities as Black in the more immediate and personal level of their friendship groupings had to be worked on that much harder. This is illustrated in the following transcript, where the other boys teased Jordan and claimed he was an 'Indian':

PC: What about the girls in your classroom? Do you play with any of them?
All: No-oo! No!
Daniel: Some are Indians!
PC: Are they? What, do you play with Indian girls, then?

Stephen:	No way!
Daniel:	Jordan kisses 'em!
Jordan:	No! I'm West Indian!
Daniel:	Eh?
Jordan:	I'm West Indian – I'm English and I'm half-White, ain't I?
Paul:	Yeah, but then if you say that – d'you know what? – you're an *Indian*!
Jordan:	No! . . . Are you still my friend, then?
Paul:	Not if you talk like India! No – talking like an Indian!
Jordan:	I bet I am!
Paul:	If you do, I'm not, we're not playin' with ya!
P C :	Why's that, Paul? Don't you like/
Paul:	/We don't like Indians!
P C :	Why?
Paul:	We don't like Indian talkers!
P C :	Why?
Jordan:	[*indignantly*] Well, I ain't a Indian!

The contradictory and fluid nature of these racialised identities is certainly evident in the above, especially in the way that Paul, who himself is of dual heritage, led the teasing of Jordan. Here it can be seen how the symbolic capital claimed by Jordan was arguably being denied by his other peers. This contingent nature of 'race' is also evident in the following transcript taken from an argument between Jordan and Stephen. Here, Jordan was trying to reverse the above process by calling Stephen a 'Paki'. However, as can be seen, Stephen cleverly reclaimed the racist abuse directed at him and ironically turned it on its head:

Jordan:	[*sharpening pencil*] I'm going to do this very sharp!
Stephen:	Shut up, will you, Jordan!
Jordan:	Shut up, you, you Pakistan!
Stephen:	That's why Pakistan beat England! At cricket! Init? [*to PC*]
P C :	What?
Stephen:	Pakistan beat England at cricket?
P C :	Yeah.
Stephen:	[*to Jordan*] Ahhh! 'Cos I'm a Paki!
Jordan:	[*laughs*]
Stephen:	Init? I'm half-Paki and he's half-Paki!
P C :	Are you?
Jordan:	I'm half-Indian 'cos I'm a West Indian!
P C :	You're a West Indian?
Jordan:	I'm a little bit English and I come from Jamaica with my dad. Like this: chill out, man!
Stephen:	I bet!

What the above transcripts tend to illustrate above all else is the contradictory and contingent nature of racialised identities and the ability of these 5- and 6-year-old boys actively to work with, appropriate and successfully rework these discourses within their own experiences. It is interesting here to note how the field of masculine peer-group relations provides one of the central dynamics, not only for the appropriation and reproduction of racist discourses but also for their contingent and contested nature.

WESLEY AND THE DE-SIGNIFYING OF 'RACE'

The case study of the Bad Boys has been discussed here in detail as it draws attention to a range of racialised discursive processes that can articulate in the construction of some Black boys' masculine identities. In this it alludes to the power of discourses in influencing and shaping an individual's very sense of identity. As I made clear when introducing the case study, however, it was the fact that the Bad Boys were regularly seen together as a *group* of Black boys that arguably tended to increase their likelihood of being drawn into these processes. As such, they are not being held up as representative of all Black boys, but rather as being located at one end of a continuum which charts the influence of these broader racialised discourses on Black boys' emerging identities. Towards the other end of the continuum lay Wesley, the only Black boy from Mrs Brogan's class. As I want to suggest below, it was the fact that he was an individual Black boy who played with White boys that appeared partially to explain his ability to remain largely untouched by the discursive processes so central to the Bad Boys' lives.

Partly as a result of being the only Black boy in his class, Wesley had developed a close friendship with two White boys, Karl and John. In contrast with the Bad Boys, these three boys largely played among themselves and only occasionally involved themselves in other social networks. They could be seen most days sitting together in the classroom or playing together in the playground. Their games often involved a degree of fantasy and would revolve around creating 'secret bases' in the bushes and trees at the sides of the playing field, and/or role plays where one would be a monster chasing the others. Even their games of tick and races were much less conspicuous than the Bad Boys', often being located on the peripheries of the playground and round the bushes.

This general context of invisibility seemed to enable the boys largely to evade the more public struggles and contests over masculinity that the Bad Boys had been enmeshed within. Their notions of masculinity, and the various forms of capital that went with it, seemed to be far more related to the fantasy games which they often played. Alongside discussions of who was the fastest and who could 'batter' whom, they also had elaborate discussions over such characters as Superman and Spiderman, and whether they were going to get their costumes for Christmas. The following transcript, taken from an interview with the three boys, is typical of the forms of masculine interaction found among them:

Clive: My hamster died, so I'm going to get a little tiny guinea pig.

Wesley: My dad is going to get me a big Rottweiler soon!/

Clive: /Uhhh!

Wesley: When I'm older, and he's going to chase you and you. [*indicating Clive and John*]

John: I'm going to get an Alsatian tomorrow!

Wesley: Awwhhh!

Clive: I'm going to get a Doberman!

Wesley: Don't you dare bring your dogs near me or I'll beat you!

John: I'm going to bring my dogs tomorrow!

Wesley: Ohhh! I'll definitely be hiding right by my mum then!

It could be argued that, as opposed to the Bad Boys, the more private and exclusive nature of this friendship grouping enabled the construction of masculine identities to evolve much more around the appropriation of a range of alternative masculine symbols, fantasy figures and games. Their lack of involvement in the wider social arena of the playground, including the games of kiss-chase, meant that while they also came to define themselves in opposition to girls they appeared to do so in a different way from the Bad Boys. In this, there seemed to be no contradiction, as found with Stephen, between notions of girlfriends and girls-as-friends. Any association with girls for Wesley and his friends was questionable. This is evident from the following discussion, taken from the same interview with the three boys:

PC: What girls do you play with?

Clive: Urrr!

John: No one!

PC: Why?

Wesley: We don't like girls! We won't even go near them.

PC: Why?

Wesley: Don't like them.

Clive: 'Cos they might chase us/

Wesley: /And they might kiss us!

Clive: Yeah, that's why we stay away from them, don't we?

John: Yeah.

Wesley: I definitely don't like girls.

Clive: Nor me!

Wesley: 'Cos they chase me every time and I have to go speeding round the playground.

Clive: Well, I'm glad I ain't got a sister!

Wesley: Well, I have, but she can't chase me 'cos she's only eight weeks old.

I therefore observed no struggles and fights over girlfriends; as a consequence, the central dynamics through which girls became sexualised and objectified in the specific way that they did among the Bad Boys appeared to be missing for Wesley and his friends. Arguably, as a result, these specific discourses on girls, so evident with the Bad Boys, never really permeated into the language and cusses of these boys. Rather, typical cusses used by Wesley and Clive were: 'fat banana dog', 'fat motorbike' and 'mardy piece of cheese', all indicative, again, of the prominence of fantasy within their friendship group.

This friendship group, therefore, appeared to provide Wesley with a largely effective barrier to being drawn into the broader racialised processes so evident for the Bad Boys. His invisibility within the school generally, and therefore as a Black boy specifically, arguably meant that he was rarely physically or verbally challenged by other boys, nor encouraged into games of kiss-chase by girls. 'Race' seemed to be most prominent for Wesley within the more formal modes of discipline within the school, where he was slightly more likely to be chastised for the misdemeanours of the three boys in comparison to John and Clive. However, this appeared to be mostly confined to social arenas such as assemblies and the dining hall, involving teachers and other school staff who did not personally know Wesley. For Mrs Brogan, 'race' had been subsumed by gender, and Wesley and the other two boys were very much seen as 'typical boys'.

For the boys themselves, the salience of 'race' appeared also to have been significantly down-played. While Wesley was therefore acknowledged as being Black by his friends, they would often also simultaneously de-emphasise the significance of this, and, as illustrated in the following quote, at times redefine him as White. Here, the boys had just been talking about another boy:

PC: What boy?

Wesley: Kevin.

John: Kevin, a Black boy, same as him. [*pointing to Wesley*]

Wesley: I'm not Black, I'm brown, you silly boy!

PC: You're brown?

Wesley: Yeah.

PC: Well, what are you two [*Clive and John*] then?

Clive: We're White.

Wesley: You're kind of pink, though!

PC: Aren't we all the same, though? What's the difference?

Clive: No, 'cos he's the odd one out and us two are the same.

PC: But why is he the odd one out?

Wesley: 'Cos I'm brown!
Clive: He's changing into White, though, 'cos look at his skin!

CONCLUSIONS

This chapter has been concerned with charting the position of Black boys within the field of masculine peer-group relations. Rather than attempting to offer a comprehensive and representative account of the schooling experiences of all Black boys, the chapter has drawn attention to some of the more prominent racialised processes that articulate, to varying degrees, in the construction of Black boys' masculine identities. It has highlighted the potential power of discourses in coming to influence and shape a young child's very sense of self. Through the use of case studies, the chapter has highlighted some of the particular contexts within which Black boys appear more or less likely to be drawn into these processes. In this the notions of visibility and territory were central to our understanding. For the Bad Boys, they were rendered visible as a *group* of Black boys whose simple presence, and tendency to play with White girls, seemed to be regarded as invasions of the territory of some of the other boys. In contrast, Wesley, within his small friendship group with two White boys, appeared largely able to evade both of these.

Above all, the chapter has drawn attention to the importance of the children's peer-group relations in understanding Black boys' schooling experiences. In this it helps to develop and broaden out the important insights offered in relation to a now substantial body of work focusing on 'teacher racism'. What I want to suggest from this chapter is that teacher–pupil and pupil–pupil relations form a complex feed-back cycle where the actions of each tend to influence and exacerbate the other. In this sense it could be argued that the over-disciplining of Black boys tends to construct an image of them, among their peers, as being 'bad' and quintessentially masculine. This, in turn, provides the context where Black boys are more likely to be verbally and physically attacked. As a consequence, Black boys are more likely to be drawn into fights and to develop 'hardened' identities, which then means they are more likely to be noticed by teachers and disciplined for being aggressive. The cycle is thus complete.

It is an understanding of this complex set of processes that helps to overcome the increasingly intense debates surrounding 'teacher racism' that have emerged over recent years.[3] To crudely oversimplify, it has been argued by Foster, Gomm and Hammersley, in their reviews of a number of the studies cited above, that this work has not offered evidence beyond reasonable doubt that the teachers' actions can be understood simply as expressions of their own racist stereotypes (Foster *et al.* 1996). Rather, in Foster's (1990a) own work, and also more recently in that of Hurrell (1995), it has been argued that the teachers may well have been reacting to what was actually a 'real' tendency for Black boys to be, on the whole, more disruptive in class. The point is that, with the incorporation into our analysis of peer-group relations as set out in this chapter, we do not need to embrace the notion of teacher racism exclusively nor fall into the rather spurious and arguably ethically dubious conclusions offered by Peter Foster *et al.* The evidence from this present study is that some teachers did appear to reproduce a series of racialised assumptions about Black boys, often in a very subtle and unintended way and largely with the best intentions. However, these teachers also found that some Black boys were more likely to be 'troublesome' and involved in fights. As regards the latter, a focus on peer-group relations helps us to contextualise the boys' behaviour within a broader set of racialised discursive processes. As such it helps us avoid the tendency to draw the conclusion that this behaviour is somehow an inherent part of the Black boys' nature.

7

INVISIBLE MASCULINITIES?
SOUTH ASIAN BOYS AT EAST
AVENUE

Compared to Black male students, the schooling experiences of South Asian males have received relatively little research attention (Bhatti 1995). Some of the work that has been done on teacher/student relations has tended to suggest that they have been rendered 'invisible' within the school (Mac an Ghaill 1988; Gillborn 1990). However, as some of the previous chapters have already suggested, at East Avenue they often appeared to have been highly visible and the subject of significant levels of racist abuse. In this chapter I want to explore the nature of that visibility and the particular forms of racist discourses that surround it. In particular the chapter will draw attention to the ways in which many South Asian boys have been constructed as 'effeminate' through a range of discursive processes and practices within the school. This will form the context within which the chapter will go on to explore the general position of South Asian boys within the field of masculine peer-group relations. As will be seen through the use of a number of case studies, this provided the social backdrop against which many South Asian boys came to negotiate and develop their sense of masculinity.

As before, the chapter makes no claims to be representative of the schooling experiences of *all* South Asian boys. Rather, it is concerned with drawing attention to some of the more prominent racialised processes evident within the school that came to affect South Asian boys, to one degree or another. The use of case studies will highlight the agency of these boys and the very different ways in which they have either been drawn into these processes or have struggled to resist them.

TEACHER DISCOURSES ON SOUTH ASIAN
BOYS

In Chapter 4, I drew attention to the relatively high incidence of racist attacks experienced by a significant proportion of South Asian people living on Manor Park. In part I suggested that this could be understood through the way in which local people were encouraged to understand their sense of isolation and communal loss through discourses on 'race'. For some of the White and Black residents on the estate, it was suggested that they came to contrast their own sense of isolation with the perceived 'community spirit' enjoyed by South Asians. Their cultural and linguistic distinctiveness and what was thought of by some as their traditionalist approach appeared to set them apart from the rest of the community. While there was a general sense of community decline felt by many White and Black residents, this was to be contrasted, by some, with what was felt to be a growing and thriving South Asian community on Manor Park. For some of these residents, therefore, South Asian people appeared to represent an 'alien wedge' which had become the scapegoat for their broader experiences of social and economic decline. It was this, I suggested, that quite possibly lay behind the significant amount of racist abuse meted out to many South Asian residents on the estate.

These discourses that were being generated and reproduced on the estate appeared to provide the medium through which some teachers at East Avenue came to make sense of their own relationships with the South Asian children in their classes. What seemed to be particularly drawn out and emphasised by these teachers was the perception of the tight-knit, strict and traditional way of life practised by South Asian families on the estate. They were seen by some of the teachers as being one of the only sources of a 'normal' two-parent family structure on Manor Park (see also Wright 1992). I want to suggest that these discourses can, in part, be understood as rooted in the teachers' experiences of working at East Avenue. Here they were faced with children they generally perceived to be difficult to motivate and hard to control. As we saw in Chapter 5, one way of understanding this was through the dominant discourses on the inner city and familial decline, where it was widely felt that local working-class children were simply not being raised properly by their predominantly 'immature' single mothers. Within this discourse, the South Asian community were held up as an example of what a 'good' family should be. This is illustrated in the following quote from an interview with Mrs Campbell:

> I personally feel that the majority of White children are left behind more than the Asian and West Indians. [. . .] We've got three kinds of standards of living. [. . .] We find that the Asian community, the majority of the Asian community, are more caring on how much each child is learning. The West Indians want to get their child to learn, I mean I'm not saying they don't, but their values are entirely different to what the Asian community is. The Whites, as long as they're at school, they're doing something.

It is arguably within this context that a perception existed among some of the teachers of South Asian children as 'model pupils'. This is illustrated in the following extracts taken from the school reports on South Asian boys written by the three reception/Year 1 infant teachers. Their consistent emphasis on the positive nature of these boys was remarkably representative of the reports on other South Asian boys and stood in stark contrast to many of the teachers' reports on others.

Ms Patterson's class:

Malde   A very enthusiastic boy who is keen to do well. [. . .] He enjoys lots of work and is very industrious in the classroom.

Mrs Brogan's class:

Amit   Amit takes a great deal of pride in his presentation. He works slowly and carefully. [. . .] Amit is a friendly happy child.

Mrs Scott's class:

Prajay   Prajay [. . .] is a very agreeable boy. Very obedient also. [. . .] He is well behaved generally. His mother is very keen on his doing well.

The problem with this discursive framework, however, was that it failed to explain fully the teachers' own experiences of some South Asian boys who were difficult either to teach or to control. Ironically, in relation to their teaching role, it was the very discourses on their perceived traditionalist and strict family structure that were sometimes employed by these teachers to help make sense of this situation. Mrs Scott, for instance, often complained about her inability to motivate Irfan, a Muslim boy who had been in her class the year before. This, she explained to me, was due to his general tiredness, brought on, she felt, by his family who sent him to the mosque every night and whose high expectations he was continually struggling to meet. Similarly, Ms Patterson complained on several occasions about the way that some South Asian parents would spend a lot of time trying to teach their children but would do it incorrectly. She explained that many of her South Asian children would therefore be taught to memorise particular reading books from cover to cover without understanding and/or recognising the meaning of individual words. More generally from these experiences, some teachers seemed to have arrived at the belief that while many South Asian parents were perceived to adopt a 'good' traditional family life, they also tended to lack appropriate parenting and social skills.

Moreover, the difficulties that some teachers occasionally faced in motivating particular South Asian boys were not generally seen as reflecting an inherent stubbornness or challenging style – as was often the case with the Bad Boys in the last chapter. Rather, it was interpreted as little more than simple laziness and/or tiredness. This was not only the case for Irfan, as discussed above, but appeared to be used by some teachers for other South Asian boys. As Mrs Scott wrote in a school report of Prajay: 'When doing his written work he tends to dream and talk too much. This results in his being slow to complete work. [. . .] Prajay does not volunteer himself to any group discussions but will sit back and let other children do the work.'

This underplaying of the significance of particular South Asian boys' lack of motivation was also true in relation to incidents of their more direct challenges to authority. Here, many teachers appeared to make sense of the transgressions of South Asian boys in two main ways. First, as the following quote taken from an interview with Mrs Brogan illustrates, the significance of discourses on 'race' were downplayed and replaced by those on gender:

> Amit's a bright boy as well, very conscientious worker, neat in his work, works very methodically and he seems happy when he has achieved it. He likes to achieve, to have good results at the end of it. Again, he's a boy and when he gets together with, er, it's really Wesley, Amit, Clive [. . .] they can get a bit silly really – that's what it is.

As can be seen in the above, not only was gender used to explain Amit's 'silliness' but it was also used to imply that the source of the misbehaviour was the peer group, and more specifically the *other* boys. This was also a fairly common explanation offered by some of the other teachers. The following extracts taken from Mrs Scott's school reports on Bhavin and Prajay were both fairly representative of this. In relation to Bhavin, she wrote that he 'unfortunately [. . .] tends to befriend the most immature boys in the class', while for Prajay she felt that 'when he gets with other boys he gets rather boisterous'. The significance of the behaviour of South Asian boys, rather than being seen as a serious threat to order and control, would tend to be downplayed by the use of words such as 'silly' and 'immature', thus seemingly maintaining the teachers' perceptions of them as hardworking and helpful.

For the most part, however, the behaviour of South Asian boys tended to go unnoticed by the teachers (Mac an Ghaill 1988; Gillborn 1990). As we saw in the previous two chapters, at times when a teacher felt that order and control were being challenged she/he appeared to be more likely to single out Black boys to be publicly chastised. In this it was suggested that the particular perception of Black boys as aggressive and troublesome had possibly become part of the teachers' habitus. At times when a teacher was in a stressful situation and had to make snap decisions in order to regain control, these discourses did sometimes appear to lead her to identify Black boys as being the most likely to be the cause of the trouble. As other research has shown, the more the Black boys were publicly chastised for misdemeanours that they were not involved in, the more they came to resist this, and the more teachers perceived this resistance as reinforcing their initial beliefs that the Black boys concerned were indeed aggressive and troublesome (Wright 1986; Mac an Ghaill 1988).

This form of self-fulfilling prophecy also appeared to be evident for the South Asian boys, but with very different consequences. Here, it could be argued that the general perception of South Asian boys as hardworking and helpful also came to be incorporated into some teachers' habitus. For these teachers, at times of crisis, it would encourage them to overlook the South Asian boys in the belief that they were probably not the cause of the trouble. As discussed in Chapter 5, whoever the teacher did single out for public chastisement – whether that child was essentially 'innocent' or not – did not matter in the sense that it always resulted in the regaining of order and control in the classroom. This practice of making an example of particular children therefore served as a warning to others who, generally, would desist from their behaviour, for the time being at least. And it is here that the self-fulfilling prophecy for South Asian boys is complete. For the more that the teachers overlooked South Asian boys in the search for the ring-leaders of particular misdemeanours, and the more they regained control by publicly chastising those they thought were involved, then the more their decision to overlook South Asian boys appeared to be vindicated. In this way it was a decision that, over time, could possibly be seen as becoming part of some of the teachers' taken-for-granted practice: that is, their habitus. While it is difficult to state just how often such a process was evident in the classrooms I observed, it was certainly the case that on a significant number of occasions disruptive behaviour on the part of South Asian boys did appear to go unchallenged – behaviour that teachers often appeared to address in other boys. In these instances the teacher observed would either ignore the situation altogether or, when the misbehaviour involved a number of children and was difficult to avoid, she would tend to single out and discipline another boy.

TEACHER DISCOURSES AND THE FEMINISATION OF SOUTH ASIAN BOYS

There were two immediate and essentially inter-related effects that these particular teacher discourses, as manifest within the school, had on the children's peer-group relations. The first related to the apparent tendency for the seriousness of South Asian boys' behaviour to be either downplayed or overlooked altogether by some teachers. As outlined above, many of these boys were rarely disciplined in school. Indeed, when they were, the perception of their misbehaviour was often such that it was far more likely to be addressed as an individual private matter between teacher and pupil rather than in a more public way. One of the central processes that operated to produce and reproduce the masculine status of Black boys in the school was therefore largely denied to South Asian boys. In some respects, therefore, theirs was a masculinity that could be argued to be largely 'invisible' (Mac an Ghaill 1988; Gillborn 1990).

However, and this is the second point, it could be argued that it was not so much that they were simply rendered invisible by teacher discourses but, rather, they were actively 'feminised' by them. I have already alluded to the relatively high number of occasions the South Asian boys were praised for their hard work and eagerness to please in class. Moreover, and as will be seen below, references to them 'all being the same', to being quiet and 'little' and therefore needing to be befriended and looked after, all acted to bestow upon these particular boys some of the central characteristics often associated with femininity. The following two incidents, both of which took place in the Infants' Birthday Assemblies, illustrate these processes quite vividly. The first took place as the head of the Infants, Mrs Christie, stood at the front and was awarding stickers to those nominated by the class teachers for 'being good'. She had just finished awarding stickers to the nursery children and had moved on to Ms Patterson's class, reading out the names that Ms Patterson had added to be awarded stickers:

> Class 1, Anand and Malde. Anand's in the band I think [. . .] I always get those two confused. Anand's the one with the smiling face and Malde . . . it says in the book you are in this book for trying hard, both of you, well done, go and choose your stickers.

This apparent objectification of South Asian boys, in that they were all seen as the same and devoid of individuality, was also something that tended to be appropriated and reproduced by some of the children. Anand, for example, came to me during one playtime and complained that, 'Everyone's calling me Amit and I'm not!' Alongside this objectification, as I have mentioned, was the tendency for some South Asian boys to be referred to as little, passive and in need of 'looking after'. This is illustrated in the following incident, also taken from a Birthday Assembly, where Mrs Christie was at the front. The children had just finished singing a song. Note also, towards the end of the transcript, how Mrs Christie inadvertently reproduced the notion of the strong and extended South Asian family:

Mrs Christie: The prayer this morning was all about being good friends. The reason I mention that is because we have had quite a few new children start school over the last fortnight. I've got one little girl in my class, Beenal, who was new just the

121

	end of last week. Mitesh is new in Mrs Jones' class, and I bet the other teachers have got quite a few new children/
Mrs Brogan:	/Yesterday, Mrs Christie!
Mrs Christie:	Somebody yesterday, who's that?
Mrs Brogan:	Satpal.
Mrs Christie:	Satpal in Mrs Brogan's class. That little lad down there? [*pointing*]
Mrs Brogan:	The tiny one.
Mrs Christie:	The tiny little one? [*puts her hand out to summon him to the front, he stands up a little apprehensively and walks up to her*] He's brand new?
Mrs Brogan:	Brand new; ever so quiet!
Mrs Christie:	Now when you start a new school, especially very late in the year, it's ever such a big change because you've left all your old things behind; your old friends, your old school, your old house or flat, perhaps even his relatives – perhaps he's moved, a long way away, perhaps *he won't see his aunties and uncles for a while* so, when you start a new school it's lovely if everyone at that new school tries to be your friend. It makes you feel so much more happy. So [. . .] I hope you're going to be a good friend to Satpal. Help him, and if he looks confused or if he looks unhappy, take him by the hand and show him you're a friend. [*emphasis added*]

These broader discursive processes that tended to construct some South Asian boys as 'feminine' also appeared to be exacerbated by those associated with the school's approach to multiculturalism, which seemed to reinforce the objectification and alienation of South Asian children generally. In Chapter 5 I drew attention to the school's celebration of Diwali, which was held up as the main 'multicultural' event of the school year. The chapter highlighted how there was not only a whole Family Gathering given over to the celebration of Diwali, but also how it had become increasingly embedded within the school over recent years, as various activities were organised in classes during the weeks prior to the assembly. For the infant classes, this included: the reading of relevant stories, learning specific songs (often in Gujerati), the colouring in of pictures, and the preparation of displays on the walls each with a Diwali theme. During the Diwali assembly the children would display their pictures to the rest of the school and sing one of the songs they had learnt. Older children would also contribute to the assembly with some re-enacting traditional stick dancing, others reading out stories and others presenting a puppet show relating to the story of Diwali, all of these being prepared within their respective classes.

The general message that teaching staff conveyed to the children was that Diwali represented the South Asian children's Christmas. This was used to explain the general celebratory mood of Diwali and the giving of presents. However, beyond this many of the teachers had only a very sketchy understanding of the festival (see also Tomlinson 1983). This was illustrated by one of the full-time Section 11 staff, Mrs Coombs, who had chosen to read the Diwali story to Mrs Scott's class one morning before the Diwali assembly. The children all sat together on the carpet and a number of them were called to the front to hold puppets depicting the various characters referred to in the story. However, Mrs Coombs, to the amusement of some of the children, experienced problems in pronouncing some of the characters' names and looked for help to a South Asian female student who was on placement at the school and sitting in on the class. When Mrs Coombs picked up the puppet of the ten-headed monster, she asked the children what its name was. No one replied. After a while spent trying to encourage a response, she turned to two South Asian girls sitting on the carpet and asked them, saying: 'Come on, Beenal, Poonam! What's his name?' The two girls sat there quietly, looking rather awkward and refused to reply. After a period of silence, Mrs Coombs told the children it was Ravana or Ravan, saying she could not remember, and looked again to the South Asian student, who told her it was Ravan.

It could be argued that this example, which was by no means unique, tended to downgrade the importance of Diwali in the children's eyes through the teacher's lack of knowledge and her inability to pronounce and/or remember the names of some of the main characters. Arguably this latter point was particularly true given the comparisons that teachers encouraged between Diwali and Christmas. While the latter came to dominate the whole of the school during the last two to three weeks of term in December, the celebration of Diwali came to revolve around one assembly and a few particular activities in class during the days leading up to the assembly. The detailed knowledge of and enthusiasm for Christmas shared by most of the staff and children meant that comparisons with Diwali would quite possibly only help to reinforce the latter's 'second-rate' status.

The way in which this approach to Diwali appeared to reinforce further the discourses tending to objectify and set apart South Asian children as the 'Other' is illustrated in the following interview with three girls (two White and one Black) from Mrs Brogan's class. It illustrates the way in which aspects of the Diwali celebration (notably the dancing and singing) provided the means with which the girls were able to reproduce the discourses on the 'alien' and inferior status of South Asians:

PC: What's Diwali?
Stacey: It's Indian!
Zoe: I don't like Indians very much!

Kylie: I didn't like the Indian Diwali things. We didn't even do anything
        – we didn't do no dancing, we didn't do nothing – the Juniors
        did!

Zoe: All they do is get their sticks and done that. [*gesturing*]

PC: Did they? [*turning to Kylie*] What is it, Kylie? What do you think
        Diwali is?

Kylie: Diwali lights!

PC: So why don't you like Diwali then, Zoe?

Zoe: 'Cos I'm not related to it/

Kylie: /I know 'cos we don't do nothing/

Zoe: /She's not related to it [*pointing to Kylie*], I'm not related to it.

PC: Related to it? What do you mean?

Zoe: I am not Indian.

[. . .]

PC: But why can't you like Diwali then?

Zoe: We don't.

Stacey: Because it's Indian.

Kylie: 'Cos it's Pakis! I don't like Pakis/

Zoe: /I don't like Pakis/

Kylie: /because they are horrible.

PC: Why? Why are they horrible?

Kylie: They get some sticks and dance with 'em.

Zoe: I like the show but I don't like them doing dancing.

[. . .]

PC: So tell me what Diwali is about?

Kylie: Pakis have circles on [*pointing to her forehead*], red things, I hate
        'em.

Zoe: And them! [*pointing to posters of South Asian children on wall*] and
        them and them!

PC: But why do you hate them?

Kylie: Because they're horrible.

PC: But why are they horrible?

Kylie: 'Cos they chatterbox all the time.

PC: But don't we all chatterbox?

Kylie: Yeah.

[. . .]

PC: But why are they horrible [then]?

Zoe: They're Indians.

Kylie: And Indians stink!

Zoe: And they're chatterboxes and they chatterbox all day.

PC: But Indians don't smell.

Zoe: They do stink! They do!

PC: No they don't! Who told you that?

Zoe: My brother said so.

It can be seen from the above that the girls played a central and active role in appropriating, weaving together and reworking a whole range of discursive themes associated with South Asian children. Here they had drawn upon more general and popular stereotypes learnt from one of their brothers relating to the way that South Asians 'stink' [*sic*] and had woven this together with more particular concerns relating to what they perceived as the South Asian children's peculiar forms of dancing and talking. Arguably, these latter elements emphasised the importance of the children's own experience in their appropriation and reproduction of these racist discourses. The fact that these girls were denied the opportunity to get involved in the dancing that took place in the assembly, together with the more general concern (and one which will be returned to later) related to the threat they appeared to feel in not being able to understand the language used by South Asian children, were experiences that seem to have been understood through the medium of 'race'. It could be argued that this signifying of 'race' was also reinforced by the discourses on the inferior and 'alien' nature of South Asian people reproduced on the Manor Park estate. As will be remembered from Chapter 4, these manifested themselves primarily through a significant number of verbal and physical assaults on South Asians often meted out by children from the school. It is within this context that we can begin to understand how, for some of the children, the school's multicultural approach, while developed for the most laudable reasons, tended ironically to provide the basis for the development and reproduction of particular racist discourses.

MASCULINE PEER-GROUP RELATIONS AND SOUTH ASIAN BOYS

So far I have purposely focused on some of the broader processes in operation within the school, manifest both in particular teacher discourses and in the school's overall multicultural policies. What I have highlighted is the way in which these appeared discursively to constitute South Asian boys as ultimately effeminate. This femininity can be understood along a number of axes: the way that their invisibility operated to deny them access to the public sphere and hence tended to restrict them to the private; the constitution of them as being small, defenceless, eager-to-please and helpful; and the objectification of them through the discourses that tended to render them alien and different. The effects of this on the field of masculine peer-group relations appeared to create a tendency for South Asian boys to be forced into the role that has been traditionally associated with girls (see, for instance, Best 1983; Clark 1990), that is, being what boys 'are not'. I want to suggest that South Asian boys had therefore partially become the focus through which other boys were able to develop and reassert their own masculine status. Arguably, being masculine could be reinforced by some boys through distancing themselves from South Asian boys just as much as it could from girls more generally (see also Connell 1989).

As a result there was a marked tendency for some South Asian boys to be both verbally and physically attacked and excluded from wider social networks (see also Bhatti 1996). As regards the former, there were regular, at least weekly, incidents observed during the fieldwork involving White and Black boys attacking South Asian boys. These forms of racist attacks, however, were of a different order to those experienced by Black boys. Many White boys, as will be remembered from the previous chapter, appeared to hold a grudging respect for Black boys and would attack them in essentially public spaces seemingly to reaffirm their own sense of masculinity. In this it was assumed that Black boys would fight back, and what was therefore sought appeared to be no more than a public duel in which White boys could 'flex their muscles'. In contrast, the attacks on South Asian boys seemed not to be based on any form of respect, grudging or otherwise, but on contempt. There was no prolonged 'sparring match' entered into by those White and Black boys who chose to attack South Asian boys. Rather, the attacks were often observed to be quick and brutal, with the possible goal of White and Black boys sending immediate signals to close friends about their own masculinity without appearing to give South Asian boys any legitimacy through prolonging the encounter. They were attacks more reminiscent of fleeting 'raids', where certain boys would swoop in, assault, and swoop out again. It could be argued that the style of such confrontations prevented South Asian boys from effectively defending themselves and, therefore, 'proving' themselves as competent fighters. In many ways, the boys' general racialised perceptions of South Asian boys meant that they did not expect a response from them. This style of assault was certainly evident from observations in the playground. Periodically throughout the year, small groups of boys would be seen seeking out South Asian children, boys in particular, calling them names and/or hitting them before walking off. This was certainly true of Prajay's experience, which was fairly representative of that of a number of South Asian boys. As he explained to me in one interview:

Prajay: When I play outside, Jordan hits me and Jordan's big friends hit me.
PC: Did they? Why did they do that? Did they call you anything?
Prajay: They call me Paki!

The fact that Prajay also played football with Jordan and the other Bad Boys draws attention to the complexities of South Asian boys' identities and the need to understand them within their particular contexts.

In many ways, these attacks appeared to be symptomatic of a broader process whereby Black and White boys were actively policing their own masculine identities (see also Mac an Ghaill 1994). As part of their identity is developed through their distance from South Asian boys, not only did they need to show their direct contempt for these boys but they also needed to ensure that they were not associated in any way with them. It is here that we can also begin to understand the general exclusion of South Asian boys from wider social networks. The extent to which some South Asian boys are excluded depends upon the specific context. As will be discussed later, a number of friendships between Black, White and South Asian boys did occur, although these were more likely to have been formed and maintained in more private and enclosed friendship groups. In contrast, social activities that were highly visible and public in their nature were much harder for South Asian boys to access. Two such activities were noted in the last chapter: kiss-chase and football. Both of these were highly public affairs being played out across the whole of the playground and inviting much attention and gossip from other children. As I outlined, kiss-chase appeared to be a prominent expression of the children's gender identities. As we saw, for Black and White boys to be associated with South Asian girls would invoke derision from their male peers. Interestingly, this also appeared to be true for Black and White girls. A South Asian boyfriend was seen by some girls as at best a joke and at worst placing a serious question mark over their own feminine identities (see also Hatcher 1995). This is illustrated in the following incident, where a group of Black and White girls were playing 'Orange Balls'. This was a game involving singing and the progressive selection of one girl, who was then asked by the others whether she loved a particular (unnamed) boy. The boy's name was chosen by the other girls out of earshot from her. She would then indicate whether she loved him or not, at which point his name would be revealed. On this occasion, the boy chosen by the other girls was Jayesh, a South Asian boy who had just moved up to Mrs Brogan's class from the nursery. When the girl said that she loved him, the others burst out laughing and told her who it was and began to tease her. A couple of the girls then ran off to Jayesh, laughing, telling him how their friend loved him.

It appeared that Jayesh was used by the girls collectively to reassert their own sense of taste and feminine identity. It is also interesting to note how, because of this general discourse on South Asian boys shared by some of the White and Black girls, these girls were never observed encouraging South Asian boys to play games of kiss-chase with them. As with the issues of discipline and racist assaults discussed above, these processes therefore appeared to reinforce further some of the South Asian boys' sense of invisibility and, as a result, denied them another public arena through which they could otherwise attempt to construct and assert their masculine identities.

This process of exclusion was also evident in relation to games of football in the playground. By its very nature, football was a highly public affair and competency at it appeared to provide an important means through which boys could assert their masculine athleticism. Moreover, who a boy played football with also reflected back upon his own level of competency. This is illustrated by the following interview with Irfan, from Mrs Brogan's class, which illustrates the way in which football had become a heavily guarded affair among the boys:

PC: Do you ever play football at school in the playground, Irfan?
Irfan: I don't play in the school football; I play in the home football.
PC: Why don't you play football at school?
Irfan: Because they will batter me!
PC: Who?
Irfan: I don't know their name.
PC: Why won't they let you play?
Irfan: Because they won't play with me and the ball [. . .] Stephen won't let me play.
PC: Stephen? Why not?
Irfan: Stephen in Mrs Scott's class. [. . .] He won't play with me – I play in the bushes.
PC: Who do you play in the bushes with?
Irfan: Nobody!

The nature of these exclusions and some of the underlying reasons for them can be seen in the following interview with the Bad Boys who featured in the previous chapter. Here, they were struggling with the contradictions of racism, and the way that they allowed Prajay to play but wished to justify their continued exclusion of Ajay and Malde from Ms Patterson's class. As before, it illustrates quite clearly the active role that the children themselves appeared to play in the reworking and reproduction of racist discourses. Moreover, it highlights their relatively sophisticated cognitive ability to appropriate and use a number of racial stereotypes in the line of prolonged questioning.

PC: So I'm just trying to figure out who plays [*football*] – so Prajay plays, does he?
Paul: Yeah.
PC: He's one of yours/
Daniel: /Yeah/
PC: /What about, er, Ajay and Malde? [*both in a parallel Reception/Year 1 class*]/
Daniel: Urrr no!
Paul: Nah!
Daniel: They're rubbish!
Jordan: They're always playing crap games!

PC: Why are they rubbish, though, Daniel?
Daniel: Because they're Paaa-kis!/
Stephen: No, no, no! Because they can't run fast!
PC: They can't run fast?
Stephen: Yeah, and say we've got the ball and we just, we just burn it and they're, they're, still near their, near our bloody goal, and we, and we've got the goal.
PC: Why can't they run fast?
Paul: Because they're small! [Laughs]
Stephen: No!
PC: Stephen, you tell us, why can't they run fast then?
Stephen: 'Cos 'cos they're Pakis and Pakis can't run fast!
PC: But they're the same as everybody else, aren't they?
Stephen: No!
PC: Why? Why aren't they the same as everybody else?
Daniel: Don't know!
Stephen: 'Cos . . .
PC: Well, they are, aren't they?
Stephen: [shouting frustratedly] 'Cos they're slow and everything!
Jordan: An' they want to be on your side 'cos you're fast, ain't it Stephen?
PC: [. . .] Would you let Ajay and people play if they wanted to?
Daniel: No!
PC: No? Why not?
Stephen: I wouldn't let slow people play!
PC: But you let Prajay play – is he slow?
Paul: No!
Stephen: He's quite fast!
PC: Yeah, but he's Indian!
Stephen: Yeah, so, he ain't got a dot on his head!
Jordan: His mum has!
PC: Yeah, but Ajay hasn't got a dot on his head!
Stephen: Yes he has!
Daniel: No he hasn't!
Stephen: He's got a black one, so there!

It is apparent from the arguments put forward above, especially in relation to South Asian boys' perceived inability to run fast, that they were not simply taken and reproduced, word for word, from older peers or parents, but seemed to have been actively re-formed and moulded to justify their particular actions. Above all, the conversation illustrates the way in which the nature and form of these discourses related quite directly to the boys' lived experiences. What is also interesting from the above discussion is the way in which the Bad Boys defended Prajay and his ability to play while, as seen before, they continued in other contexts to verbally and physically assault him. It is to the contradictions inherent within the schooling experiences of South Asian boys as they came to negotiate, resist and challenge these broader racialised discourses that I now want to turn for the remainder of this chapter. In doing this I will use three different case studies to highlight the variety of ways in which South Asian boys within the school have come to respond to these broader racialised processes. As we will see, some tried to avoid these broader processes and develop their own alternative space. Others chose to resist them and attempt to gain status within the broader field, while others still came to find that their identity as South Asian was significantly downplayed. We will look at each of these responses in turn.

AJAY, MALDE, VIGNESH AND PRITUL

Ajay, Malde, Vignesh and Pritul were four South Asian boys who began the academic year together in Ms Patterson's class. With the partial exception of Pritul, who will be returned to shortly, their experience of schooling, and particularly of relations with their peers, was nearest to the broader picture outlined above. Arguably, their tendency to sit together in class, play together in the playground and sometimes talk among themselves in Gujerati meant that they were the most likely group of South Asian boys in the Infants to attract the attention of their peers. As a result, they appeared to be more likely to be attacked by some of their male peers and were also almost uniformly excluded from the most prominent and public social activities including football and group games such as tick and play-fighting and kiss-chase. It was because of this general exclusion, together with the ever-present threat of attack, that their tendency to associate together should arguably be seen more as an inevitable response to these broader experiences than merely a matter of choice. In other words, it appeared to represent a strategy of survival. Part of this strategy could be seen in their tendency to inhabit the more private and protected spaces within the playground. They were more likely to play in the bushes and round the edges of the playground, congregate around the entrance to the school building where teachers and/or dinner supervisors usually stood and, when on their own, to follow teachers and other adults (including me) around the playground.

Their response appeared therefore to be essentially one of avoiding, as far as possible, the threat of attack and the humiliation of being excluded, by developing their own protected spaces. Here, over time, they seemed to have developed, valued and struggled over their own forms of social, symbolic and cultural capital, and it was through this that they appeared to have developed their own sense of masculine identity. However, it could be argued that, being excluded from the more public arenas within the school, including football and kiss-chase, their masculinity came to organise itself around various forms of capital that were more likely to be based upon role-plays and fiction. Thus, alongside the more common practices of kick-fighting and racing that they indulged in, they were also more likely to play 'super-hero' games such as Superman or Thunderbirds (see also Davies 1989; Jordan 1995). Moreover, while the notion of girlfriends was also a significant strand to the maintenance of their masculine identity, it was more likely to take the form of picking various girls' names and teasing one another, rather than finding expression through actual games of kiss-chase. As such it was arguably less likely to have turned more directly to themes of ownership and control in comparison with the Bad Boys in the last chapter.

What we find with these four boys, then, is that while the struggles they engaged in between themselves in relation to the successful acquisition and maintenance of masculine identities were as keenly fought as with other boys, their struggles took place in more private and self-contained spaces within the school. Their masculine competencies went largely unseen by other boys, who rather saw only a group of South Asian boys playing together in the corner. This, in turn, appeared simply to reinforce the perception of them as different and alien.

Within this, the role adopted in the group by Pritul was an interesting and contradictory one. While a significant proportion of his time was spent with these boys, he also engaged in a struggle to be recognised by the other boys in his class, especially the two Black boys, Peter and Devan, who were considered by many of the boys to be the hardest and strongest. Ironically, both of these boys appeared to be also among those most likely to verbally abuse and hit and kick South Asian boys. However, while Devan very rarely entertained Pritul's company, Peter did at times play with him. Their games were often based around the acquisition and display of competencies involved in wrestling and kick-fighting, and as such involved mutual play-fights among themselves, as well as directing their attention to others in the playground who did not wish to get involved, including other South Asian boys. Peter appeared to play the dominant 'minder' role in their relationship, and at times would step in to defend Pritul and/or enact retribution if he was hurt. This occurred, for example, on one occasion when Pritul had run up to Prajay and kicked and pushed him before running away. Prajay followed him and kicked him quite hard in retaliation, causing Pritul to cry. On seeing this, Peter ran over and pleaded with Pritul to tell him who it was so that he could 'batter them'. After being told, Peter ran directly towards Prajay with the intention of enacting revenge, but failed to catch him.

The contradictory nature of Pritul's sense of identity can be seen in the following extract where Pritul was forced to accept that Peter and Devan did, on occasion, hit and kick the group of South Asian boys, but also attempted to distance Peter from this and defend him.

PC: Do you play with Peter?

Ajay: NO! He keeps hitting us!

Pritul: Yeah! Yeah! Peter's my friend! If someone comes to hit me, Peter just hits them.

Ajay: [. . .] I don't like them any more. [*meaning Devan and Peter*]

PC: Why?

Ajay: 'Cos they keep hitting us.

[. . .]

Ajay: Peter is nasty to me and Devan is nasty to us!

PC: What do they do?

Ajay: Kick us sometimes!

Pritul: No! Not me! – only Devan! When I kicked the ball he hit me round here!

PC: Did he?

Pritul: Yeah, one time!

[. . .]

PC: Does anybody call you horrible names?

Ajay: Yeah! [. . .] Devan and Peter do!

PC: Do they? What do they say?

Ajay: Stupid!/

Pritul: /NO! Not Peter! Not Peter – Peter's my friend!

Ajay: No, he's not!

Pritul: Yeah, he is!

PC: Peter's friends with you, Pritul?

Pritul: Yeah.

PC: And is he friends with Ajay?

Ajay: YEAH! Yes, he is – sometimes!

Pritul: Yeah, but why sometimes does he say dirty things to you?

What is interesting from the above is the contradictions that unfold in Pritul's attempts successfully to bridge his friendship with these South Asian boys and with Peter. In developing a friendship with Peter, it appeared that he had to distance himself, at least in part, from the other boys, and this can be seen in the way he closely guards Peter's friendship at the end of the transcript and reminds Ajay that Peter had said 'dirty things' to him (including racial abuse). Moreover, it was possibly through this act of distancing that Pritul also told me during this interview how he wanted to change his name to 'Jason', because: 'I don't like my name now.'

The problem was, however, that in attempting to compete successfully within the broader, more public field of masculine peer-group relations, Pritul was more likely to run the risk of being racially identified and abused. For, as was discussed earlier, to be seen associating with 'Pakis' in such public spaces seemed only to cast doubts on the other boys' claims of masculinity. Moreover, it could be argued that to be seen to be being beaten by South Asian boys in football, racing or fighting could only exacerbate all of this; hence Pritul's admission in the above interview that Devan hit him when he kicked the ball.

PRAJAY AND FOOTBALL

These problems faced by South Asian boys, in attempting to compete successfully within the more public field of masculine peer-group relations and the problems and contradictions that result, can be illustrated by the case of Prajay. Prajay started the academic year as the only South Asian boy in Mrs Scott's class. The foregrounding of gender and of classroom loyalties appeared to have the effect of downgrading the significance of 'race' for Prajay in the classroom, and meant that he was, albeit only partially, accepted into the friendship groups that evolved and developed around the four Bad Boys (Stephen, Jordan, Paul and Daniel). The transcript discussed earlier, from an interview with the Bad Boys where they attempted to justify the exclusion of Ajay and Malde from their football games while allowing Prajay to play, appears to demonstrate the way they had downgraded the significance of 'race' in their relationship with Prajay.

However, as with Pritul, this was not without its contradictions; within the more public arena constituted through games of football, Prajay was more likely to be verbally and physically assaulted. This can be illustrated by the following two incidents that happened during playtime. The first occurred when Prajay made the mistake of picking up the ball midway through a game and interrupting its flow, for which he was called a 'stupid Paki' by one of the boys, who proceeded to grab the ball from him, push him and tell him to 'go away'. The second related to the time Prajay had been successful in winning the ball from another boy, who then decided to chase after him, push him to the ground and mutter the word 'Paki' before regaining the ball and running off again.

It was not only public spaces that provided the contexts within which Prajay was more likely to experience racist abuse, but also in competitive situations. An example of this can be seen in an incident that occurred at the end of morning break, when Mrs Scott's class were asked to line up in pairs ready to be led over to the sports hall for a PE lesson. This was ten minutes' walk away, on the other side of the estate. Stephen, Jordan, Paul and Daniel were arguing among themselves and jostling with each other as to who should stand at the front. Behind them, Prajay stood on his own. Mrs Scott asked me to lead the way and so I took Prajay's hand, walked to the front and led the children off. Seeing this, Stephen appeared to become a little frustrated and said, in a slightly raised voice, 'That's it, let the *Paki* go first!' On hearing this I stopped, turned around and asked him what he had said, to which he refused to reply, simply repeating his assertion that he should have gone first. What this tends to illustrate is the way that broadly competitive situations, where masculine status and identities are at stake, have a tendency to become racialised as those involved vie for position and use 'race' to try and make sense of their success or, as in this case, failure.

Above all, what these incidents involving Prajay and Pritul tend to illustrate is the context-specific nature of racist incidents and how the salience of 'race' at any particular time can only be understood by the specific nature of the field of social relations that have developed. They illustrate how two particular, although by no means exclusive, contexts created a climate within which racist incidents were more likely to occur. In many ways this has been more than adequately highlighted and discussed elsewhere (see Troyna and Hatcher 1992). What I am interested in drawing attention to here is the inherent irony that football, in particular, presented at East Avenue. As outlined in detail in the previous chapter, this was a sport that had been positively encouraged and developed by many of the senior staff. It was seen by them as a way of reaching out to and engaging the Black boys at the school to overcome what was perceived to be their disaffection with schooling. As a result, not only had it flourished among the older juniors, who were the main target group for the strategy, but it had also significantly increased in its popularity among the younger boys. However, the irony arises in that this particular multicultural/anti-racist strategy had also created the contexts within which racist incidents were more likely to flourish. For football, more than many other group activities, was not only an inherently public affair but also a highly competitive one. It could be argued that games of football among the boys therefore provided one of the predominant social arenas in which masculine identities were lost and won. Within this context, we saw that not only were South Asian boys almost systematically excluded from football but, for those few who were able to play, such as Pritul and Prajay, they were more likely to be at the receiving end of racist abuse. The irony, then, is that while football was used as a distinct multicultural/anti-racist strategy aimed at trying positively to engage Black boys in the school, its effects had unwittingly been to increase the likelihood of South Asian boys being either socially excluded and/or racially abused. Above all, it is an irony that highlights the need to come to terms fully with the complex relationship between 'race' and gender relations before embarking on particular multicultural/anti-racist strategies, a point highlighted all too vividly by the Burnage Report (Macdonald *et al.* 1989).

AMIT: 'HE AIN'T A PROPER PAKI!'

The final case study is that involving Amit, a South Asian boy in Mrs Brogan's class. As with Prajay, he was the only South Asian boy in his class at the beginning of the academic year, and in a similar way he developed close friendship ties with three other boys: Wesley (Black) and Clive and John (both White). As with the four South Asian boys discussed earlier, it was a friendship group that was relatively closed, and one which appeared to create its own private spaces within which the boys could develop and express their own sense of masculine identities. In the last chapter I spent some time outlining some of the central dynamics of the group as they related to Wesley's position within it, highlighting the fact that their similar emphasis on role-plays, fantasy and super-heroes seemed to have had the effect of downgrading the significance of 'race' for the boys within the group. Thus, while they would at times define themselves as a group in opposition to South Asians through a number of racialised and derogatory discourses on 'Pakis', they would nevertheless downplay the significance of skin colour within their group. The contradictions inherent within this are illustrated quite clearly in the following extract taken from an interview with Amit, Clive and another White boy, Mark, where Amit's identity as South Asian was not only denied altogether, but Amit, himself engaged in reproducing racist discourses on 'Pakis':

Clive:	I don't like Pakis!
Amit:	You do like Pakis, stupid!
Clive:	No, I don't – I only like you!
PC:	Why don't you like them?
Mark:	'Cos they speak Gujerati!
[. . .]	
PC:	Clive, why don't you like them?
Clive:	Because they smell horrible.
Amit:	'Cos they smell like a clock!
Clive:	Yeah, like Amit does!
Amit:	I don't smell!
PC:	You like Amit, don't you Clive?
Clive:	Yeah.
PC:	You like Amit, and yet Amit's an Asian as well, isn't he?
Clive:	Yeah.
PC:	So, you said you don't like them – why not?
Clive:	'Cos he don't smell like a clock!
PC:	No, seriously, why?
Clive:	'Cos he ain't a proper Paki!
PC:	Why isn't he a proper one?
Clive:	Because he don't smell right!
[. . .]	
PC:	Do you think people like being called 'Paki'?
Clive:	Yeah.
PC:	Yeah? Do you think so really?

Clive:	Yeah.
Amit:	Sure!
PC:	Do you think so, Amit?
Amit:	I hate a big boy!
Clive:	I hate a big Paki – he pushed me in the playground.
Amit:	I hate a big, giant Paki! When he kicks me I whack him on the nose!
PC:	Amit, you said that you don't think people mind being called 'Paki'?
Amit:	I think a big boy needs to be called a Paki and he needs to call himself Paki!
Clive:	[*laughs*]
PC:	But would you like to be called that?
Amit:	No.
PC:	No? So, Clive, if he doesn't like to be called that, why do you call him that? Would you like to be called names like that?
[. . .]	
Clive:	I would mind but I'd batter them if they called me it.

CONCLUSIONS

The focus of this chapter has been the position of South Asian boys within the field of masculine peer-group relations. What I have argued is that, in contrast to Mac an Ghaill's (1988) notion of 'invisible' masculinities, many South Asian boys were visible and appeared to be discursively constituted through teacher discourses as 'effeminate'. This, I have shown, could possibly be seen in the way they were denied access to the public sphere, perceived as small, helpless and eager-to-please, and objectified through racialised discourses that construct them as 'all the same'. The effect of this on their position within the field of masculine peer-group relations has consequently been to construct a role for them traditionally given to girls, that is, being what 'we' (as boys) 'are not'. In this sense they had become cultural symbols or representations in opposition to which many other boys had come to define and reassert their own sense of masculinity. The consequences of this generally for the field of masculine peer-group relations appeared to be that South Asian boys experienced a tendency to be excluded from social activities and also to be verbally and physically assaulted. This exclusion, together with the nature of the assaults, seemed to have had the effect of denying South Asian boys access to a number of central social processes through which they could have come to develop, express and reaffirm their own masculine status.

It was against this broader discursive background that the chapter used a number of case studies to illustrate the variety of ways in which South Asian boys came to develop their sense of masculinity. Some were seen to come together to develop an alternative defensible social space within which to explore and experiment with their sense of masculinity, while others were shown to try and gain status within the broader field of masculine peer-group relations, with varying degrees of success. As highlighted, however, this latter strategy tended to be fraught with risks.

8

THE FIELD OF FEMININE PEER-GROUP RELATIONS AND BLACK GIRLS

Very little research has been conducted into the schooling experiences of young Black girls. That which has been done has either tended to focus on 'race' and has largely overlooked the gendered nature of their experiences (Wright 1992; Nehaul 1996) or, when incorporating an analysis of gender, has tended to focus almost exclusively on the way that teacher discourses influence and shape their gender identities (Grant 1992). Unfortunately, we therefore still know very little about young Black girls' experiences of schooling and, in particular, the influence of peer-group relations on this.

This chapter will explore the schooling experiences of the young Black girls at East Avenue and locate them within the context provided by the field of feminine peer-group relations. The first half of the chapter will set out some of the main characteristics of this field and the particular forms of capital associated with it. This will provide the context within which the chapter can then go on to examine the position of Black girls in relation to this. As with the other chapters, case studies will be used in the final section to highlight the agency of these Black girls and the diverse strategies they have employed in responding to this position.

RESEARCHING YOUNG GIRLS: A NOTE ON REPRESENTATION

Before beginning with an exploration of the field of feminine peer-group relations, I want to make a brief but important point about representation. This and the following chapter have been very difficult ones both to research and to write. The very nature of the girls' friendship networks, located in more private and intimate groupings (Grugeon 1993), meant that I, as both an adult and a male, found them almost impossible to access (see also Jenkins 1983). This was partly due to my own approach, in tending to fore-ground and in part identify with the essentially public nature of the boys' field. It was through this interest in the public nature of the children's social worlds that I also came to study the girls. The majority of data forming the basis of this chapter therefore relates to the particular discourses the girls chose to appropriate and reproduce in more public arenas. It was not until well into the fieldwork that I came to realise the importance of the girls' more private friendship groupings. This, together with my inability to gain access to these, meant that the conclusions reached below can only ever be read as a partial account of the girls' social lives.

Moreover, the fact that much of the data relating to the girls' talk and behaviour took place in my presence warrants a further note of caution. In this, as we have seen with the boys, my presence as an adult male more than probably came to mediate and inform the particular nature of the discourses that these girls chose to reproduce (see also Davies 1982). As active and strategic agents, they could possibly be seen as appropriating particular discourses either that they came to associate with me as an adult male and/or that they believed would most effectively usurp the predominant discursive relations of adult/child that provided the background for my relationship with them.

Arguably, the centrality of discourses on boyfriends and on kiss-chase to be highlighted below can be understood within this context: not only my almost exclusive focus on the public arena of the girls' lives, but also my presence in that arena as an adult male. Possibly even more than in the previous two chapters, therefore, this should stand as a warning against any attempt to generalise. However, the data used below is still important in the way that it highlights quite vividly particular forms of capital that some girls within the field of feminine peer-group relations came to value and strive for in public spaces. Moreover, these forms of capital will be shown to provide an important context for understanding the general position of Black girls within that field.

YOUNG GIRLS AND SCHOOLING

Before we look in more detail at the way that the field of feminine peer-group relations was structured, it is worth contextualising this within the young girls' more general experiences of schooling. In this we can identify two broader discursive processes that appeared to reinforce the notion of gender difference. The first related to the gendering of order and control in the school. As highlighted in Chapter 5, gender provided a significant organising principle with which teachers came to organise their classes. Boys and girls were often asked to line up at the door; finish their work and tidy up, get changed for physical education, and enter and leave the classroom, hall and playground separately (see also Deem 1978; Clarricoates 1981; Best 1983). It was through this that gender differences appear to have been reinforced and routinised within the very practices of the school.

Reproducing gender differences in public

However, not only did these processes appear to reinforce and underline the social divisions between boys and girls, they also arguably said something about the respective gender roles associated with these two groups. This seemed to be evident, for example, in the way that boys were most prominently drawn into the disciplinary modes of the school. As we saw in Chapter 5, it was boys, and Black boys in particular, who were most frequently singled out and publicly chastised and who therefore became increasingly associated with the public sphere. Moreover, the use of sport, particularly football, to try and positively engage certain groups of boys only appeared to help reinforce this positioning of boys within the public sphere. In addition, as we saw in Chapter 5, the masculine banter that at times developed out of this between these boys and some male members of staff during assemblies can be argued to have further underlined the prominence of a masculine ethos within the school.

The particular expectations that teachers held of boys and girls were not only expressed through school assemblies, however, but also appeared to influence relations in the classroom. Here, as we also saw in Chapter 5, many teachers were often faced with situations where they were being bombarded by children who had finished the work set for them and had nothing to do. These teachers often had to think quickly in deciding what other task to allocate which they felt would interest the children and keep them occupied for an appropriate length of time. It was here that the teachers' habitus, in apparently being shaped by their taken-for-granted assumptions about gender differences, was more likely to be influential. From my observations, girls were more likely to be encouraged in drawing and creative writing while boys were directed towards maths, science and computing. This was certainly the case in Mrs Scott's class: for instance, she would often encourage certain boys to work on the computer in the classroom. The consequences of this in terms of the marginalisation felt by some of the girls and their sense of frustration is captured in the following transcript taken from an interview with two of the White girls from Mrs Scott's class:

Margaret: [*frustratedly*] All the time! Daniel and Paul play on the computer, all the time!

Stephanie: Yeah, and Priti and me doesn't play – never! All the boys do, don't they?

PC: Would you like to play on the computer?

Margaret: Yeah!

Stephanie: Yeah!

Margaret: But they don't let us.

[. . .]

Stephanie: The boys always go on the computer – the same boys!

PC: Who are they?
Stephanie: Daniel and Paul and Stephen and Jordan!

Of course, it is not surprising that the boys these girls were referring to were the Bad Boys, from Chapter 5, who had a specific reputation for being troublesome. Here, it could be argued that Mrs Scott's decision to allow them to play on the computer could also be seen as a strategy of containment – allowing them to do something they enjoyed to keep them out of 'trouble'.

Girls and public spaces

The above incident involving the Bad Boys also alludes to the central role played by the boys themselves in actively developing and consolidating their monopoly over resources and public spaces. As a growing number of important studies have shown, boys not only tend to exclude girls from a number of their activities and dominate many of the public spaces within the school, but they also actively engage in harassing girls and invading their own more private social spaces (Wolpe 1977; Mahoney 1985; Clarricoates 1987; Dixon 1997). It can possibly be best understood as 'boundary work', as Thorne (1993) calls it, where the boys are purposely constructing their own masculine identities in opposition to girls. This certainly appeared to be the case at East Avenue, and is illustrated in the following interview with Jemma and Lyndsey, Black and White respectively, from Ms Patterson's class. The way in which their games seemed to be regularly interrupted by particular boys was quite a common experience for many of the girls at the school . Here, I was asking them about an incident I had witnessed the previous day, where two boys from their class approached them while they were playing a clapping game and proceeded to push, kick and thump them:

PC: I saw you playing the other day, and some of the boys came up and
           stopped you playing your game, didn't they?
Jemma: Yeah, and battered us – [*to Lyndsey*] remember?
Lyndsey: [*nods*]
Jemma: They hit us in the belly.
PC: Who was that?
Jemma: Devan and Peter – they battered me and Lyndsey.
PC: And why do they do that?
Lyndsey: 'Cos they always pick on us.
PC: On you? What do they do to you?
Lyndsey: They just hit us.
Jemma: And they just punch us.

On another occasion, Nicky and Emma, from Mrs Brogan's class, came up to me in the playground and complained that two infant boys, also from their class, had been 'spoiling our game'. They explained that they kept making groaning noises while thrusting their pelvises up against them. The salience of discourses on heterosexuality among boys, especially when harassing girls, appeared to be a relatively common theme (see also Mahoney 1985; Lees 1993; Dixon 1997; Kenway and Fitzclarence 1997). In the following incident, I was seated adjacent to a table where three White infant children were working in Mr Wallace's class: Sean, Hannah and Michaela. Hannah and Michaela had just been talking about Michaela's new boyfriend, which appeared to frustrate Sean as he had previously expressed an interest in Michaela as a girlfriend. Hannah was now turning her attention directly to Sean and trying unsuccessfully to engage him in conversation:

Hannah: That's a nice name – 'Sean'!
Sean: I hate my name! [*his head remains focused on his work and he slightly turns away from her*]
[. . .]
Hannah: [*carries on with her own work for a short while before looking up again and turning her attention to Michaela*] You're only five and he's six! [*referring back to Michaela's boyfriend*]
Sean: [*looks up and stares at Michaela. Frustratedly*] He sits on your knee and pulls your clothes off! [*stands up and leans over the table to Michaela, staring her directly in the face*] He sits on your knee and licks your [*whispers the rest – inaudible*].
Michaela: [*appears upset and jumps up, pushes her chair under the table and walks towards Mr Wallace*]
Hannah: [*anxiously sits up straight, folds her arms and momentarily puts one of her fingers over her lips in anticipation of Mr Wallace's attention*]
Michaela: [*as she made her way towards Mr Wallace, he looks up and asks her to go over and have her turn making a bumble bee with the classroom assistant. She does this, deciding not to tell Mr Wallace*]

It could possibly be argued from the above that it was Sean's sense of 'rejection' that underlay his decision to sexually harass Michaela. It is also interesting to note Michaela's decision not to complain about Sean's behaviour to Mr Wallace. Indeed, this was not uncommon among the girls, who appeared to find it difficult to complain about such matters to some teachers. It was the way that notions of heterosexuality came at times to influence and shape the public experiences of many girls at East Avenue that helps us to understand the significance of discourses on boyfriends within the field of feminine peer-group relations, as will now be seen.

THE FIELD OF FEMININE PEER-GROUP RELATIONS

Girls, resistance and friendship groupings

The foregoing discussion, especially in relation to the role that boys played in policing and trying to maintain their dominant social position, should not be read as simply implying the passive compliance of the girls. There were numerous incidents observed throughout the fieldwork where girls would actively challenge and effectively resist the behaviour of boys (see also Grugeon 1993). Some forms of resistance were highly organised and imaginative, involving upwards of eight or ten girls who would develop a concerted challenge to specific boys. Here, at times, they were observed either to verbally chastise and humiliate them or physically take hold of them and exact some form of retribution (see also Epstein 1997a). One example of the former was observed when six girls turned on Daniel and Paul, from Mrs Scott's class, who had been pestering some of them during an earlier playtime. Here the girls were following them around, with their arms crossed over their chests, singing, 'If you want to marry him, cross your heart!' While the boys were becoming increasingly irritated by this, their attempts to push individual girls away were in vain and the girls persisted for nearly twenty minutes, laughing, joking and teasing as they continued. Another example involved Ben, a White boy from Ms Patterson's class, who seemed to have acquired a distinct reputation for being troublesome and was often disruptive in the playground, directing his attentions primarily at girls and certain South Asian boys. On this occasion around eight girls, led by Lyndsey, Lisa and Sheetal, had chased and caught Ben and were now holding on to him and parading him around the playground. Initially, Ben was seen to be enjoying the attention, but this soon changed with his concern not to get his clothes 'mucky'. Unfortunately for Ben, his concern appeared to have been picked up by the girls, who then proceeded to tease him about their intentions to dirty his clothes and tried to wrestle him to the floor.

It appeared, however, that direct forms of resistance were more likely to be reactive, as some girls had to respond to the often regular incursions of boys into their social spaces. Nicky, Emma and Lyndsey, for instance, were observed one day being harassed by Jason, who repeatedly tried to disrupt their game by running 'through' them. When his shoe came off during one encounter, they saw their opportunity and threw his shoe over the school fence into the road. Not surprisingly, Jason became quite upset and ran off. Emma explained to me that Jason was 'spoiling our game', to which Nicky added defiantly: 'So we spoiled his stuff!'

On another occasion, Debbie and Levi, the younger brother of Stephen, who had moved up to Mrs Brogan's class from the nursery in the spring term, were arguing at a table. Levi seemed to have been frustrated that Debbie wanted to 'go out with' his brother rather than him and appeared to have been pestering her in the classroom for the best part of the afternoon. Debbie was becoming increasingly frustrated by this as I moved over to the table:

Debbie:	[*in a slightly raised voice to Levi*] So what if I want to go out with Stephen?
PC:	What's the matter?
Debbie:	He said to me last week: 'Would you go out with me or Stephen?' I said Stephen. He said: 'So I'll go out with Reshma, then.' [*a South Asian girl who had also just started in the class, at the same time as Levi*]
Levi:	No I never!

A little later I overheard the two children still arguing about the issue while sitting on the carpet:

Levi:	I just don't want you to be a two-timer.
Debbie:	I go out with Stephen!
Levi:	[*a little frustratedly*] And Paul and Daniel.
Debbie:	[*assertively*] Stephen!
Levi:	Paul and Daniel and Jordan!
Debbie:	Stephen!

Later that afternoon, Debbie, Levi, Zoe and Reshma were all in the home corner. It appeared that Debbie had exhausted her patience with Levi. She looked up to me and said:

Debbie:	Mr Connolly, he were touching her back.
PC:	Who was?
Debbie:	Him, Levi, when she was reading.
PC:	Touching who?
Debbie:	Reshma – touching her bum and things.
Levi:	No I weren't!
Debbie:	Yes you were – touching her bum-bums!
[. . .]	
Debbie:	[*taunting Levi*] Kiss your girlfriend! Levi! Kiss your girl-friend! Levi, I said kiss your girlfriend!
Levi:	[*to Debbie, pushing her*] ·Kiss your boyfriend! Kiss your boyfriend! Kiss your boyfriend!
Debbie:	I ain't even got a boyfriend!
Levi:	Yes you have!
Debbie:	Well, who is it then?

Levi:	My brother!
Debbie:	What's his name, then?
Levi:	Stephen.
Debbie:	Reshma's your girlfriend.
Levi:	Stephen's your boyfriend.
Debbie:	Reshma's your girlfriend! Reshma's your girlfriend!
Levi:	Stephen's your boyfriend.
Debbie:	[*looking towards* PC] Reshma for Mr Connolly!
Debbie and Zoe:	Reshma for Mr Connolly! Reshma for Mr Connolly! [*laughing*] Reshma for Mr Connolly!
Debbie:	[*singing and now directing her attention back to Levi*] In bed with Reshma, kissing her in bed!
Debbie and Zoe:	[*chanting to Reshma*] Kiss the Prince! Kiss the Prince! Kiss the Prince!
Reshma:	[*covers ears and runs out of the home corner*]
Levi:	[*also leaves home corner at this point*]

A number of points can be drawn from the above. First, Levi's accusations of 'two-timing' illustrate the importance of discourses on boyfriends and girlfriends to the public relations between boys and girls (see also Epstein 1997a). As we saw in earlier chapters and as I will shortly develop further, it was through these discourses on gender differences that some girls and boys came to develop their sense of identity. It also illustrates the way that some girls, once positioned within such discourses, can find themselves in a situation where they were forced to reclaim these discourses to resist the unwanted attention of certain boys. Third, it also serves as a good example of my role, not only in terms of how the children came to perceive me as a male but also in what appeared to be their desire to undermine my authority as an adult. More fundamentally, however, it also places me firmly within the research frame and speaks of my presence and inevitable influence on the particular way in which these young children decided to appropriate and reproduce specific discourses on sexuality.

For the majority of the girls, however, it could be argued that their most effective form of resistance to boys was through seeking out and developing alternative and manageable social spaces which they could effectively defend against their incursions. Because of the prior dominance of public spaces by boys, this meant that some girls were left with little choice other than to carve out more personal and private spaces, that neither drew the attention of boys nor could be easily disrupted by boys. In relation to the field of feminine peer-group relations, then, what was found was a complex network of small friendship groupings, seemingly providing the modal point for relationships within the field. These were then often linked to one another by a complex latticework of relationships. Thus, while individual friendship groups typically included only two or three girls, these relations were devel-

145

oped and expanded through the coming together of various groups at certain times (as was seen, for instance, in the organisation of resistance to Daniel and Paul and to Ben, outlined in the examples above). This tended to create a complex network of relationships where individual groups would periodically come together to form extended social groupings, but would also as easily break up again. Thus, while it appeared that the immediate reference point for individual girls in the field was their often involved and intimate relationship(s) with one or two other girls, there was a wider, more public social network that they could key into. Arguably, it was here that the dominant forms of cultural, social and symbolic capital were developed, learnt and reproduced. In this sense, it could be argued that a hierarchy existed within the field between the various friendship groupings in terms of the successful acquisition and competent display of certain forms of capital. It would appear that the more dominant friendship groupings within the field would, at times, act as role models for others, who would try to learn from and mimic their behaviour. It was, therefore, through these complex strands of relations that some common forms of capital tended to be valued, to varying degrees, by some of the more private groupings, and it is to these forms of capital, as manifest in the public spaces of the field, that the chapter will now turn.

It needs to be reiterated here that the discussion to follow can only offer a partial and inevitably incomplete account of the young girls' social worlds and the forms of capital they came to value and struggle over. The specific forms of capital that they focused on, and the ways they came to rework these, tended overwhelmingly to use the medium of particular friendship groupings. While we can therefore gain some insight into the importance of gender difference and the power of heterosexuality in the formation of young girls' sense of identity (Epstein 1997a), this absence of a focus on their more private worlds means that we can infer very little in relation to the precise ways in which these discourses came to structure those identities. To the extent that this present study does move on, in this and the next chapter, to use particular case studies of Black and South Asian girls, then it does serve as a reminder of the dangers of overgeneralising, and the need to take little for granted in relation to the resourcefulness of these young girls in being able to appropriate, rework and/or resist the broader themes set out below.

Boyfriends, kiss-chase and relationships

As alluded to above, within the more public domain of the field of feminine peer-group relations, having a boyfriend appeared to invest some girls with a significant degree of social capital (Hatcher 1995; Epstein 1997a). This was certainly the case for Emma and Nicky, from Mrs Brogan's class. It was these two White girls, as will be recalled from Chapter 6, who were at the heart of the fights between groups of Black and White boys, both laying claims on them as girlfriends. The status that this seemed to invest in the two girls can be seen in the following quote from Nicky, where she was 'complaining' about the attention she was receiving from the boys. Her 'complaints' were framed in such a way as to attract the attention and respect of the others in the room, including me. In this, it could be argued that the introduction of these essentially 'adult' themes needs to be understood in the context of my presence and their ability to undermine, at least partially, the predominant discursive relations of adult/child:

Nicky: Everyone keeps saying they go out with me!
PC: Do they?
Nicky: Yeah.
PC: Who says that?
Nicky: Don't know their names, but they know my name.
PC: Why do they keep saying that, do you think?
Nicky: Don't know.
PC: Do they just say it about you or do they say it about anybody else?
Nicky: About me!
PC: Paul and Daniel from Mrs Scott's class – they play with you a bit, don't they?
Nicky: Yeah, he says he goes out with me.
PC: Which one?
Nicky: Daniel.
PC: There's also somebody from Mr Wallace's?
[. . .]
Nicky: No, that's Emma's boyfriend [. . .] Emma goes out with James and Michael [*both Black*] . . . I hate Black boys!
PC: You hate Black boys?
Nicky: Yeah.
PC: Which Black boys do you hate?
Nicky: Kylie said to me that Michael and Devan go out with her!
Kylie: No, James goes out with me! [. . .]
PC: But why do you hate Black boys, Nicky?
Kylie: Because they're always around us, ain't they, Nicky?
Nicky: Yeah! . . . What? Kissing?
Kylie: [*laughs*] No, chasing!
Nicky: Well, Daniel's always chasing me!
PC: But Daniel's White, isn't he?
Nicky: Yeah.
PC: So it's not always Black boys that are around you, is it?
Kylie: Yeah.
Nicky: No!
PC: So which Black boys don't you like, then, Nicky?
Nicky: Michael.

PC: So why don't you like Michael, then?
Nicky: 'Cos I hate him hanging around Emma.
PC: Why does he hang around Emma, do you think?
Nicky: I don't know! – I don't know everything!

It is interesting to note from the above the way that Kylie appeared to try and associate herself with Nicky, and thus gain some social capital for herself, even though they rarely played together in the playground (see also Denmark 1995; Reay 1995). It is also interesting to note the way that the conversation became racialised, as Nicky developed her complaint to focus on Black boys. In Chapter 6 we noticed how Black boys were positioned in a certain way within discourses on boyfriends that seemed to emphasise their perceived athletic and sexual nature and thus increased their attractiveness to some. Indeed, Nicky and Emma's boyfriends, at the time of the interview, were two of the Bad Boys discussed in that chapter: Daniel and Paul respectively. Arguably, Nicky's comments should therefore be seen more in the way of an expression of resentment at Emma successfully gaining the attention of these Black boys.

This position that some Black boys have been given in discourses on boyfriends by some girls is also illustrated in the following transcript taken from an interview with Lisa and Sheetal from Ms Patterson's class. We had been having a conversation about which boys in the class they played with, and I had offered them a number of names before suggesting Peter, a Black boy from their class:

PC: What other boys are in your class? Peter? Do you play with Peter?
Lisa: Yeah – I'm going to marry him! [. . .] We're going to marry each other! [. . .] Well, I want to marry two boys.
PC: Who's the other one?
Lisa: Devan. [also Black]
PC: Devan and Peter? But he [Devan] was kicking you.
Lisa: Yeah, but he's stopped that now and he's my friend.
PC: What other boys? Pritul – do you play with Pritul?
Lisa: No! [. . .] Well, Pritul wants to marry Lyndsey!
PC: Does he? Why?
Lisa: Because they love each other – they went to each other's house.

While Lisa rarely played with either Peter or Devan, and indeed was more likely to be attacked by the latter, she appeared to use them symbolically as a way into the themes of love and marriage. It is here that we can see how these discourses on boyfriends seem to have provided the medium through which a host of other discursive themes on intimacy, love and marriage were expressed (see also Grugeon 1993; Epstein 1997a). In this respect it is interesting to contrast the way that the boys came to perceive their relationships with girls, through the medium of kiss-chase, with the girls' own perceptions. For the former, as we saw in Chapter 6, many of the Bad Boys' readings of girlfriends, including Daniel and Paul, were inextricably bound up with notions of ownership, control and sex. However, for their girlfriends, Nicky and Emma, their perceptions of the same relationships were, interestingly, run through with notions of love. In one interview Emma talked about making a card for her boyfriend, 'because I love him so much!'

Girls' games and femininity

Importantly, these discourses on boyfriends and the various discursive themes interwoven into them in relation to love, marriage, relationships and intimacy, as Grugeon (1993) and Epstein (1997a) highlight in their respective studies of older girls, also appeared to become embedded within the very games that some of the girls played among themselves. Here, the popular games, such as 'Mummies and Daddies', 'Doctors', 'Mummies and Babies' and 'Shops', all seemed to be primarily concerned with the routine playing out and exploration of (heterosexual) relationships. Alongside games of kiss-chase, girls' games provided one of the central dynamics through which these discourses on boyfriends and their related discursive themes were reproduced within the public sites of the field of feminine peer-group relations. Moreover, it could be argued that these not only provided a medium through which some girls came to explore and develop relationships, but also arguably provided an important arena for the expression of feminine competence. As such, the games were often taken seriously and were heavily guarded. The following transcript, taken from an interview with Aisha, Poonam and Beenal, in Mrs Scott's class, illustrates the importance given to competently carrying out the roles allocated in particular games:

PC: So who do you play with in the playground, then? Who do you all play with?
Aisha: Whitney, Jemma, Lyndsey/
Beenal: /And me!
Aisha: Not you!
PC: Beenal doesn't play with you, Aisha? Why not?
Aisha: I don't know why! 'Cos I don't want her to play with me! She does it wrong!
PC: Does it wrong?
Aisha: Yeah – what I say!

Here, Aisha was referring to the games that she organised and controlled, and to what she perceived as Beenal's failure to successfully play out the feminine roles given to her.

Together with these forms of role-playing games, clapping games were popular among some of the girls, where two or three girls would clap hands together while singing certain rhymes. As Grugeon (1993) also found, these were essentially public games, where a great deal of status was attributed to the successful recounting of various rhymes. A number of girls could regularly be observed watching and learning from others engaged in clapping games. What is interesting about the rhymes is the way they appeared to be embedded with the dominant discursive themes of love, marriage and attractiveness. And as Epstein (1997a: 42) argues, while it is difficult to judge exactly how girls read and understand the content of these rhymes, they do tend to provide a key cultural moment through which 'heterosexuality is normalised/naturalised'. The following three rhymes, very popular among the girls, illustrate this quite effectively:

My boyfriend gave me an apple,
My boyfriend gave me a pear,
My boyfriend gave me a kick up the bum and threw me down the stairs.
I gave him back his apple,
I gave him back his pear,
I gave him back his kick up the bum and threw him down the stairs.
I threw him over Scotland,
I threw him over France,
I threw him over Workingham and he lost his underpants!
When I wasn't looking, he kissed another girl,
When I wasn't looking, he kissed another girl.
Hypnotise her! Paralyse her! Turn around and faint!

My mummy told me,
If I was goody,
Then she would buy me
A rubber dolly.
My aunty told her
I kissed a soldier,
Now she won't buy me
A rubber dolly.

Co-Co Cola, Co-Co Cola,
Makes you burp, makes you burp,
Have another bottle, have another bottle,
Burp-burp-burp, burp-burp-burp!
Co-Co Cola, Co-Co Cola,
Minus, minus,
Boys got the muscles, teachers got the brains,
Girls got the sexy legs walking down the lane.

Most of the girls, at one time or another, played these clapping games. It was a very creative process as girls seemed to spend a lot of time adding new verses, adapting old ones and mixing existing verses from different songs together. After all, it could be argued that knowing a 'new' song attracted much status from the other girls.

It is interesting to note, however, the salience of gender differences within these rhymes and the emphasis placed on boyfriends, love and marriage. These were themes that appeared to run through other games involving songs. The popular game Orange Balls was played by a larger group of girls, where one girl was picked and the others huddled in a group out of earshot and picked a boy's name. They would then form a ring and dance around her, singing:

Orange balls, orange balls, here we go again bum! bum!
Orange balls, orange balls, here we go again bum! bum!
Stamp your feet if you hate him,
Stamp your feet if you hate him,
Stamp your feet if you hate him,
E-i-e-i-oh!
Cross your heart if you love him,
Cross your heart if you love him,
Cross your heart if you love him,
E-i-e-i-oh!
Michael [or whatever name is chosen] says he loves you,
Michael says he loves you,
Michael says he loves you,
E-i-e-i-oh!

Because of the relatively large numbers of girls usually playing this, together with those who stood and observed, this was also a very public affair and one which enabled the girls publicly to explore particular relationships by attaching specific names to each other and gauging the reactions of others. Arguably, a great deal was at stake, therefore, as reputations and status were forever being made and remade. In many ways, it could be argued that because of its public nature, this game not only enabled them to probe the desires of particular girls but also acted to reinforce a collective sense of taste. It is in this sense that we can more fully understand the incident in the previous chapter involving Jayesh, the South Asian boy who had just moved up to Mrs Brogan's class from the nursery. In this, the girls chose his name when playing Orange Balls, and then took delight in not only teasing the girl who was 'on' afterwards but also Jayesh himself. This could possibly be seen as an example of the increased salience of racialised discourses in public spaces where, at this more general level of abstraction, much more was at stake in terms of the maintenance of reputations.

Attractiveness, identity and the feminine habitus

It was through the daily struggles over these particular forms of cultural capital and the routine playing out of specific games that these dominant notions of femininity appeared to become embodied by some of the girls to form part of their habitus. For instance, successful participation in many of the girls' games, whether at home or at school, required the adoption of a caring and nurturing demeanour, and it was this which seemed to be positively rewarded. At this point, the power of these discourses takes on what Foucault (1980: 39) referred to as their 'capillary form of existence', which reaches 'into the very grain of individuals, touches their bodies and inserts itself into their actions and attitudes'.

An example of the way in which some girls' sense of self was constituted in and through these discourses on boyfriends can be seen in terms of the particular understanding many of them had of attractiveness. Here, the discourses on boyfriends and girlfriends had a tendency to frame the attractiveness of girls in relation to the needs and desires of boys. We can see this, for instance, in the way that it was boys who chased girls when playing kiss-chase, and in the rhymes quoted above where it was the girls who had the 'sexy legs' and the boys who were tempted, through their attractiveness, to kiss other girls. Arguably, the acquisition of the relevant forms of cultural capital associated with boyfriends within the field of feminine peer-group relations was therefore related to the skills necessary to attract boys. The status that this tended to bring was evident with the cases of Nicky and Emma and Debbie, discussed earlier. Debbie, for instance, after finishing her argument with Levi over his brother Stephen, told me how 'I'm going to have my hair cut right round here and have it curly a bit. When I have my hair done, Stephen's going to really like me!' Similarly, in the following transcript taken from an interview with Aisha, Beenal and Poonam, Aisha showed not only how she had come to define her own attractiveness in relation to boys, but also how she had understood their hostility to her South Asian friends in this discursive frame as well:

PC: Why don't they play with Poonam and Beenal, Aisha? Why are the boys nasty to them?
Aisha: Er, their hair's not long!
PC: Because their hair's not long?
Aisha: Yeah.
Beenal: Mine's long!
PC: Beenal's hair's long.
Aisha: Yeah, but she does plaits and I hate plaits and boys hate plaits like that! And boys like this [touching her own hair] and a hair-band.
PC: How do you know they like that? Who said they like that?
Aisha: Stephen in our class, yesterday.

PC: Did he? What did he say?
Aisha: He said I was very, very nice.

It is within this context that girls came to value and gain symbolic status through the acquisition of what were perceived as 'grown-up' or adult fashions. This was where the particular way that some of the mothers on the Manor Park estate came to clothe their children, as outlined in Chapter 4, tended to intervene in the particular forms of symbolic capital that were generated. Here, the latest skirts, tops and shoes, together with ear-rings and other jewellery items, all appeared to invest particular girls with symbolic capital, and hence status, within the field of feminine peer-group relations. Moreover, girls were also seen to bring make-up that had been bought for them into the school. Aisha, for example, had gathered quite a large group of girls around her one day in the playground, where they sat in the bushes applying face cream she had brought in with her. On other occasions, girls were seen to bring in lipstick and jewellery, which they would then invite an exclusive network of friends to use and try on.

BLACK GIRLS AND THE FIELD OF FEMININE PEER-GROUP RELATIONS

So far, I have drawn attention to some particular aspects of the field of feminine peer-group relations that have predominantly come to be expressed in the more public spaces of the school. In the omission of any extensive study of the private worlds of these young girls, it offers only a partial, essentially incomplete and overgeneralised account of the field. As before, while making no claims to be representative, the chapter has drawn attention to the apparent salience of gender difference and the importance of heterosexuality in the construction and reproduction of particular notions of femininity within the public sphere. It is against the background of the reproduction of discourses on boyfriends and their associated discursive themes that we can begin to understand the influences of particular discourses on 'race' as they affect the general position of Black girls in the field. It is with this in mind that the remainder of the chapter will be concerned to explore the schooling experiences of the Black girls at East Avenue.

What I want to argue here is that the particular discourses on 'race', highlighted in Chapter 6 in relation to the perceived tendency for Black children to be troublesome, athletic and sporting, have resulted in a contradictory positioning of some Black girls within the field of feminine peer-group relations. While their perceived athleticism afforded these girls a level of symbolic capital within the field, it also had the effect of inhibiting their ability successfully to acquire some of the dominant forms of capital associated with the discourses on boyfriends. Through the use of particular case studies, the chapter will explore the diverse ways in which Black girls have come to respond to these broader racialised discursive processes.

One of the problems in doing this, however, relates to the relatively small number of Black girls – four – present at East Avenue in the three sample classes for the whole of the year. While there were other Black girls in the three sample classes during the year, they either left halfway through the fieldwork or moved up to the classes from the nursery only at the start of the final term. As such, I was able to get to know only four girls well: Annette, Naomi, Charlene and Whitney. It is with this in mind that an extra note of caution needs to be added in relation to the following, where I intend to use these girls' experiences of schooling to tentatively draw attention to some of the broader and more general discursive processes, evident within East Avenue, that appear to affect Black girls.

Teacher discourses and Black girls

A review of the official and internal school reports relating to the four girls indicates the existence of a number of common discursive themes that resonate quite closely with those outlined in Chapter 6 in relation to Black boys. Just as Grant (1992) found that teachers tended to encourage young Black girls' social competence at the expense of their academic skills, so the teachers at East Avenue also tended to underplay the Black girls' educational achievements and focus on their social behaviour. In this, notions of disruptiveness, aggressiveness and athleticism were found to underlie some of the teachers' perceptions of many of these girls. This is illustrated in Mrs Scott's school report on Annette, which was very typical of the other Black girls' reports:

> Annette is very popular and has many friends. She is very good at games and athletics. She excels in PE and at the Sports Hall. [. . .] She acts silly and prevents others from working. [. . .] The one thing that she loves and excels at in the classroom is beautiful colouring.

What is interesting in the above is the way that gender appears to carve out important distinctions in the schooling experiences of Black boys and girls. Thus, while a perception of Black boys as being troublesome and aggressive was found to predominate among the teachers at East Avenue, it was found that, with the girls, their perceived creative side tended to be foregrounded instead. Indeed, in reading other school reports it appeared that the disruptive activities they did get involved in were much less likely to be seen as overtly confrontational and threatening, as was the case with the boys, and more likely to be merely the result of the girls' tendency, *as girls*, to 'chatter' and be 'quarrelsome' and 'silly'.

These discourses were inevitably woven into the practices of some teachers and the dominant processes within the school. There was, for instance, a greater likelihood that Black girls would be publicly singled out for discipline and chastisement by teachers than other girls within the school. This was a common experience for Charlene, from Mrs Scott's class, for instance, who was regularly singled out and publicly disciplined for 'chattering' and disrupting others. The reputation for being disruptive was one that came to precede some of the girls and created a level of expectation among the teachers. Ms Patterson, for example, was taking the register one morning with most of the children sitting on the carpet. As she went through the register, she called out Naomi's name and then looked up, leant forward in her seat and said to her, 'I hope you're going to be good this week – not like last week!' The way she tended to be singled out by Ms Patterson was something of which Naomi herself appeared to be acutely aware. In the following transcript, taken from an interview with Naomi, Lyndsey and Jemma (a Black girl who left the school towards the end of the autumn term), Naomi complained of being unfairly picked on by Ms Patterson:

Lyndsey:	I like Miss Patterson 'cos she lets us play with toys and on the computer.
Jemma:	She gives us hard work.
Naomi:	And she don't let me and Jemma play on the computer – [*to Jemma*] I never had a go, did you?
Jemma:	She won't let us sit together.
PC:	She won't let who sit together?
Jemma and Naomi:	Us!
Lyndsey:	Sometimes they be naughty, that's why.
Jemma:	We don't fight!
Naomi:	We talk!
PC:	And she won't let you sit together?
Naomi:	No.
PC:	What do you think about that?
Jemma:	But when we were over there [*pointing to a table in the classroom*] we said we won't talk and just carried on with our work, we weren't talking, right, between ourselves, and Ms Patterson said, 'Sit on a different table, Naomi!' – [*to Naomi*] Didn't she?
PC:	And you weren't talking?
Jemma:	Yeah.
PC:	So why did she say that?
Naomi:	'Cos we were sitting together.
Jemma:	Sitting at our table.

What is particularly interesting from the above conversation is the way other girls came to take on board the discursive frame of the teacher. Here, Lyndsey was seen readily to reproduce the view that Naomi and Jemma were naughty at times, even though, in relation to this incident, they were in fact getting on with their work and not talking any more than other children. This is a theme that I will return to shortly.

As highlighted in relation to the school reports, however, some teachers tended to focus more on what they perceived to be the Black girls' abilities in music, dancing and athletics rather than their disruptive behaviour. This was also true in relation to their practice, as was illustrated in Mrs Scott's class. Here, during the few minutes before dinnertime, she would often have all the children sitting on the carpet while certain individuals were chosen to come to the front and sing their favourite songs. There was a distinct tendency for Mrs Scott to choose Black girls and Stephen, a Black boy, more often than the other children. On a couple of occasions, she was observed to ask these children to come to the front and show the other children how to do it. This was also the case during one morning where she had the class in the main hall for Music and Movement. The children were asked to march around the hall in a big circle while singing a song. Some appeared reluctant to do this, so Mrs Scott asked Whitney and Stephen to do it on their own while the other children stood at the sides of the hall and watched.

These processes also appeared to be true in relation to some of the teachers' perceptions of the girls' athletic abilities. This was particularly the case with Annette, from Mrs Scott's class, who was positively encouraged in PE and other sporting activities by Mrs Scott and publicly praised for her achievements. As Mrs Scott explained to me:

> She's a tomboy. You see, she's got a big brother called Luke, do you know him? He'll be twelve now and I had him years ago. His father was in prison at the time. But, erm, he was the best runner in the school. But he's totally dizzy otherwise. [. . .] But I think having a big brother has had an influence on her and she's very good at sport – have you seen her? She can do anything. If we have to practice sports, like we did the other day, she could go along, we had an obstacle course, and most of them couldn't do some of it. We only had a skipping rope, bat and ball, and a hoop to go over your head. She could go through it – and she's the fastest runner – she's brilliant, really, at athletics. If it was channelled in the right direction, it would be. [. . .] She plays football, she's very nifty with her feet.

Teacher practices and the field of feminine peer-group relations

This tendency for some Black girls to be seen as disruptive, musical and athletic by particular teachers within the school inevitably had an influence on the position of Black girls within the field of feminine peer-group relations. Most prominently, it appeared to invoke contradictory responses towards some of the Black girls from others within the field. On the one hand, their perceived musical and athletic abilities endowed these Black girls with a certain amount of status. It represented a form of symbolic capital that was almost universal among boys and girls and which, particularly through racing and games of tick and chase, seemed to afford the holder a certain privileged position among their peers. For Black girls, then, it could be argued that what was seen to be their quickness and agility was also perceived, in the eyes of the others, as making them good at certain popular games played by the children, and so required a certain level of respect.

However, this appeared to be much less the case for other aspects of capital within the field that centred around the discourses on boyfriends, and the related discursive themes on intimacy, love and marriage. Here, their discursive positioning as athletic and, moreover, as troublesome, seemed to act in severely limiting their ability to acquire these particular forms of capital in the eyes of the other girls. In this sense, the particular notions of femininity had arguably been constructed at the public level within the field around gender differences and in opposition to boys. This 'tomboy' identity gained by some of the Black girls appeared to severely limit their ability to acquire a feminine identity within these discourses on boyfriends. Moreover, this seemed also to act to reduce their attractiveness to the boys *as girls*. Especially for Naomi and Annette, while they played with boys for a relatively high proportion of their time, they were never seen to be engaged in games of kiss-chase with them during the whole of the fieldwork. Annette's reputation for being sporting and troublesome, then, while gaining her status within the field of masculine peer-group relations, also seemed to limit the possibility of the boys seeing her as a prospective girlfriend.

Not only were some Black girls excluded from games of kiss-chase, but they also appeared to be restricted in relation to their ability to enter into the more general girls' games that came to reproduce these discourses on boyfriends. As will be remembered, these games were essentially public affairs and there was thus a lot at stake in terms of girls' status and reputations. As they were seen as essentially public expressions of a girl's feminine competence, it was therefore arguably important for girls to choose carefully who they played these games with (Denmark 1995). It could be argued that being so publicly associated with a girl not seen as particularly 'feminine' would therefore reflect as much on the other girls' status. As illustrated by the earlier quote in relation to Aisha's games, those girls who were thought not to be able to play the games properly (i.e. who lacked the relevant level of feminine competence) were therefore excluded.

It is here that we can at least partially understand the tendency for some

Black girls to be excluded from particular public games relating to notions of boyfriends and love and marriage. As the following quote illustrates, it was Naomi's reputation for being disruptive and troublesome that led Chloe and Lisa to decide not to play with her. Chloe had just said that she did not like to play with Peter, a Black boy, in her class:

PC: Why don't you like to play with Peter, Chloe?
Chloe: 'Cos he's naughty, ain't it! Peter makes Ms Patterson shout.
PC: Makes Ms Patterson cross? Is that why you don't like him?
Chloe: Yeah.
PC: Does anyone else make Ms Patterson cross?
Lisa: Yeah!
PC: Who?
Lisa: Naomi!
PC: Naomi? Why do you think Naomi makes her/
Chloe: /Devan! [another Black boy]
Lisa: Yeah, Devan as well.

As we will see shortly when examining the case of Naomi in more detail, it was certainly true that Naomi was actively excluded from many of the girls' games, even though she valued and continued to adhere to some of the more prominent notions of femininity defined through these discourses on boyfriends.

BLACK GIRLS' STRATEGIES OF CONFORMITY AND RESISTANCE

So far, then, I have explored the nature of teacher discourses and practices in relation to some of the Black girls in the three sample classes at East Avenue, and how these appeared to have generally impacted upon the field of feminine peer-group relations. I have tentatively suggested that, at a relatively broad level of abstraction, the discursive positioning of Black girls as disruptive, musical and athletic afforded them a certain level of status among their peers. However, this also appeared to act in excluding them from acquiring and successfully maintaining a dominant position within the field of feminine peer-group relations. Of course, it would be wrong to assume from this that these broader discursive processes affected all Black girls equally and in the same ways. Nothing is predetermined. The four Black girls forming the focus of this present discussion adopted very different strategies in response to these processes, with very differing consequences for their resultant sense of identity. To illustrate this, we will briefly look at each of the girls in turn.

Annette

One response to these broader discursive processes was to reject the field of feminine peer-group relations altogether, and to seek out alternative social spaces within which to carve out a sense of identity. In this, Annette, from Mrs Scott's class, appeared to be the most successful. She had positively rejected her positioning within the field and had capitalised upon her reputation for being disruptive and athletic to gain a prominent position within the field of masculine peer-group relations. Moreover, not only did she seem to have been accepted within this field, but she had apparently acquired considerable forms of capital, to the extent that she had gained a dominant position within it. The respect that she had gained was considerable, and is illustrated in the following interview with her classmates, Stephen, Paul and Jordan – the Bad Boys from Chapter 6. Here, they were talking about Jason and his 'gang', a group of Year 2 boys they were having a prolonged conflict with:

Stephen: They think we're scared of them!
Paul: We're not scared of them!
Stephen: Daniel is!
Paul: But Annette won't! Annette scares them off!
Jordan: Yeah! Annette, Annette is brave, right, and me and Paul and Stephen/
Paul: /But not Daniel!
Jordan: 'Cos Annette, because Annette just stands there and lets this boy just kick her and, like, and, like, don't cry!

Annette's strength and her competence at athletics and football, as alluded to earlier in the interview with Mrs Scott, therefore seemed to afford her a dominant position within the field of masculine peer-group relations. Indeed, it was a position consolidated in the fact that she very rarely associated with girls at all and refused to be identified with them. Such was her apparent position within the field that she would regularly take control of games and carve out a position where she could pick and choose which boys could and could not play. This is illustrated in the following discussion that I had with Prajay, a South Asian boy, in the playground. I had earlier noticed him with a group of children, including Annette, who were playing 'Beezo', a variation of tick. As I approached him, he was stood on his own, looking at the other children who were running around the playground chasing each other:

PC: Hello, Prajay. I thought you were playing Beezo. [. . .] Why have you stopped playing it?
Prajay: Because Annette said I couldn't play.

PC: Why did she say that?

Prajay: [shrugs his shoulders]

PC: Has she said it to anyone else?

Prajay: [nods]

PC: Who?

Prajay: Harry – but he's playing it again!

In fact, as with the other boys, Annette was more likely to exclude South Asian boys than others. On another occasion, for example, she was seen to be quite violently pushing Bhavin, another South Asian boy, away from the group.

However, while Annette had gained a strong position for herself within the field of masculine peer-group relations, it was not without its contradictions. There was always a risk that she would be repositioned within discourses on gender. As the following incident illustrates, this was something that boys could draw upon at times as a resource to maintain their own position. In this I was sitting at a table with Paul and some other boys in Mrs Scott's class, helping them with their work. The incident began with Daniel, who approached the table rather excitedly and sat down:

Daniel: Miss! Miss! Miss! [referring to PC] Me and Annette, we broke off Stephanie's peg! [in the cloakroom] When we're upstairs [i.e. for an interview] we'll tell you!

PC: What peg?

Daniel: Annette saw it wobbling and Annette broke it off! [Annette walks over to the table and remains standing] Annette, didn't me and you break off that peg?

Annette: [nods and smiles before calmly putting her work on the table]

Paul: And me!

Annette: [shakes head]

Paul: Yeah I did, didn't I, Daniel?

Daniel: [no response]

Paul: Come and sit here, Annette. [pulling back the chair next to him for her to sit on]

Annette: [walks over and sits next to Paul]

Daniel: [to Paul and Annette] Are you two going to have sex? [. . .] He pinches your bum!

PC: Who pinches your bum?

Daniel: Paul!

PC: You've just said they're going to have sex – who do you mean?

Daniel: Yeah, them two are going to have sex! [pointing to Paul and Annette]

Paul: No! Them two! [pointing to Annette and another boy sat at the table]

Daniel: No! Her and him [*pointing to Annette and then* PC] are going to have sex!

Annette: Nnoooo!

Three main points can be drawn out from the above. First, it alludes to the ongoing respect that Annette had gained from the boys, witnessed here in Daniel's enthusiasm to relay the story concerning Annette and Stephanie's peg. Second, and most important for the present discussion, it also illustrates the way that the boys were able to introduce alternative discourses in order to reposition other children to their own advantage (see also Walkerdine 1981). Here, Daniel appeared to regain some of the status he had lost through Annette choosing to sit next to Paul by discursively switching from regarding Annette as 'one of the boys' to repositioning her within discourses on heterosexuality as a sexualised object. While this was quite rare, it does point towards the contradictions in Annette's strategy and the ultimately precarious nature of the position in which she found herself. Finally, the incident also reinforces my position within the research and the role I inevitably played in shaping and influencing relations. Arguably, Daniel's reference to me as 'Miss' and his comment about Annette and me having sex both allude to the children's perception of me as an adult male, with all that signifies. Within the context of the complex interplay of discourses and contested subject positions, it also possibly signified another attempt to undermine the dominant discursive frame on childhood and the positions of adult and child within this.

Naomi

It is useful to contrast Naomi briefly with Annette. As outlined earlier, Naomi's reputation for being disruptive had the effect of excluding her from particular aspects of the field of feminine peer-group relations. Her response, similar to Annette's, appeared to be to try and create an alternative space within the field of masculine peer-group relations with which to develop and maintain her sense of self. The problem that Naomi faced, however, was that she was not particularly strong, nor was she competent at sports. She did not, therefore, seem to have the appropriate cultural capital necessary to gain status among the boys, as Annette did. Moreover, the reputation that she did have for being disruptive and which positioned her within the public sphere was also significantly gendered, in that the discourses associated with this, as reproduced by Ms Patterson, revolved around her being 'moody' and 'manipulative' rather than aggressive and confrontational. The potential she had for gaining a certain amount of masculine capital among the boys for being aggressive and confrontational was therefore denied her because of this redefinition.

Naomi was therefore essentially 'caught between two fields', being partially excluded by the field of feminine peer-group relations but lacking the appropriate forms of capital to successfully position herself within the field of masculine peer-group relations. She appeared to aim towards the boys but had neither the interest nor the ability to take part successfully in the games that they were playing. Many of the boys came to regard her presence in their group negatively – as someone who was getting in their way. As Mrs Adams, an ancillary teacher working in Ms Patterson's class, observed:

Mrs Adams: I think the boys get irritated by her [. . .] but she's bored by the girls – the boys are a bit too rough with her.
PC: And why do you think they get irritated with her?
Mrs Adams: Because she's a girl, and she wants to play the girly games but she doesn't want to play with the girls.

It appeared that while Naomi was often seen hanging around boys she was rarely observed playing with them. In essence, she identified more closely with the forms of capital associated with the field of feminine peer-group relations – what Mrs Adams rather condescendingly referred to as 'girly games' – but could not identify with the girls in that field. Unfortunately for Naomi, what was regarded as capital among the girls (which Naomi identified with) was viewed quite negatively within the field of masculine peer-group relations; after all, the dominant forms of capital here seemed to have been developed in direct opposition to notions of femininity.

Charlene

The predicament that Naomi found herself in and the contradictions she ultimately experienced were also those that seemed to underlie Charlene's experiences of schooling. She too had little ability or interest in sports and athletics, and she too was drawn into the public sphere by being frequently chastised by her teacher, Mrs Scott, for being disruptive. Moreover, the way in which Mrs Scott publicly chastised Charlene, by couching it within gendered discourses on her 'chattering' and being argumentative, also appeared to limit the potential Charlene had for capitalising on this within the field of masculine peer-group relations.

However, in contrast to the strategy adopted by Naomi, Charlene befriended another girl in her class, Melanie, a White girl who had also gained a particular reputation for being stubborn and troublesome. They were effectively seen as inseparable, and would regularly attract the attention of Mrs Scott, who spent much of her time trying to keep the two girls apart in the classroom. As with Naomi, because of the girls' reputation for being troublesome they found themselves on the fringes of the field of feminine peer-group relations and were rarely invited to participate in various games and activities. Indeed, their reputation was such that many other girls appeared actively to avoid the two at times, for fear of the disruption they could cause.

However, in contrast to Naomi, Charlene did not choose to try and create an alternative space within the field of masculine peer-group relations but, with her friend Melanie, carved out a space within the field of feminine peer-group relations. It was from this space, albeit at the fringes, that they appeared actively to struggle to be accepted and included within the broader network of relationships found in the field in relation to discourses on boyfriends. While they were often seen to play games on their own, including Mummies and Babies, Doctors and Tick, they also made regular attempts to access broader friendship groups within the field. As we saw earlier, one particular friendship group, that of Nicky and Emma, from Mrs Brogan's class, appeared to attract a great deal of status. To be associated with them would therefore tend to offer a significant level of social capital. This was similarly the case for the four boys from Mrs Scott's class, the Bad Boys discussed in detail in Chapter 6, two of whom – Daniel and Paul – regularly played kiss-chase with Nicky and Emma. To be associated with these particular boys as boyfriends also seemed to offer girls within the field of feminine peer-group relations a degree of social capital. The following transcript, taken from an interview with Charlene and Melanie, illustrates the way that they came to value and reproduce these discourses on boyfriends, through ascribing status to having Paul and Daniel as boyfriends as well as being friends with Nicky and Emma. While they were never actually seen to play with these children, it is the fact that they fantasised about associating with them that demonstrates their subscription to these particular forms of capital within the field of feminine peer-group relations:

Charlene:	Anyway, do you know Daniel? Daniel, er, kissed us!
Melanie:	Yeah and snog us!
PC:	Did he?
Melanie:	Yeah.
[. . .]	
Charlene:	I like Daniel.
Melanie:	I like Paul – he's my best.
Charlene:	Daniel's my best, I know he's my best.
PC:	What girls do they play with?
Charlene:	Emma/
Melanie:	/Me! Charlene, Emma and Nicky and kiss all four of us.
Charlene:	And Stephen.
Melanie:	Yeah.
Charlene:	They batter each other, you know!
PC:	They batter each other?

Charlene:	And Jordan.
Melanie:	And I kick Jordan straight in the mouth, don't I?
Charlene:	Yeah, and I kick him in his rude!
Melanie and Charlene:	[*laugh*]

What is also interesting about the above transcript is the way it alludes to the contradictions in these girls' identities. For alongside their struggle to be feminine and acquire the various forms of social, cultural and symbolic capital associated with this, through their discussion of how they would fight with Jordan, the transcript also alludes to the way they valued what were considered to be traditionally more masculine traits. It is arguably indicative of their contradictory positioning – being discursively constructed as disruptive and troublesome while also striving for a more feminine identity and acceptance within the field of feminine peer-group relations. It is the inherent struggles that Charlene and Melanie faced in trying to reconcile these contradictory positions that seemed to characterise their experiences of schooling, and which ensured their positioning on the periphery of the field of feminine peer-group relations.

Whitney

Finally, I want to mention Whitney, a Black girl from Mrs Scott's class. Whitney could be seen as being towards the other end of a continuum drawn by the other three girls. For not only did Whitney appear to subscribe to some of the dominant forms of capital associated with the field as outlined above, but she had also been largely successful in gaining acceptance within it. She had developed a relatively close relationship with a small group of (mainly White) girls, and as a group they were regularly encouraged to participate in various games by other girls in the field. Although she had not acquired a dominant position within the field of feminine peer-group relations, she did seem to have gained a strong position and was routinely accepted by others.

To understand Whitney's position we need to go back to her positioning within the discursive practices of teachers. Whitney's mother was working full time and she was brought to and from school by her grandmother. Mrs Scott spoke of how she was helped at home with her academic work and how she had become a pleasure to have in class. As her school report stressed: 'Whitney [. . .] is a very friendly, studious girl – very agreeable and pleasant. A pleasure to have in the class. [. . .] Very helpful, lovely to talk to. Very mature.' While the report also stressed how she 'enjoys dancing and the sports hall activities as well as singing and playing instruments', she was also seen as academically bright.

It is Whitney's 'studiousness' that at least partially helps us understand her differing experiences of schooling from that of the three other girls.

Whitney had not come through the school's own nursery classes, but had recently arrived on the estate and moved directly into Mrs Scott's class from another school. The reports that accompanied her were as glowing as Mrs Scott's. Observations in the classroom confirmed that she was, to all intents and purposes, a 'model' pupil: attentive, hard-working and progressing extremely well, especially in reading and writing. In fact, it is precisely this fact that she was seen as a model pupil that helps us to understand Mrs Scott's differing perceptions of her. As discussed in Chapter 5, a significant part of teachers' status among their professional peers is the production of competent pupils. Just as Sharp and Green (1975) found, in a school such as East Avenue with all the social problems that are believed to accompany it, part of the strategy adopted by some teachers, which becomes part of their habitus, is the academic grooming of a small number of children – small enough to leave time to control the majority of children in the class, but of sufficient numbers to parade them – and, more important, their work – around the school. And it was here that Whitney could be located within Mrs Scott's teaching practices. Whitney's identity, as coming from a higher social class background than the other Black girls and therefore being perceived as a model pupil, came to predominate for Mrs Scott over and above her identity as a Black girl. Whitney was therefore not exposed to the broader disciplinary modes of the school, deriving from the racialised perceptions held by some teachers about Black children generally being disruptive; she was therefore not constructed in such a way as to hinder her successful negotiation of the field of feminine peer-group relations. Indeed, in the praise she publicly received from Mrs Scott concerning her academic work, she actually gained status among the girls.

CONCLUSIONS

This chapter has been concerned with exploring the field of feminine peer-group relations and the position of Black girls within it. Through an examination of particular aspects of the field, principally its more public spaces, the chapter has drawn attention to the apparent prominence of gender differences and the importance of heterosexuality in the formation of certain aspects of the girls' sense of feminine identity. Through discourses on boyfriends, the chapter highlighted how a number of other discursive themes on intimacy, love and marriage were appropriated and reproduced among some of the girls, not only through their involvement in kiss-chase but also through a wide range of essentially public games. It was against the background of these discourses on boyfriends that some girls came to develop their own sense of feminine identity.

While the chapter raised a number of concerns about the partial and incomplete nature of this particular aspect of the study and the need to avoid drawing any detailed conclusions from the data in relation to its generalisability, it was argued that this coverage of particular aspects of the field of feminine peer-group relations provided an adequate context for understanding the position of some Black girls within it. It was found that, on the one hand, some Black girls' perceived musical and athletic abilities appeared to invest them with a certain amount of status among their female peers. However, their discursive construction, through teacher discourses, as disruptive did act to severely limit their ability to negotiate a position successfully within the particular discourses on boyfriends within the field. Through a number of case studies the chapter then explored the variety of responses of the Black girls at East Avenue to this partial exclusion. While some chose to try and carve out an alternative space within the field of masculine peer-group relations in which to develop a sense of self, others struggled to gain status through these discourses on boyfriends within the field of feminine peer-group relations. While the focus in this latter part of the chapter has been on Black girls, it does provide a useful corrective to the more general discussion on the salience of kiss-chase and boyfriends within the field. The diversity of these four girls' responses is an important reminder in maintaining an active notion of agency and resisting the temptation to draw out overgeneralised conclusions about the reach and impact of these more public discourses.

9

THE 'SEXUAL OTHER'? SOUTH ASIAN GIRLS AT EAST AVENUE

Of all the groups of children so far discussed, South Asian girls appear to be the least researched of all. The few pieces of work that have been done have tended to focus on older South Asian female students (Brah and Minhas 1985; Stopes-Roe and Cochrane 1990; Ghuman 1994). Even in the light of this work, however, we still know relatively little about the detailed schooling experiences of these women. With this in mind, it is not surprising to find that younger South Asian girls seem, at present, to have been overlooked altogether. One possible reason for this could be that South Asian female students, especially very young girls, often seem to be perceived as 'model pupils'. Being quiet, hard-working, obedient and helpful, they therefore appear to represent some of the quintessential characteristics of femininity and are thus believed to present very few demands upon teachers. Within such a view it is not surprising that they tend to become 'invisible' to both teachers and researchers. Some of the data to follow certainly appear to support this view.

However, for the young children at East Avenue, South Asian girls are anything but invisible. In the previous chapters, we have seen what an important role South Asian girls seem to play in the discourses of young boys and girls. Here, some of the South Asian girls appear to have been constructed as the 'Sexual Other' (see also Brah and Minhas 1985) where, as we have seen, a significant number of boys and girls within the school seemed to develop their own gender identities in opposition to these girls.

This chapter will explore some of these themes further. A central concern will be to try and understand how many South Asian girls have been perceived as the Sexual Other by some of their peers, especially when many teacher discourses seem to have constructed them as quintessentially feminine. After looking at teacher discourses and the field of feminine peer-group relations, the chapter will conclude with a number of case studies. As before, it will illustrate the active role that South Asian girls play in responding to these broader discourses.

TEACHER DISCOURSES AND SOUTH ASIAN GIRLS

To begin with, it is important to explore briefly the role that some teachers have played in developing and reproducing discourses on particular South Asian girls. I will do this by first looking at these teachers' perceptions of South Asian girls from the three sample classes before moving on to some of the ways in which these perceptions appear to be woven into their classroom practices. This will then provide the context, in the next section, for exploring how these discursive practices came to influence and shape the general position of South Asian girls within the field of feminine peer-group relations.

Teacher discourses and school reports

What is striking, when looking at all of the school reports on South Asian girls, is their apparent similarity to those of the South Asian boys. What, in Chapter 7, we found perceived as the helpful, quiet, hard-working and obedient nature of South Asian boys is almost indistinguishable from that attributed to the girls. This is illustrated by the following extract taken from Mrs Scott's school report on Priti, which was representative of the other South Asian girls' reports: 'Priti listens attentively to all our discussions. . . . She has worked very hard and is making excellent progress. . . . She is most helpful in the organisation of the classroom and with tidying up at the end of the day.'

It could be argued that the noticeable similarity between these reports and those on the South Asian boys and the apparent lack of any significant gender distinction can be understood by the feminisation of South Asian boys, discussed in detail in Chapter 7. It was this discursive positioning that appeared to act significantly to reduce any distinctions that some teachers (and other children) may have made between the South Asian boys and the girls. What was found with the teachers' reports on the South Asian girls, therefore, was an overemphasis on the South Asian girls' perceived obedient and hard-working manner compared to that of White and Black girls. These reports stood in contrast with what I actually observed, however, where the behaviour of South Asian girls pointed towards a similar mix of work and avoidance of work and obedience and disruption, making their behaviour largely indistinguishable from that of their female peers.

I want to argue, in a similar way to the arguments on South Asian boys in Chapter 7, that the appropriation and reproduction of these broader racialised discourses on the passive, obedient and eager-to-please nature of South Asian girls can possibly be located in the broader field of education and the teachers' struggles to maintain status and a competent image among their peers. The two key elements to this, as discussed at length in Chapter

5, were the successful maintenance of discipline and learning in the class-room. One aspect of the cultural capital that has been learnt and habitualised by many teachers in relation to discipline is the practice of publicly chastising individual children as an example to others. As we have seen in previous chapters, this appears to have become a highly gendered affair, involving frequent confrontations between teachers and boys, particularly Black boys. A result of this was that a strong tendency existed for the behaviour of girls generally (and South Asian boys as a result of their discursive constitution as 'effeminate') to be overlooked. It appeared that, for some teachers, making an example of certain boys was usually enough to attract the attention of the girls and bring their behaviour back into line. For South Asian girls, however, this process seemed to be even more exacerbated, as their particular construction as being passive, obedient and eager-to-please arguably transformed them into the epitome of femininity in the eyes of some teachers. Even more so than with their White peers, then, this quintessential femininity had relegated South Asian girls to the private sphere where their actions and behaviour were more likely to be overlooked.

Moreover, this invisibility was also evident in relation to the teacher's other main role – that of teaching (see also Brah and Minhas 1985; Wright 1992). Here, as has also been argued in Chapter 5, teachers periodically needed to prove their teaching competence among their peers by exhibiting 'good' pieces of work that had been completed by their children. While the perception of South Asian girls as hard-working meant that their work was often included in this and came to be displayed on the walls of school corridors and held up at assemblies, it appeared to be relatively down-played in comparison with the work of other pupils. South Asian girls were observed to attract less praise and attention from some members of staff than other children. This was especially true in relation to boys generally, whose work would be especially singled out and highlighted around the school. In many ways this could be seen not only as an attempt to encourage the boys' positive experiences of schooling and reduce what was perceived to be their greater likelihood of disaffection, but also as a way of underlining the class teacher's own skills, in terms of their ability to derive good work from what were seen as difficult pupils. For South Asian girls, however, as suggested above, good work was almost expected of them, and the status derived from this therefore tended to be devalued.

South Asian girls and teachers' classroom practices

One of the main consequences of the teachers' discourses on the quintessentially feminine nature of South Asian girls was their effective removal from the public sphere and their invisibility. In relative terms, teachers rarely called out to them in the classroom and/or publicly chastised them for misbehaviour. Indeed, some of the teachers commented that South Asian girls were a 'pleasure to have in the class', the sub-text of which can also possibly be understood as meaning that they presented very few behavioural problems requiring the teacher's intervention. Moreover, as explained above, their brief entry into the public sphere in relation to praise for their academic work was also relatively less marked and overt in comparison with their peers.

This lack of presence in the public sphere was also commonly represented among some teachers through references to South Asian girls as 'quiet, little' girls. One day, when I was accompanying Mrs Scott's class back to the school after a visit to the local park, Mrs Pringle, a classroom assistant, complained to Mrs Scott that some of the children had been swearing. Mrs Scott turned round to see a group of South Asian girls near Mrs Pringle and said, in a loud, disbelieving voice, 'Pretty little girls don't swear!' In reply, Mrs Pringle explained that she was not referring to the South Asian girls but to Charlene, a Black girl in the class. Ironically, even more proactive attempts aimed at encouraging South Asian girls into the public sphere often only tended to discursively reinforce their marginal position in the eyes of the other children. One example of this was in Mrs Scott's class, where Mrs Scott had just been talking to Reena's mother about Reena staying for school dinner for the first time that day. Her mother explained that Reena was a little apprehensive and had asked her to stay with her for dinner. Mrs Scott summoned the children to sit on the carpet and, while the mother was still present, called Reena to the front:

Mrs Scott: What is it that's upsetting you? Is it playing out after dinner or what? [*no answer, Reena just stands there looking a little apprehensive*] Or the dinner? What is it? [*still no answer*] [. . .] [*looks to the mother*] They choose what they want, they walk along and choose. [*looking back to Reena*] Why do you want your mummy to come along at dinnertime? You don't know? [. . .] Do you play with somebody after dinner? Who do you play with? [*no answer. Mrs Scott turns round to whole class*] Sit down everybody! Does anybody play with Reena at dinnertime? [*Stephanie and Sonia put hands up*] Oh, do you, Stephanie? Thank you! You do, do you? Oh, good girl, Sonia!

Mother: [. . .] There are girls from other classes; you know Kamaljeet and Deepti? [*two girls from the Juniors*] They play with her.

Mrs Scott: Oh, I see, yes, I do, they're very nice!

Mother: They play with her.

Mrs Scott: Well, the thing is, she should try to make friends in here.

Mother: That's what I'm telling her; she should try/

Mrs Scott: /Listen, girls, you must try to look after Reena because she's *very* quiet! And she doesn't talk to anybody very much. Poonam will look after her, won't you? She's friendly! And Beenal.

Mother:	[*to Reena*] They're all so friendly, look!
Mrs Scott:	And Sonia. This is the danger, actually, Mrs, erm, Woods wrote in her report that she works on her own and doesn't talk to people.
Mother:	Yeah, that's the dan/
Mrs Scott:	/That's the danger, because when you go out you're lonely. [. . .] [*to Reena*] Who would you like to sit with today? [*points to Poonam*] Poonam! Well, you go and sit over there and Poonam will look after you.

It could be argued that not only did this incident help to publicly rein-force the perception of South Asian girls as quiet, passive and dependent among the other children but that it also, through Mrs Scott's assumption that Poonam and Beenal would 'look after' her, arguably reproduced the assumption that South Asian girls 'stick together'. Indeed, later that day, these discursive themes were publicly underlined by Mrs Scott when most of the children were sitting on the carpet having their drinks. Mrs Scott noticed that Poonam did not have a drink and called her to the front:

Mrs Scott:	Have you brought your own drink today?
Poonam:	[*looks a little apprehensive and shakes head*]
Mrs Scott:	Well, you're supposed to; isn't it in your packed lunch?
Poonam:	[*shakes head*]
Mrs Scott:	Where is it, then? You're supposed to bring your drink up here! Is it in the fridge?
Poonam:	Yes.
Mrs Scott:	Well, you must bring it here, because if you're on a packed lunch then you bring your own drink. Go [*looks to PC*], will you go down with her to the fridge and get it please? I don't think she understood that! [*Poonam and PC leave the classroom and walk down the corridor*]
[. . .]	
Poonam:	I told my mum to bring two drinks, one at the school and one for packed lunch, but my mum said no!
PC:	She said no? So you've only got one drink then?
Poonam:	Lots of drinks, but she don't let me have two drinks.
PC:	She doesn't let you have two?
Poonam:	No.
[. . .]	
[*PC and Poonam return to classroom*]	
Mrs Scott:	Now drink all of it; just drink a bit! See, Aaron knew that. If you bring sandwiches, you have to bring your own drink. OK?

This incident tends to illustrate how Mrs Scott's perceptions of South Asian girls can at times set the agenda for interaction with them. Here,

Poonam was quite clear why she did not have a second drink – her mother did not listen to her requests – and yet she was unable to offer this explanation because Mrs Scott did not allow it. Arguably, it was as if Mrs Scott had already convinced herself that Poonam would not have an explanation other than that she was too passive and dependent to carry out Mrs Scott's instructions. Moreover, the fact that Mrs Scott expressed concern to me that Poonam had not understood her was also testimony to the way in which she had convinced herself that there would be no answer forthcoming, and so failed to create the appropriate space to enable Poonam to offer one. For the children who witnessed these types of incidents, it could be argued that they were left in little doubt that South Asian girls were quiet, passive and dependent, especially given the fact that they rarely entered the public sphere of the classroom in any other capacity (see also Ross and Ryan 1990).

SOUTH ASIAN GIRLS AND THE FIELD OF FEMININE PEER-GROUP RELATIONS

Bearing in mind the above discussion, I want to look more closely at the general location of South Asian girls within the field of feminine peer-group relations, and the influence of the discursive practices of some of the teachers and the organisation of the school more generally upon this. Here there appeared to be an inherent contradiction: on the one hand, South Asian girls had been discursively constituted by teachers as quintessentially feminine in certain respects, being perceived as quiet, passive, obedient and helpful. However, when looking at the predominance of discourses on boyfriends and the related discursive themes of love, marriage and relationships within the field of feminine peer-group relations, this identity did not appear to enable them to gain access to the field through these particular discourses. On the contrary, as we will see, at a general level they seemed to be largely excluded from these discourses. Their feminine identities so constituted do not appear to have been recognised by other girls or translated into appropriate forms of capital. It is this contradiction that provides the focus for this section. What I want to do is to highlight the nature of that exclusion, before exploring other aspects of the discourses on South Asian girls that can possibly help us understand this paradox.

The social exclusion of South Asian girls from the field

The previous chapters have been punctuated with examples of how South Asian children have been adversely positioned within some children's discourses. Here, I am concerned with exploring how and why these discourses were reproduced within the field of feminine peer-group relations. As Wright (1992) has argued, underlying many of these discourses was the constitution of South Asian girls as the Other: as inferior and 'alien'. This is illustrated in the following extract, taken from an interview with Charlene and Melanie, from Mrs Scott's class. Charlene had just noticed some posters depicting South Asian children on the walls of the interview room:

Charlene: They're all Indians! [*pointing to pictures on the wall*]
Melanie: No – some of 'em are White people, some of 'em!
Charlene: That baby is – but they're all Indians. Urrr, I don't like Indians!
PC: Why?
Melanie: Urrrhhh! They're Pakis – I don't like Pakis!
[. . .]
PC: Why don't you like Indians. then?
Charlene: [. . .] I don't like Pakis!
Melanie: Urrrhhh! I don't like Indians!
[. . .]
Melanie: Paki-Paki-Paki!
PC: Is that a nice word – saying 'Paki'?
Charlene: Nah.
PC: No?
Melanie: No!
PC: Why isn't it a nice word?
Charlene: Because it's naughty.
PC: Naughty? Why is it naughty?
Melanie: I don't know! Now shut up!

Moreover, this construction of South Asian girls as the Other in relation to the field of feminine peer-group relations could arguably be seen in the way that White and Black girls would also refer to and tease each other as being 'Pakis'. One playtime, for instance, Zoe, a girl from Mrs Brogan's class whose mother was White and father Turkish, came up to me in a rather distressed state and pointed to a group of girls she had been playing with. She complained that they had called her a Pakistani, and added defiantly: 'I'm White, aren't I?' Later, in the classroom, I was able to ask her about this incident:

PC: What did they call you?
Zoe: I'm a Pakistani.
PC: Did they?/
Zoe: /But I'm not! [*defiantly*]
PC: You're not? What are you?
Zoe: I'm half-English and I'm half-Turkish! I'm *not* Pakistani.
PC: You're not? Don't you want to be?
Zoe: [*shakes head*]
PC: Why?

Zoe: I'm not, anyway; my daddy's not Pakistani, and we are allowed to eat meat but not pork meat.

PC: Oh! Didn't you like them calling you that?

Zoe: No.

PC: Why?

Zoe: Because it's horrible!

PC: Is it?

Zoe: Because I'm not a Pakistani, anyway. [. . .] And if they call me Pakistan I'm going to tell my dad, because I'm not even one anyway.

A similar process could be seen operating in an interview with Debbie and Kylie, two White girls from Mrs Brogan's class. Here, Debbie talked about her half-sister whose father was Black:

Debbie: You know Stella, she's my sister/

Kylie: /She's Black!/

Debbie: /And she's still my sister!

PC: She's your sister? What do you mean she's Black?

Kylie: She's a Paki!

Debbie: [*angrily*] No, she's not a Paki! She's a *normal* girl!

[. . .]

PC: What do you mean, she's a normal girl, Debbie?

Debbie: You know how she's a normal girl like that – just got Black on her.

PC: But Indian people are normal, aren't they? Debbie?

Debbie: No – not like Indian people!

PC: But Indian people are normal as well, aren't they?

Debbie: Indian people are normal.

Kylie: She's a Paki!

Debbie: No, she *ain't* a Paki!

PC: Do you think it's nice saying 'Paki', Kylie?

Kylie: [*shakes head*]

PC: So why do you say it, then?

Kylie: I don't know!

PC: If you were an Indian, would you like to be called a Paki?

Kylie: No.

PC: No? Why not?

Debbie: [*shouts at Kylie*] So why do you call other people Pakis?

What is interesting from the above was how, in the course of the conversation, Debbie shifted from an implicitly racist stance, in referring to her sister as a 'normal girl' in comparison to South Asians, to a more anti-racist stance in the last line, where she criticised Kylie for using the term 'Paki'. It could be argued that one of the dynamics underlying this shift related to Debbie herself and the way she was struggling to locate her Black sister in relation to herself, and struggling with the appropriateness of racist terms.

South Asian girls, the Other and attractiveness

To understand this discursive construction of some South Asian girls as the Sexual Other within the field of feminine peer-group relations, and especially to make sense of how this occurred against the backdrop of their constitution as quintessentially feminine through teacher discourses, we need to return to some of the other elements of the discourses on South Asian children, manifest within and beyond the school, that have been outlined in previous chapters. Here we found that discourses being reproduced on the Manor Park estate in relation to what was perceived to be the 'alien' and inferior nature of South Asian people appeared also to be appropriated by some of the children and reworked into their own experiences of schooling. As we saw in Chapter 7, this was a process that ironically appeared to have been aided by the school's approach to multiculturalism, which acted to underline and reinforce this construction of South Asian children as the Other. We also saw that, for some of the boys, the association with South Asian girls, especially as girlfriends, had come to be regarded extremely negatively and signified a fundamental attack on a boy's masculinity. This is illustrated in the following argument between Stephen and Paul and Daniel, where South Asian girls were introduced into the argument as the Sexual Other. It is interesting to note that the argument began with Paul and Daniel teasing Stephen about having Annette, a Black girl from their class, as a girlfriend. As we saw in the last chapter, while Annette had been extremely successful in negotiating a prominent position within the field of masculine peer-group relations, the contradictions in this meant that, at times, the boys could switch discourses and adversely position her within those on heterosexuality as a girl. In relation to the following, this appeared to have been done primarily out of Paul's jealousy that Stephen associated with her, and the struggle to countenance the social capital that he had gained:

Paul:　　Annette does love you! Annette does go out with you!

Stephen:　I bet! Is that why . . . ? All right then, if Annette goes out with me then Nazia goes out with Daniel!

Paul:　　You have two girlfriends – Nazia, Kelly [*dual heritage*] and her, Annette.

Stephen:　And I know, and I know you go out with Rupal, Rakhee and [*saying last name slowly and pulling face*] Neelam!

[. . .]

Daniel:　You've got a Paki girlfriend!

175

Stephen: Who?
Daniel: That one there with that dot! [*on another poster*]
Paul: [*laughs*]
[. . .]
Stephen: You go out with Neelam!
Daniel: And so do you!
Stephen: You go out with all the girls in our class!
Daniel: You go out with all the Pakis! [*laughs*]
Stephen: I said you go out with everyone in the whole world, mate!
Daniel: So do you! [*laughs*]
Stephen: How can you say I do when I've already said you do?
Daniel: You do!
Stephen: You do!
Daniel: You go out with all of the Pakis, I go out with all the Whites. [*laughs*]
Stephen: You go out with all of the Pakis! Because I, do I look like a Paki though – you do! You go the mosque, mate, where all the Pakis go!
[*general laughs*]

The specific ways in which South Asian girls came to be defined as the Other, as set out above, offer us clues as to the particular discourses in play. Here I want to suggest that attractiveness, so embedded in the dominant forms of capital within the field of feminine peer-group relations generally and within the more specific discursive themes of boyfriends and girlfriends in particular, could possibly provide a medium through which South Asian girls were constituted as the Sexual Other (Brah and Minhas 1985). What we found was that there was no positive and shared understanding of what being attractive was, *per se*, but simply of what it was not. While we found a few references in the previous chapter relating to how some of the girls came to associate attractiveness with long hair and with the use of make-up, it was more common to find that children simply asserted their own tastes in relation to their distancing from South Asian children. This was certainly the case in the interview quoted above, where the boys associated South Asian girls with 'bad taste'. It could be argued that while South Asian girls may be discursively constructed as quintessentially feminine by many teachers, this did not translate into feminine notions of attractiveness. It was here that we can see the salience of the more general discourses on the perceived 'alien' and inferior nature of South Asian people being appropriated, reworked and reproduced by some of the children. This was also seen to be the case for girls within the field of feminine peer-group relations, as highlighted through some of the incidents described above. Here one of the central dynamics involved was the struggle over one of the more significant public forms of capital in the field – that relating to boyfriends – which was underpinned by the discursive theme of attractiveness. Arguably, the teasing of each other as being a 'Paki' could therefore be seen, at least in part, in relation to these struggles.

The discussion so far has drawn attention to the complexities of feminine identities and the way that they were not simply closed around a certain number of easily identifiable – and transferable – characteristics, but were highly contingent and contradictory. South Asian girls appeared, therefore, to be located within a discursive position that defined them as both feminine and the Other in relation to femininity. The association of the former with passivity, obedience and dependency and the latter with sexuality, as implied so far, was also not that simple in practice. Their constitution as the Other sexually was also imported by some girls to justify their exclusion from more general games of tick and Mummies and Daddies. Similarly, their perceived passivity and 'alien' nature appeared also, at times, to render them sexual among the boys, as is illustrated by the following transcript, taken from an interview with two Year 2 boys, from Mrs Jones' class. Here, the traditional discursive themes of South Asian girls as sensual and exotic were alluded to. The extract begins with Dean's frustration at Jason's inability to understand him:

Dean: He don't know what I mean, he don't know what I mean, he talks English.

Jason: English, I'm talking English now!

Dean: Yeah, like Paki! [*laughs*]

Jason: You talk French!

Dean: You talk like Paki language. [*laughs*] You talk . . .

PC: What's that language?

Jason: You talk French.

Dean: When you got a girlfriend, no way you want to play with them [*South Asian*] girls, right? They might, you might, you might, you might [*in soft voice*] 'come on baby want to suck you off'.

PC: You want to what?

Dean: [*embarrassed*] Nnaaahhhh, not . . .

PC: What girls are those? What do you mean by them girls?

Jason: Downstairs.

Dean: In our class

Jason: Like Reema. [*laughs*]

PC: You don't want to play with those, then?

Dean: No.

PC: Why?

Dean: She's a Paki!

This theme was also apparent in the following transcript, taken from an interview with Daniel, Paul and Stephen, from Mrs Scott's class. Here,

South Asian girls appeared to be constructed as mysterious and unpredictable:

Daniel: I don't like 'em. [*Asian girls*]
PC: Why don't you like 'em?
Daniel: Because they're tigers! [*laughs*]
PC: They're tigers?
Daniel: Yeah! They've got a mask on their face like a tiger!
Paul: Daniel, if there, if you go with one of them – you know what will happen, you know what, what they'll do?
Daniel: What?
Paul: Bite ya!
Stephen: Eat you!
Daniel: Bite your bum off!

STRATEGIES OF CONFORMITY AND RESISTANCE

What we have seen so far is the contradictory discursive positioning of South Asian girls. On the one hand, they appeared to be constructed as feminine through teacher practices which highlighted their perceived passive, obedient and helpful manner. On the other hand, however, they were also discursively constituted as the Other by their peers in relation to notions of attractiveness. While these competing themes inevitably emerged through a range of contradictions, some of which have been highlighted above, it was this latter process that tended to predominate and appeared to be behind a tendency for South Asian girls to find themselves excluded from the field of feminine peer-group relations. It was the variety of responses adopted by the South Asian girls at East Avenue to this tendency for exclusion which provides the focus for this final section. As we will see, these responses varied from the carving out of alternative social spaces to the struggle to gain acceptance within the field of feminine peer-group relations.

Sheetal

Sheetal was the only South Asian girl to begin the academic year in Ms Patterson's class. Her general experience of the field of feminine peer-group relations appeared to be one of exclusion, as the following extract, taken from an interview with Naomi, Devan and Peter, illustrates:

Naomi: I don't like playing with Sheetal.
PC: Sheetal? Why not?
Devan: I don't like playing with Sheetal and I play with Robert.

Peter: I play with Robert! No one likes playing with her [*Sheetal*] – just Lisa!
PC: Why doesn't anyone like playing with Sheetal?
Naomi: 'Cos she's horrible!
PC: Why's she horrible?
Devan: Everyone thinks she's, erm, horrible just 'cos she's a Paki.
PC: Do they? Do you think that's true?
Devan: No.
Naomi: Yeah.
Devan: No.
Peter: Yeah.
Devan: No, I don't.

The general sense of isolation that Sheetal seemed to experience as a result of this exclusion was something recognised by Mrs Ashton, a supply teacher who took Mrs Patterson's class for one day a week:

Mrs Ashton: Sheetal's [. . .] a bit introverted and a bit shy, but she's coming out. [. . .] I think in a way she could do with an Asian girl to be friends with, because quite often she's a bit on her own, and quite often it's nice if they've got another Asian girl to be pals with and she hasn't got anybody, and I feel a bit sorry for her. Doesn't seem to bother her overmuch, but I think that perhaps she'd be more confident with another girl which she could be particularly friends with.
PC: Who does she play with, then, usually?
Mrs Ashton: Sort of hangs about, around different ones in the playground.
PC: So she doesn't hang around with the girls and that?
Mrs Ashton: She does, but she's not as accepted as, erm, as if she'd been White there's a definite difference there. She sort of hangs around with them but she doesn't seem to be as part of the game as she might be if she had another little girl to be with. The Asian girls often just walk round together with arms linked or holding the teachers' hands. They're not always madly involved in games like the others.

While Mrs Ashton's explanation of Sheetal's isolation, largely in relation to 'race', was partly supported by the children's perceptions of her as a 'Paki' as highlighted earlier, a number of other factors could well also be in play, including, most prominently, the possibility that she was simply shy. In the absence of more detailed biographical information about the children, these other factors can only be assumed. Whatever the final mix of causal factors, Mrs Ashton's general observations were quite accurately representative of my own. Sheetal did not appear to be firmly rooted in friendships with others.

While she did periodically play with Lisa, a White girl from her class, she tended to find herself on the periphery of social relations. The lack of a strong nucleus of friends meant that she was often left to float from one group to another, playing only a marginal role in the games or activities that the children were involved in. In other words, the absence of one or two close friends meant that she was unable to carve out an alternative social space for herself. Having said that, however, it was arguably because of this that she found herself located in a very contradictory position. In the classroom, for instance, this lack of an alternative social space made it almost inevitable that she would come into direct contact with other children as they worked, and that those children would come to relate to her on a personal level to a certain degree. This was certainly true for Devan, a Black boy from her class, who, as we saw in earlier chapters, had actually been observed picking on and harassing South Asian children. And yet, possibly because they regularly worked together on the same table, he had come to relate to her on a more personal level and therefore, as we could see in the transcript above, set her apart from the more general derogatory discourses on South Asian children he frequently engaged in in other contexts. Albeit to a lesser extent, the same was true for Lisa, who would periodically play with Sheetal in the playground but at other times would equally engage in more generalised, racist discourses on South Asians. Part of the reason for the development of these particular friendships, especially in relation to Devan, appeared to be the ability of Sheetal to trade in the cultural capital she had acquired in terms of her academic work. This ability to complete particular assignments quickly and successfully was something that was valued equally among girls and boys.

Sheetal's inability to access some of the dominant forms of capital related to discourses on boyfriends in the field of feminine peer-group relations, together with the lack of close friends with which to experiment with these forms of feminine capital in an alternative social space, meant that she was far less inclined to embody within her own habitus the related discourses on love, marriage and attractiveness that underlay these forms of capital. Rather, as already alluded to, she tended to gain status and develop her sense of self through her academic work, which provided one channel that enabled and encouraged her to acquire, develop and express other aspects of her feminine identity.

Poonam, Beenal, Priti and Stephanie

Poonam, Beenal and Priti, three South Asian girls from Mrs Scott's class, shared a close friendship grouping that Sheetal lacked. While they were also largely excluded from the discourses on boyfriends within the field of feminine peer-group relations, they were able, with Stephanie, a White girl, also from their class, to carve out their own alternative social space, which did not tend to rely on the recognition of others and appeared to provide the basis from within which they were able to explore and develop their sense of identity. In some ways, the creation of their own social space and its relative distance from that of the field of feminine peer-group relations meant that they were less likely to be influenced by the dominant forms of capital associated with the discourses on boyfriends. Because of this, they were arguably more able to experiment with differing activities and develop and perfect their own games, making full use of the resources available to them. They had developed, for instance, a particular game involving the numbered snake painted on the playground which was a variation of traditional hopscotch. They were also to be seen playing a game they called 'Musical Stones', which appeared to be influenced by the more established game of pass-the-parcel, while at other times they played a game they had developed called 'The Fair', where they would imitate and role-play certain fairground acts and rides. Of course, this ability of young children to appropriate, rework and amend games was one shared by most of the children and provided a staple ingredient of their playground lives. The point I want to stress here, however, is that it appeared to be a more common pursuit among these four girls in comparison to others. Many other children seemed to have their lives in the playground more structured by the complex set of pre-given games, whether these were football for the boys, clapping and skipping games for the girls, or kiss-chase, tick and racing more generally. The South Asian girls' tendency to be absent from this public sphere, therefore, appeared to give them a space and freedom to express themselves not available for others to the same degree.

However, they were also seen to value and struggle over some of the more predominant public forms of capital associated more specifically with these discourses on boyfriends within the field of feminine peer-group relations. Most commonly this took the form of playing games such as Mummies and Daddies or Babies, and also games which involved more creative, expressive skills, such as picking and arranging daisies in the playground and combing and plaiting each other's hair. As we saw in Chapter 8, one of the more significant dynamics underlying these discursive themes of love, marriage, relationships and attractiveness was the more general discourses on boyfriends and girlfriends, and it was primarily through Stephanie that they gained access to these discourses. Stephanie's involvement in this friendship group did not preclude her from other social networks and, in a similar position to that in which Emma and Nicky found themselves as detailed in previous chapters, she was also central to a number of fights between boys from her class who wanted her as a girlfriend. Not only did she appear to gain a significant amount of social capital from this but it also enabled Beenal, Poonam and Priti to engage in detailed and prolonged conversations about her exploits and relationships with the boys. Arguably, it provided a way in which these girls could circumvent their exclusion from the broader discourses on boyfriends/girlfriends. It thus tended to create the medium through which they could explore their own ideas and fantasies in relation to boyfriends, which consequently came to be woven into their other games, such as Mummies and Daddies and Babies.

Stephanie's friendship with the other girls was not without its own problems or contradictions, however. To a certain extent, her ability to bridge the gap between the social world created by the South Asian girls and those of other children appeared to lay her open to racial abuse. Nicky and Kylie, from Mrs Brogan's class, were seen on a few occasions to refuse to play with Stephanie because they said she 'smelt'. They also teased her by pretending to talk in Gujerati. As we saw in relation to Daniel, the White boy from Mrs Scott's class who played with three Black boys (the Bad Boys), Stephanie's association with South Asian girls meant that some of her peers came to see her in racialised terms, as symbolically South Asian. Stephanie's attempts to distance herself from this process appeared to provide the context where a whole range of contradictions emerged, as in the following extract taken from an interview with Stephanie, Aisha and Poonam. Here Aisha had just said that she did not like playing with Beenal:

PC:	Why don't you want to play with Beenal, Aisha?
Aisha:	I don't know.
Stephanie:	'Cos she's [*Beenal*] Indian! Init?
Aisha:	No!
Stephanie:	Yeah – 'cos she's Indian!
Aisha:	NO!
Poonam:	She plays with me – she's Gujerati! She plays with me, silly! She's not Indian!
PC:	Because she's Indian, you say, Stephanie?
Stephanie:	Yeah.
PC:	Is that right, Poonam?
Poonam:	No, she's not Indian, she's Gujerati.
PC:	She's Gujerati?
Poonam:	I'm Gujerati, she's [*Beenal*] Gujerati.
PC:	But what's wrong with her because she's Indian? What's wrong with that, Stephanie?
Stephanie:	I don't know.

Here, Stephanie approvingly introduced the cultural marker that Beenal is Indian to explain why Aisha did not want to play with her, even though Aisha strongly denied this. It is interesting to note how Poonam also tried to distance herself from these more general derogatory discourses on Indians and 'Pakis' by claiming that she and Beenal were Gujerati.

Aisha

The above interview conveniently leads us on to Aisha, who provides the final case study to consider here. What is worth noting in relation to Aisha is the way that Stephanie felt able to introduce the racialised discourses on Indians so directly in her presence. I want to suggest that this was made possible partly because of the success that Aisha had in downplaying the significance of her identity as South Asian and gaining a prominent position within the field of feminine peer-group relations. One of the main reasons she appeared to be so successful in doing this was as a result of the cultural and symbolic capital she had acquired through her mother. Her mother seemed to be positioned relatively prominently in those discursive practices discussed in Chapter 4 where, because of her sense of isolation, she was more likely to focus on her children and use them as the medium through which to express her own identity and desires. As a result, Aisha came to school in very fashionable clothes and often wore jewellery. She was also one of the main sources of face creams and other make-up for her friends to experiment with, and would often bring in her favourite games, such as Pretty Princess and My Little Pony, to play with and parade in front of others. Aisha therefore came to acquire a significant amount of status among her female peers as well as some of the teaching staff, who would also comment on her attractiveness. At Christmas, for instance, she was given the much-sought-after role of an angel, along with Debbie, a blonde-haired girl from Mrs Brogan's class, who was also considered by some of the teachers to be an attractive child.

While Aisha did, periodically, play with Poonam, Beenal and Priti, principally because she was in their class, she also appeared to spend much time socially distancing herself from them. It is within this context that we can understand her comments reported in Chapter 8, where she tried to explain why boys did not like the other three girls because of their short hair, and how boys liked long hair like hers. This social distancing and its underlying racialised nature can be seen in the following extract, taken from an interview with Aisha and Poonam. Here they were talking about Stephen, a Black boy from their class, when Aisha corrected and made fun of Poonam's accent and her pronunciation of 'Stacey':

Poonam: Stephen hates girls!
Aisha: Yeah, the only ones he likes is Jemma and Marcia.
Poonam: And Stacey.
Aisha: [*frustratedly to Poonam*] Not 'Stazeee' – Stacey! You can't even speak properly!
PC: Stacey?

Aisha: Yeah – not Stazeee. Stacey! She can't even say it, Mr Connolly. [*laughs*]

PC: That's all right!

It is interesting how, in the act of distancing herself from Poonam, Aisha seemed to try to implicate me, a White person in authority, as someone she may have identified with more closely and/or deferred to within that specific argument.

Arguably, part of the reason for Aisha's attempts to distance herself from the other three South Asian girls was related to age and her feeling that they were immature. In this she made a specific attempt to associate with older children from 'upstairs', meaning the higher infant and junior classes situated on the top two floors of the school. This is illustrated in the following interview with Aisha, Beenal and Poonam, where the latter two had just complained that Aisha never played with them:

PC: So why don't you play with Beenal and Poonam, Aisha?

Aisha: They're boring!

PC: They're boring?

Aisha: Yeah.

[. . .]

PC: Why don't you two play with Aisha, then?

Poonam: She don't let us!

PC: Why?

Aisha: Because I've got so many friends to play with.

PC: But why don't you want [. . .] more friends?

Aisha: I've got loads of friends in the Juniors and upstairs in the middle class.

What was interesting with Aisha was the way that her position as attractive appeared to have been developed primarily through the symbolic and cultural capital gained via her mother. In contrast to other girls, she neither played kiss-chase with boys nor spoke of having a boyfriend. This could well be the result of Aisha's own decision to distance herself from boys. Equally likely, it could be because, as we have seen in earlier chapters, boys had also constructed South Asian girls as the Other in terms of attractiveness, and so to be associated with a South Asian girl as a girlfriend would risk the loss of a considerable degree of status. Within this context, Aisha was as likely as the other South Asian girls to be singled out for abuse and harassment from the boys in her class. This is illustrated in the following quote, taken from an interview with Aisha, Poonam and Beenal, where they were complaining about the harassment they received from the Bad Boys in their class featured in Chapter 6:

Aisha: Stephen's horrible to me at school.
PC: Stephen from your class?
Aisha: Yeah.
PC: How's he horrible? What does he do?
Aisha: He pushes me and all that stuff.
Poonam: And Paul.
Aisha: I don't do anything to him, init?
Poonam: No, you don't, ain't it? You don't.
Aisha: No, but he does it back to me – he thinks I done it.
PC: [. . .] What else do they do? Anything else?
Poonam: And Paul, I think! Ah! Jordan! And Jordan, ain't it?
PC: What does Jordan do?
Aisha: Pushing me.
Poonam: Kicking!
Aisha: Yeah, kicking me, punching, fighting, karate.
[. . .]
PC: Why do you think they do it to you, Aisha?
Aisha: I don't know – because they hate me!

I have quoted this at length so as to contrast it with the following, also taken from an interview with Aisha. Here she talked of how Stephen had commented favourably about her hair:

Aisha: [. . .] And boys like this [*touching her own hair*] and a hair-band.
PC: How do you know they like that? Who said they like that?
Aisha: Stephen, in our class, yesterday.
PC: Did he? What did he say?
Aisha: He said I was very, very nice [. . .] just because I helped him because he can't do take-aways.

To understand this contradiction articulated by Aisha in terms of a boy who physically assaulted her and 'hated' her while also saying she was 'very, very nice', we need to remind ourselves of how attractiveness is constructed within discourses on boyfriends and heterosexuality. In this, while Aisha never spoke directly of boyfriends in relation to herself, she was located within a discursive frame that constructed attractiveness in relation to the desires of boys. Thus, although Stephen, in other contexts, was thoroughly nasty to her, he was a boy, and one with a lot of status among his peers. Arguably, therefore, his judgement was valued by Aisha and other girls. It is also interesting to note the conditions within which Stephen chose to associate with Aisha: in a relatively private space and with the benefit of being helped with his work. It is this contrast between the private and more personal setting and the public and more status-ridden arena that also helps us partially understand Stephen's radically different treatment of Aisha.

CONCLUSIONS

In this chapter I have explored the position of South Asian girls within the field of feminine peer-group relations. While the chapter has drawn attention to the way that some teachers have come to discursively construct South Asian girls as quintessentially feminine, such discourses did not tend to invest these girls with significant forms of capital within the field of feminine peer-group relations. Rather, many South Asian girls appeared to be constructed as the Sexual Other in relation to discourses on boyfriends and the related discursive themes of intimacy, love and marriage. Here, it was argued that the broader discourses on the 'alien' and inferior nature of South Asian children came to predominate. In this sense the chapter has helped to develop our understanding of the ways in which South Asian girls have been discursively constituted as the Sexual Other (see also Brah and Minhas 1985). It was within this context that the chapter went on to examine the differing ways in which South Asian girls came to respond to these broader discursive processes. Some chose to carve out their own more private alternative spaces within which to explore and develop their gender identities. In contrast, others were shown actively to resist these processes and to gain appropriate forms of capital within these discourses on love, marriage and attractiveness.

10

CONCLUSIONS

This book has been concerned with exploring the significance of racism in young children's lives and, within this, how discourses on 'race' came to influence and shape the gender identities of Black and South Asian children. What I want to do in this concluding chapter is to draw out and discuss four main themes that have been addressed in the book. These are: methodological implications that have arisen in relation to researching young children; a reassessment of the theoretical framework used in the study of racism in young children's lives; the implications of the study for anti-racist practice in schools; and, finally, some of the broader research questions that remain to be addressed in future work.

RETHINKING APPROACHES TO THE STUDY OF YOUNG CHILDREN

One of the main themes to emerge from the book is the social competence of children as young as 5 and 6 in reflecting upon and intervening in their social worlds. It has focused on the skill with which some young children were able actively to appropriate, rework and reproduce discourses on 'race', gender and sexuality in quite complex ways. It draws attention to their ability to interact with their social environment and adapt and reconstitute their behaviour from one context to the next. Above all, this emphasis on the agency of young children has helped bring into focus what has been termed their decentred selves. Their identities were therefore not simply determined by their age but also by their ethnicity, gender, class and sexuality. These all came together within specific contexts to provide the background against which the children developed their sense of identity. More fundamentally, the book has brought into question the appropriateness of making assumptions about children's cognitive ability or their level of awareness on matters of 'race', gender or sexuality simply by their age. While the case studies used in this book make no claims to be representative, they do quite vividly draw attention to the ability of some young children to acquire a relatively sophisticated and active understanding of their social worlds. It is this that brings into question the usefulness of research that simply focuses on the level of racial awareness among young children, as if this can easily and unproblematically be measured. Rather, the questions underlining this book have been concerned with identifying some of the complex sets of discursive processes and practices that articulated in the construction of a particular child's sense of identity. In relation to explorations of the salience of 'race' in young children's lives, this will be a theme returned to shortly.

It is this realisation of the social competency of young children that has a number of implications in relation to methodology. In this, the book has not only demonstrated the ability to research the subjectivities of young children, but has also drawn attention to the particular methods that appear to be most suitable for this. The main point I want to advance here is that, once researchers have come to accept the social competency of young children, then they should approach the study of them as they would any other socially defined group. In particular, if we want to increase our understanding of their social worlds, we need an ethnographic methodology with a prominent role given to in-depth, largely unstructured interviews with the young children. As the previous chapters are testimony, this approach seems to be the most effective means with which to unravel the complexities of young children's social identities.

Of course, this should not be read as simply encouraging researchers to ignore the particular effects of discourses on age and childhood on the research process. Indeed, the book has been punctuated with examples emphasising the role I have played as an adult in shaping and influencing the conduct of the young children. More particularly, this influence was most obvious along a number of axes. The principal one was my age, in relation to which it appeared that some young children actively introduced 'adult' discourses, possibly in order to undermine and subvert my authority as an adult. However, gender also seemed to provide a crucial variable, as the way that girls and boys would relate to me often appeared to reflect their own expectations of what I, as an adult male, would value. Of course, this and the former point would often come together, as some of the boys and girls would introduce particularly gendered and sexualised 'adult' themes in order to overcome the adult/child distinction and try to relate to me as an adult male.

Moreover, 'race' also appeared to be a critical factor. The introduction of racialised themes by a number of children also arguably expressed an important set of assumptions that they held about my own views and social position as a White person. What was more difficult to gauge was the effect of my ethnicity on Black and South Asian children, where arguably it was more what they choose *not* to say and do that was important in their relationships with me. This is an area that needs to be developed further, but some clues were evident in the book, particularly in Chapter 9, where it will be remembered that Aisha, a South Asian girl, in seemingly wanting to down-play her ethnic identity, criticised the appearance of her South Asian friends and appeared to look to me for confirmation in this.

The point, then, is that a number of specific problems inevitably arise in relation to interviewing young children. However, I would maintain that these are principally of the same order as those problems faced by any researcher, whatever their focus. Ultimately, once it is accepted that children can talk and express themselves in a meaningful way, the problem becomes one of being critically reflexive and forever questioning your role as a researcher and your relationships with those you have researched. The problem has been that, while these issues have consistently been raised in relation to young children, principally because they still tend to be perceived as being 'gullible' and open to persuasion, they have still rarely and/or inadequately been addressed in relation to research on other socially defined groups. While significant contributions have been made, particularly in the feminist and anti-racist literature, to our understanding of the influence of gender and ethnicity on the research process (Connolly 1996b), this has still only partially been incorporated into the methodological discussions of large sections of empirical work.

The main implication for this in relation to young children is that, rather than questioning the 'validity' of the data in terms of representativeness, researchers need to read and interpret it within the particular context in which it was collected. The young children's appropriation of specifically sexualised discourses outlined in this book, for example, should not be discussed in terms of how representative it was either of the particular children involved or of other children generally. Rather, the main focus of concern should be on the particular discursive processes in play, including those invoked through my presence, as an adult male, in influencing and shaping the children's behaviour. In this sense, much more attention needs to be paid to how the data are collected, interpreted and understood. The widely held perception of young children as 'vulnerable' has tended to encourage a focus on these issues in relation to research on young children. However, this should be a concern central to all research. In relation to the present study, these are themes developed elsewhere (see Connolly 1997a).

UNDERSTANDING AND THEORISING RACISM

A second theme running throughout the book has been the essentially complex and contingent nature of the young children's racialised identities. The book has drawn attention to the variety of contexts within which children were located and how, within each, discourses on 'race' came to be appropriated, reworked and reproduced in a diverse number of ways. More specifically, through the use of the case studies in Chapters 6 to 9, the book has illustrated the inherently contradictory nature of the young children's identities, as particular discourses on gender, 'race', age and sexuality were foregrounded or down-played from one context to the next. Above all, what we have seen is the centrality of experience in mediating the development and reproduction of these identities. It was here that the concept of habitus played an important role in drawing out how the routine experiences of the children tended to influence their perceptions of the social world and shape the way they came to interact with it. Furthermore, it was through the related concept of field that we were able to explore more fully the complexities of the young children's perceptions. Here we saw how children inhabited a number of fields and tended to move in and out of them relatively frequently. As such, their identities were also shown to be contingent and context-specific, dependent upon the particular field they were located in at any one time.

In highlighting the notion of the decentred self in this way, the book has also acted to refocus the research questions asked in relation to racism and young children. Rather than trying to identify and document *the* Black or South Asian 'experience' of schooling, the book has come to explore the complex nature and influence of the *processes* that provide the context for that experience. As we saw in Chapters 6 to 9, rather than making claims as to the representative nature of the experiences outlined there in relation to *all* Black boys or South Asian girls, for example, the chapters have been concerned with identifying some of the broader sets of discursive processes that can operate in relation to particular groups of children, and then with exploring the particular ways in which some of those children came to be drawn into these processes more than others. It is this approach that not only challenges the largely simple and narrowly focused accounts of young children's schooling experiences but is also one that comes to foreground agency. As regards the latter point, it offers an approach that is able to account for the diversity of young children's experiences while also resisting the slide into relativism. Each of the last four chapters, then, while tentatively drawing attention to some of the broader racialised processes manifest within the school in relation to specific minority ethnic groups, went on to use case studies to highlight the differing ways in which particular children came to be drawn into and/or resist these processes.

Looking beyond the school gates

As part of this need to draw out the essentially fluid and context-specific nature of racism, the book has also been able to demonstrate the importance of 'looking beyond the school gates' in studying racism and young children. Through the concept of field, the book has identified a number of sites throughout the social formation within which discourses on 'race' have been appropriated, reworked and reproduced in differing ways. In this the book has been particularly concerned with the fields of economics, politics, the Manor Park estate and the school, together with the fields of feminine and masculine peer-group relations. As has been illustrated, each provides a particular social arena through which discourses on 'race' are mediated, and each in turn came to influence and shape the racialised nature of relations in the others. In this the book has offered one of only a few ethnographic studies to have traced the salience of 'race' in the children's lives back to the local community and beyond (see also Troyna and Hatcher 1992). It helps to locate the reproduction of racism, not simply with teachers but within a much broader set of processes. Moreover, through the concept of capital, the book has also offered some insights into how and why these particular discourses on 'race' found within any specific field were reworked and reproduced in the way they were. As alluded to above, in drawing attention to the struggles over specific forms of capital it also foregrounds agency within the research account and the importance of experience in mediating these racialised discourses.

Theorising power in accounts of racism

Finally, the book has come to outline possible ways in which we can develop and deepen our understanding of power as it is manifest in and through discourses on 'race'. Here, as Chapter 4 illustrated in its focus on the Manor Park estate, racism appears to have an inherently formative quality in that it comes to be embedded and expressed in and through the social, spatial and/or temporal nature of particular fields. It is the way in which the field and the habitus are integrally related that we can also understand how individuals' perceptions of their social worlds are constructed, not only socially but also spatially and temporally. The field of the Manor Park estate, therefore, provided an important context within which the salience of 'race' in people's lives was constructed and reproduced.

The book has also drawn attention to the way in which racism comes to influence and shape the very identities of individuals and their sense of self. As we saw in Chapters 6 to 9, the White, Black and South Asian children did not simply stand apart from the various racialised processes but were inevitably incorporated within them. It was in this sense that the particular discourses on 'race' manifest within specific fields came to be expressed in and through the children's habitus, and ultimately provided the context within which they developed their sense of self. The point of the book has been to identify some of these racialised processes and the contexts within which they were more or less likely to be influential, and to draw attention to the diverse ways in which the children chose to respond to them. As Chapters 6 to 9 have suggested, these discursive processes at times came subtly to influence and shape the very identities of some of the children.

Above all, it is this 'formative' power of discourses on 'race' that requires much more research.

More generally, this broader focus on the range of discursive processes that influence and shape young children's lives can help us develop a more comprehensive understanding of the children's experiences of schooling. In relation to Black boys, for example, it can move beyond the rather polarised debates that cite either teacher racism or culturally deficit models of the boys' behaviour to account for their 'underachievement'. As Chapter 6 has shown, this has been done by widening the focus to include the field of masculine peer-group relations in understanding how Black boys, to varying degrees, came to develop their sense of identity. While many teachers were influenced by discourses on 'race' in their practice, they also found that some Black boys were more difficult to control. In relation to this point, however, rather than resorting to rather questionable and decontextualised assumptions about the boys' characters (see Foster 1990), the chapter has been able to locate their behaviour within a wider and more complex web of racialised processes.

MULTICULTURAL/ANTI-RACIST EDUCATION

While the primary concern of the book has been with increasing our understanding of the salience of 'race' in young children's lives and not with assessing multicultural/anti-racist practice *per se*, a number of themes have been raised in relation to this and deserve to be highlighted briefly here. In this I want to address two main issues: the potential for anti-racist work among young children, and the need to locate such work within a more whole-school approach. As regards the former, the book has clearly shown not only that many young children are capable of dealing with quite complex ideas about 'race', but that they are already doing so. In this the book offers further support to the idea that, with the right kind of analytical 'scaffolding', important work can be done in challenging children's racial attitudes and perceptions (Epstein 1993; Siraj-Blatchford 1994). While such work has already been going on with older children, the data presented here suggest that it needs to be broadened out to incorporate young children at the start of their schooling careers. As we have seen, at the ages of 5 and 6 children appear to be already actively involved in appropriating, reworking and reproducing racialised discourses. Moreover, we have also seen the contingent and contradictory nature of the young children's beliefs and identities in relation to this. And it is here, as witnessed in the book through my own role as interviewer in attempting to encourage them to think through their racialised assumptions, that much work can be done. As Carrington and Short (1989) have suggested in their work with older children, these contradictions can often be worked through to provide children with a different conceptual frame for understanding their social position.

While the possible nature and form of such work with young children is beyond the scope of the present research, the book has drawn attention to the need to develop a multicultural/anti-racist approach within a more whole-school policy. What the book has demonstrated is that the children's racialised attitudes and behaviour are inextricably bound up in experience. In this, the way they came to think about issues of 'race' was complexly woven into their experiences as being, among other things: young children, working class, White/Black/South Asian and girls/boys. It is therefore an extremely limited exercise to attempt to challenge young children's attitudes while the material processes and practices that give rise to them remain in place (Troyna and Hatcher 1992; Epstein 1993). A clear example of this was found in Chapter 6 in relation to the school's approach to football. Here, an unwritten multicultural/anti-racist policy aimed primarily at engaging Black boys had the effect of reproducing a distinct masculine ethos within the school, and this, in turn, increased the tendency for South Asian children to be racially abused. Above all, it highlighted the importance of incorporating gender equality in any strategy aimed at challenging racism. As we have seen, it was primarily through their gendered identities that children came to appropriate, rework and reproduce discourses on 'race' (Macdonald et al. 1989). Moreover, it was not just issues of gender that were implicated in the development of multicultural/anti-racist policies, but also the school's approach to discipline (see also Gillborn et al. 1993). Again, there is little point in attempting to challenge young children's racialised stereotypes about Black boys, for instance, if the school appears to continue to draw them so publicly and disproportionately into their disciplinary modes.

Of course, as Gillborn (1995) has rightly pointed out, it is very easy simply to stand back and criticise school approaches. It is in this light that the book has consistently located the teachers' and school's approach within a broader context of constraints and restrictive processes. Not least with the ever-increasing pressures being brought to bear by the 1988 Education Reform Act (see Tomlinson and Craft 1995), developing a more comprehensive approach to multicultural/anti-racist education is going to be that much harder. The book does, at least, provide some important insights that can be used in thinking through and developing such an approach. It remains for future research to focus more centrally on the complex relations between discourses on 'race', gender, sexuality, class and age, and on how these come to influence and shape the effectiveness of particular multicultural/anti-racist policies.

QUESTIONS REMAINING TO BE ANSWERED

In many ways, this book has been an ambitious piece of work. It has attempted to link a study of the local community with the school, to explore the articulations between discourses on 'race', gender, sexuality, class and age, and to develop an appropriate theoretical framework able to deal with all of this. Inevitably, many questions remain either partially or wholly unanswered, while new ones emerge. While the book has drawn attention to the interplay of a number of specific fields, it has only been able partially to uncover the complexities of the specific sets of relations found in those fields and the particular forms of capital evident there. This was especially the case in relation to the field of feminine peer-group relations. Further work now needs to be done in focusing on particular fields, and applying and developing the theoretical frame proposed here to gain a more comprehensive insight into the dynamics of specific fields. This would also serve to help refine and develop the concepts of field, capital and habitus in the way proposed.

A more detailed focus would also enable us to enhance our understanding of the habitus. In this, I am not primarily interested in trying to further delineate and define the exact parameters of the habitus. Indeed, Bourdieu never meant the habitus to be treated in such a way (see Bourdieu and Wacquant 1992). Rather, as Reay (1995) has argued, what many commentators see as its essential weakness – its imprecise and rather open and fluid nature (see Jenkins 1992) – is also its principal strength. As emphasised throughout the book, the social world is not a closed and easily definable entity but is open, fluid and diverse. This is not a call for the avoidance of analytical rigour, but rather for us to move beyond the appraisal of conceptual tools simply within strictly modernist and essentialist terms.

My concern for the future development of the concept of habitus relates to the book's inability, because of time and space, to incorporate adequately the biographies of individual children. While we have seen the very different ways in which particular young children come to respond to the broader sets of racialised processes, we are still left with questions. Exactly *why* did one child choose to conform while another actively resisted? Is it simply that a particular child is shy or are they being marginalised by their peers? What leads some children to be interested in kiss-chase, football and/or make-up while others are not? While the book has touched upon the importance of the domestic environment in relation to the latter point, there is still much work to be done in incorporating the young children's home environment more fully into an analysis of their particular forms of habitus. This is particularly true of the South Asian children where, because of the constraints of time, the influence of ethnicity and religion in the domestic environment has been largely unexplored. In doing this we can develop further the notion of the decentred self, through an analysis of the many forms of habitus that each child carries with them and how these come to shape and inform each other.

Another major theme that will stand out to many people reading the book is the lack of specific chapters on White girls and boys. At one level, this is entirely justified. As we have seen, the nature of Black and South Asian children's schooling experiences remains a relatively under-researched area and requires the continued focus of studies such as this one. Having said that, however, the present study has drawn attention to the need to include the role that White children can play in influencing and shaping the schooling experiences of their minority ethnic peers. To this end, a focus on White girls' and boys' ethnic identities has been an implicit theme running throughout the book. What we have seen is that White children's sense of identity and their ethnicity are just as socially constructed as Black or South Asian children's, and are equally fraught with problems and contradictions. What the book has highlighted, then, is the need to understand more fully the particular class-based, age-related and gendered concerns of young White children if we are to understand more comprehensively the dynamics of racialised relations (see also Macdonald *et al.* 1989). It is to this end that the insights offered here in relation to White girls and boys need to be built upon and refined elsewhere.

In conclusion, although the book will inevitably be incomplete in relation to the number of questions and issues that remain to be answered, one thing is clear: young children are socially competent. The book offers ample evidence that children as young as 5 and 6 are more than capable of appropriating, reworking and reproducing discourses on 'race'. They are, therefore, not simply empty vessels which adults can simply and unproblematically fill with their own attitudes and beliefs: they are active and strategic agents. This is the core theme that, above all else, stands out from the book, for it is the continued popularity of traditional notions of childhood innocence that constitutes the biggest obstacle to the development of a successful and comprehensive multicultural anti-racist strategy among infant children. It is only when we come to set aside our taken-for-granted assumptions about young children once and for all that we can more fully understand the nature of racism in their lives and develop and adopt more informed and appropriate strategies in order to counter it. What is so disturbing is that the children in this study came from a generation who are only just embarking on their schooling careers and on a life outside the domestic environment. While it may be a cliché, these children are the future and need to be treated as such.

NOTES

1 INTRODUCTION

1 See, for instance, Brandis and Bernstein (1974), Sharp and Green (1975), Sluckin (1981), Pollard (1985) and Hartley (1985).

2 See, for instance, Opie and Opie (1959), Clarricoates (1980), Davies (1982), Walkerdine (1981), Thorne (1993) and Opie (1993).

3 For a critical overview of this area see Aboud (1988), Denscombe *et al.* (1986) and Carrington and Short (1989).

4 This can be seen, for instance, in the foregrounding of the teacher's role in the construction of young children's identities (Grant 1992), in the focus on interviewing older children (Carrington and Short 1989; Troyna and Hatcher 1992) and in the preoccupation with observations (Grugeon and Woods 1990). While there have been some more recent exceptions to this general trend (see Wright 1992; Epstein 1993), the particular concerns and focus of this work have tended to limit its contribution to offering an (albeit very important) introductory insight into the lives and social abilities of very young children.

5 For a much more detailed discussion of the methodological issues discussed here and underlying the present study see Connolly (1998).

6 Names of all people and places have been changed in this book to maintain anonymity. All names are therefore fictitious and are not intended to relate, in any way, to real people or places.

7 'Black' throughout this book will refer to people who have at least one parent of African/Caribbean descent.

8 'South Asian' is used here, and throughout the study, to refer to people who have descended from India, Pakistan or Bangladesh. It is recognised that such a definition is problematic in that it draws together people with very different ethnic, religious and/or national identities. In relation to the present study, however, it is a definition that will suffice for two reasons. First, the children were overwhelmingly Gujerati-speaking and, for those in the three sample classes, 9 of the 13 South Asian children who started the academic year were Hindus. Second, as far as the school staff and other children were concerned, they were seen as 'all the same' [*sic*] and were forced to negotiate their sense of identity within a similar set of discourses on 'race'.

9 The fact that we still know relatively little about how minority ethnic children experience racism and how they come to develop their sense of identity partly in relation to this means that such a focus on Black and South Asian young children is necessary. It is important, however, that in adopting this focus and not including specific chapters on White children, the study should not be read as

implying that White children's identities are any less problematic or are 'the norm'. Indeed, this is far from the case. While the primary focus of the book is the experiences of Black and South Asian children, these are set in the context of the complex and contradictory nature of White children's identities. Running throughout the substantive chapters, then, is the way in which White parents, teachers and children draw upon discourses on 'race' to make sense of their own experiences and to develop their own identities. These will be themes returned to in the concluding chapter.

2 RACISM, CULTURE AND IDENTITY: TOWARDS A THEORY OF PRACTICE

1 Some of the most important work in this area can be found in: Cohen (1988), Donald and Rattansi (1992), Miles (1989, 1993), Omi and Winant (1994) and Rattansi and Westwood (1994). For a good understanding of the implications of this work for debates around 'race' and education see Gillborn (1995). Similar critiques are developing in relation to gender and the inadequacies of the sex-role models of socialisation which also tend to construct a fixed and essential view of gender. For an excellent summary and critique of this approach see Mac an Ghaill (1996).
2 For an overview see Jenkins (1992). For more detailed discussion and debate see Mahar et al. (1990) and Harker et al. (1990).
3 For an interesting and extremely useful application of Bourdieu's work to issues of 'race' and gender in education see Reay (1995, 1996).
4 In this sense the habitus is similar to Giddens' (1984) notion of 'practical consciousness'.
5 There has been much work done in relation to theorising the importance of time and space for social relations. See, for instance, Berger and Luckmann (1967), Lefebvre (1991), Giddens (1984), Massey (1985, 1993) and Keith and Pile (1993)

3 THE RACIALISATION OF NATIONAL POLITICAL DISCOURSES

1 Workingham is the city where East Avenue Primary School is located. Unless stated otherwise, much of the information drawn upon with regard to Workingham, including demographic and economic trends and statistics, has been derived from a number of publications which, because of their focus on Workingham, have not been explicitly cited in order to ensure confidentiality. Moreover, certain details relating to the estate and the city have either been removed or altered, or false ones have been added to maintain anonymity. Such details are not, however, significant to the overall arguments set out in this study.
2 A good source of these types of discourses on 'race' and the nation is the New Right journal, *The Salisbury Review*. See, for instance, Casey (1982), Ashworth (1983) and Cronin (1987).
3 See Cox and Dyson (1969a, 1969b, 1970) and Cox and Boyson (1975, 1977).
4 For a critical discussion of some of these moral panics see: Foster-Carter (1987), Randall (1988), Troyna and Carrington (1990), Connolly (1991), Richardson (1992) and Hardy and Vieler-Porter (1992).

4 LIVING IN THE INNER CITY: THE MANOR PARK ESTATE

1 This is similarly the case in relation to ethnographic studies of gender and schooling. However, recently studies have emerged which have begun to recognise and offer important analyses of the relationship between masculinities within the school and those formed and reproduced within the wider neighbourhood (see, for example, Skelton 1996, 1997; Dixon 1997)

5 TEACHER DISCOURSES AND EAST AVENUE PRIMARY SCHOOL

1 Ms Patterson differs in a number of respects from the other two reception/Year 1 teachers and will be discussed in more detail shortly.
2 Other incidents that occurred during the fieldwork in relation to this not described here can be found in Connolly (1995a, 1995b, 1996a).
3 The LEA's strategy could possibly also be understood as a response to the increasing pressures placed on them by the Black community in Workingham and their organisation of Black supplementary/Saturday schools for their children, which could be seen as progressively undermining the credibility of the formal education system (for a more general discussion of the 'Black Educational Movement' see Tomlinson 1985).

6 FROM BOYS TO MEN? BLACK BOYS IN THE FIELD OF MASCULINE PEER-GROUP RELATIONS

1 As explained in Chapter 1, throughout this book I have been using the term 'Black' to refer to both African/Caribbean children and those of dual heritage. The reason for this will now become evident as this and the following chapters unfold. What I want to argue is that both African/Caribbean and mixed-heritage children are positioned very similarly within discourses on 'race'. While there are a number of significant differences in their experiences of schooling and peer-group relations, some of which will be explored later in this chapter, the discursive themes reproduced on the Manor Park estate of Black people as street-wise and athletic come to act upon African/Caribbean and dual-heritage children at East Avenue in very similar ways.
2 This is a term that they themselves adopted in interviews with me while complaining about the way they are unfairly picked on and labelled by teachers and other children. Here they significantly reclaimed the term and reversed its meaning in referring to themselves ('bad' now meaning good).
3 These arguments are summarised in Foster et al. (1996). For a comprehensive critique see Gillborn (1995).

REFERENCES

Aboud, F. (1988) *Children and Prejudice*, Oxford: Basil Blackwell.

Anthias, F. and Yuval-Davis, N. (1992) *Racialised Boundaries: Race, Nation, Gender, Colour and Class and the Anti-Racist Struggle*, London: Routledge.

Ashworth, C. (1983) 'Sociology and the nation', *The Salisbury Review* 1, 2: 8–11.

Back, L. (1993) 'Race, identity and nation within an adolescent community in South London', *New Community* 19, 2: 217–33.

—— (1996) *New Ethnicities and Urban Cultures: Racisms and Multiculture in Young Lives*, London: UCL Press.

Ball, S. (1990) *Politics and Policy Making in Education: Explorations in Policy Sociology*, London: Routledge.

Barker, M. (1981) *The New Racism*, London: Junction Books.

Berger, P. and Luckmann, T. (1967) *The Social Construction of Reality*, Harmondsworth: Penguin.

Best, R. (1983) *We've All Got Scars: What Girls and Boys Learn in Elementary School*, Bloomington: Indiana University Press.

Best, S. and Kellner, D. (1991) *Postmodern Theory: Critical Interrogations*, London: Macmillan.

Bhat, A., Carr-Hill, R. and Ohri, S. (1988) *Britain's Black Population: A New Perspective*, second edition, Aldershot: Gower.

Bhatti, G. (1995) 'A journey into the unknown: an ethnographic study of Asian children', in M. Griffiths and B. Troyna (eds) *Antiracism, Culture and Social Justice in Education*, Stoke-on-Trent: Trentham Books.

—— (1996) ' "I asked my teacher what shall I be?" Hopes for the future, mixed feelings about the past', paper presented to the British Educational Research Association Annual Conference, University of Lancaster.

Bourdieu, P. (1977) *Outline of a Theory of Practice*, Cambridge: Cambridge University Press.

—— (1984) *Distinction: A Social Critique of the Judgment of Taste*, London: Routledge.

—— (1987) 'What makes a social class? On the theoretical and practical existence of groups', *Berkeley Journal of Sociology* 32: 1–18.

—— (1990) *The Logic of Practice*, Cambridge: Polity Press.

Bourdieu, P. and Passeron, J. C. (1977) *Reproduction in Education, Society and Culture*, Beverly Hills: Sage.

Bourdieu, P. and Wacquant, L. (1992) *An Invitation to Reflexive Sociology*, Cambridge: Polity Press.

Bowles, G. and Duelli Klein, R. (eds) (1983)*Theories of Women's Studies*, London: Routledge and Kegan Paul.

Brah, A. and Minhas, R. (1985) 'Structural racism or cultural difference: schooling for Asian girls', in G. Weiner (ed.) *Just a Bunch of Girls*, Milton Keynes: Open University Press.

Brandis, W. and Bernstein, B. (1974) *Selection and Control: Teachers' Ratings of Children in the Infant School*, London: Routledge and Kegan Paul.

Browne, N. and France, P. (1985) 'Only cissies wear dresses', in G. Weiner (ed.) *Just a Bunch of Girls*, Milton Keynes: Open University Press.

Brubaker, R. (1985) 'Rethinking classical theory: the sociological vision of Pierre Bourdieu', *Theory and Society* 14: 745–75.

Carby, H. (1982) 'Schooling in Babylon', in Centre for Contemporary Cultural Studies (CCCS) *The Empire Strikes Back: Race and Racism in 70s Britain*, London: Hutchinson.

Carrington, B. (1983) 'Sport as a side-track: an analysis of West Indian involvement in extra-curricular sport', in L. Barton and S. Walker (eds) *Race, Class and Education*, London: Croom Helm.

Carrington, B. and Short, G. (1989) *'Race' and the Primary School: Theory into Practice*, Windsor: NFER-NELSON.

Casey, J. (1982) 'One nation: the politics of race', *The Salisbury Review* 9, 1: 23–8.

Chitty, C. (1989) *Towards a New Education System: The Victory of the New Right*, London: Falmer Press.

Clark, M. (1990) *The Great Divide: Gender in the Primary School*, Melbourne: Curriculum Corporation.

Clarricoates, K. (1980) 'The importance of being Earnest . . . Emma . . . Tom . . . Jane . . . : the perception and categorisation of gender deviation and gender conformity in primary schools', in R. Deem (ed.) *Schooling for Women's Work*, London: Routledge and Kegan Paul.

—— (1981) 'The experience of patriarchal schooling', *Interchange* 12, 2/3: 185–205.

—— (1987) 'Child culture at school: a clash between gendered worlds?' in A. Pollard (ed.) *Children and their Primary Schools: A New Perspective*, London: Falmer Press.

Cohen, P. (1988) 'The perversions of inheritance: studies in the making of multi-racist Britain', in P. Cohen and H. Bains (eds) *Multi-Racist Britain*, London: Macmillan.

—— (1992) ' "It's racism what dunnit": hidden narratives in theories of racism', in J. Donald and A. Rattansi (eds) *'Race', Culture and Difference*, London: Sage.

Connell, R. (1989) 'Cool guys, swots and wimps: the interplay of masculinity and education', *Oxford Review of Education* 15: 291–303.

Connolly, P. (1991) 'Murder in the press: the Burnage Report and the assault upon anti-racism in the British press', unpublished dissertation, University of Warwick.

—— (1992) ' "Playing it by the rules": the politics of research in "race" and education', *British Educational Research Journal* 18, 2: 133–48.

—— (1995a) 'Racism, masculine peer-group relations and the schooling of African/Caribbean infant boys', *British Journal of Sociology of Education* 16, 1: 75–92.

—— (1995b) 'Boys will be boys?: racism, sexuality and the construction of masculine identities amongst infant boys', in J. Holland and M. Blair (eds) *Debates and Issues in Feminist Research and Pedagogy*, Clevedon: Multilingual Matters.

—— (1996a) 'Racisms, gendered identities and young children', unpublished thesis, University of Leicester.

—— (1996b) 'Doing what comes naturally?: standpoint epistemology, critical social research and the politics of identity', in S. Lyon and J. Busfield (eds) *Methodological Imaginations*, London: Macmillan.

—— (1996c) 'Seen but never heard: rethinking approaches to researching racism and young children', *Discourse* 17, 2: 171–85.

—— (1997a) 'In search of authenticity: researching young children's perspectives', in A. Pollard, D. Thiessen and A. Filer (eds) *Children and their Curriculum: The Perspectives of Primary and Elementary School Children*, London: Falmer Press.

—— (1997b) 'Racism and postmodernism: towards a theory of practice', in D. Owen (ed.) *Sociology after Postmodernism*, London: Sage.

—— (1998) ' "Dancing to the wrong tune": ethnography, generalisation and research on racism in schools', in P. Connolly and B. Troyna (eds) *Researching Racism in Education: Politics, Theory and Practice*, Buckingham: Open University Press.

Cox, C. B. and Dyson, A. E. (eds) (1969a) *Fight for Education: A Black Paper*, London: Critical Quarterly Society.

—— (eds) (1969b) *Black Paper Two: The Crisis in Education*, London: Critical Quarterly Society.

—— (eds) (1970) *Black Paper Three: Goodbye Mr Short*, London: Critical Quarterly Society.

Cox, C. B. and Boyson, R. (eds) (1975) *Black Paper 1975: The Fight for Education*, London: Dent.

—— (eds) (1977) *Black Paper 1977*, London: Maurice Temple Smith.

Cox, C. B. and Scruton, R. (1984) *Peace Studies: A Critical Survey*, London: Institute for European Defence and Strategic Studies.

Cronin, R. (1987) 'Myths of nationhood', *The Salisbury Review* 6, 1: 43–6.

Currie, D. (1983) 'World capitalism in recession', in S. Hall and M. Jacques (eds) *The Politics of Thatcherism*, London: Lawrence and Wishart.

Davies, B. (1982) *Life in the Classroom and Playground: The Accounts of Primary School Children*, London: Routledge and Kegan Paul.

—— (1989) *Frogs and Snails and Feminist Tails: Preschool Children and Gender*, Sydney: Allen and Unwin.

Deem, R. (1978) *Women and Schooling*, London: Routledge and Kegan Paul.

Denmark, R. (1995) 'Can I play? an anthropological entry into the play and social relationships of nine-year-olds', paper presented to Children and Social Competence Conference, University of Surrey.

Denscombe, M. (1980) ' "Keeping 'em quiet": the significance of noise for the practical activity of teaching', in P. Woods (ed.) *Teacher Strategies*, London: Croom Helm.

REFERENCES

—— (1985) *Classroom Control: A Sociological Perspective*, London: Allen and Unwin.

Denscombe, M., Szulc, H., Patrick, C. and Wood, A. (1986) 'Ethnicity and friendship: the contrast between sociometric research and fieldwork observation in primary school classrooms', *British Educational Research Journal* 12, 3: 221–35.

Dixon, C. (1997) 'Pete's tool: identity and sex-play in the design and technology classroom', *Gender and Education* 9, 1: 89–104.

Donald, J. and Rattansi, A. (eds) (1992) *'Race', Culture and Difference*, London: Sage.

Epstein, D. (1993) *Changing Classroom Cultures: Anti-Racism, Politics and Schools*, Stoke-on-Trent: Trentham Books.

—— (1997a) 'Cultures of schooling/cultures of sexuality', *International Journal of Inclusive Education* 1, 1: 37–53.

—— (1997b) 'Boyz' own stories: masculinities and sexualities in schools', *Gender and Education* 9, 1: 105–15.

Flew, A. (1987) *Power to the Parents: Reversing Educational Decline*, London: The Sherwood Press.

Foster, P. (1990) *Policy and Practice in Multicultural and Anti-Racist Education*, London: Routledge.

Foster, P., Gomm, R. and Hammersley, M. (1996) *Constructing Educational Inequality*, London: Falmer Press.

Foster-Carter, O. (1987) 'The Honeyford affair: political and policy implications', in B. Troyna (ed.) *Racial Inequality in Education*, London: Tavistock.

Foucault, M. (1979) *Discipline and Punish: The Birth of the Prison*, Harmondsworth: Penguin.

—— (1980) *Power/Knowledge: Selected Interviews and Other Writings, 1972–1977*, edited by C. Gordon, London: Harvester Wheatsheaf.

—— (1981) *The History of Sexuality, Volume 1: An Introduction*, Harmondsworth: Penguin.

Gamble, A. (1985) *Britain in Decline: Economic Policy, Political Strategy and the British State*, second edition, London: Macmillan.

Garnham, N. and Williams, R. (1980) 'Pierre Bourdieu and the sociology of culture: an introduction', *Media, Culture and Society* 2, 3: 209–23.

Ghuman, P.A.S. (1994) *Coping With Two Cultures*, Clevedon: Multilingual Matters.

Giddens, A. (1984) *The Constitution of Society: Outline of a Theory of Structuration*, Cambridge: Polity Press.

—— (1985) 'Time, space and regionalisation', in D. Gregory and J. Urry (eds) *Social Relations and Spatial Structure*, London: Macmillan.

Gillborn, D. (1990) *'Race', Ethnicity and Education*, London: Unwin Hyman.

—— (1995) *Racism and Anti-Racism in Real Schools*, Buckingham: Open University Press.

Gillborn, D., Nixon, J. and Rudduck, J. (1993) *Dimensions of Discipline: Rethinking Practice in Secondary Schools*, London: HMSO.

Gilroy, P. (1982) 'Police and thieves', in Centre for Contemporary Cultural Studies (CCCS) *The Empire Strikes Back: Race and Racism in 70s Britain*, London: Routledge.

—— (1987) *There Ain't No Black in the Union Jack: The Cultural Politics of Race and Nation*, London: Routledge.

Giroux, H. (1983) 'Theories of reproduction and resistance in the new sociology of education: a critical analysis', *Harvard Educational Review* 52, 3: 257–93.

Gordon, P. (1988) 'The New Right, race and education – or how the Black Papers became a white paper', *Race and Class* 29, 3: 95–103.

Gordon, P. and Klug, F. (1986) *New Right, New Racism*, London: Searchlight Publications.

Goulbourne, H. (1993) 'Aspects of nationalism and black identities in post-imperial Britain', in M. Cross and M. Keith (eds) *Racism, the City and the State*, London: Routledge.

Gramsci, A. (1971) *Selections from the Prison Notebooks*, trans. Q. Hoare and G. Nowell-Smith, London: Lawrence and Wishart.

Grant, L. (1992) 'Race and the schooling of young girls', in J. Wrigley (ed.) *Education and Gender Equality*, London: Falmer Press.

Grugeon, E. (1993) 'Gender implications of children's playground culture', in P. Woods and M. Hammersley (eds) *Gender and Ethnicity in Schools: Ethnographic Accounts*, London: Routledge.

Grugeon, E. and Woods, P. (1990) *Educating All: Multicultural Perspectives in the Primary School*, London: Routledge.

Hall, S. (1983) 'The great moving right show', in S. Hall and M. Jacques (eds) *The Politics of Thatcherism*, London: Lawrence and Wishart.

Hall, S., Critcher, C., Jefferson, T., Clarke, J. and Roberts, B. (1978) *Policing the Crisis: Mugging, the State and Law and Order*, London: Macmillan.

Hardy, J. and Vieler-Porter, C. (1992) 'Race, schooling and the 1988 Education Reform Act', in D. Gill, B. Mayor and M. Blair (eds) *Racism and Education: Structures and Strategies*, London: Sage.

Harker, R., Mahar, C. and Wilkes, C. (1990) *An Introduction to the Work of Pierre Bourdieu: The Practice of Theory*, Basingstoke: Macmillan.

Harris, R. and Seldon, A. (1979) *Overruled on Welfare*, London: Institute of Economic Affairs.

Hartley, D. (1985) *Understanding the Primary School: A Sociological Analysis*, London: Croom Helm.

Hatcher, R. (1995) 'Boyfriends, girlfriends: gender and "race" in children's cultures', *International Play Journal*, 3: 187–97.

Hewitt, R. (1986) *White Talk, Black Talk*, Cambridge: Cambridge University Press.

Hillgate Group (1986) *Whose Schools?: A Radical Manifesto*, London: The Hillgate Group.

—— (1987) *The Reform of British Education: From Principles to Practice*, London: The Hillgate Group.

Holmes, R. (1995) *How Young Children Perceive Race*, London: Sage.

Hurrell, P. (1995) 'Do teachers discriminate? Reactions to pupil behaviour in four comprehensive schools', *Sociology* 29, 1: 59–72.

Husbands, C. (1987) 'Introduction: "Race", the continuity of a concept', in C. Husbands (ed.) *'Race' in Britain: Continuity and Change*, second edition, London: Hutchinson.

Jenkins, R. (1983) *Lads, Citizens and Ordinary Kids: Working-class Youth Lifestyles in Belfast*, London: Routledge and Kegan Paul.

—— (1992) *Pierre Bourdieu*, London: Routledge.

Jones, K. (1983) *Beyond Progressive Education*, London: Macmillan.

—— (1989) *Right Turn: The Conservative Revolution in Education*, London: Hutchinson Radius.

Jones, S. (1988) *White Youth, Black Culture*, Basingstoke: Macmillan.

Jordan, E. (1995) 'Fighting boys and fantasy play: the construction of masculinity in the early years of school', *Gender and Education* 7, 1: 69–86.

Karn, V. (1983) *Race and Housing in Britain in Ethnic Pluralism and Public Policy*, Aldershot: Gower.

Kehily, M. and Nayak, A. (1996) ' "The Christmas kiss": sexuality, story-telling and schooling', *Curriculum Studies* 4, 2: 211–27.

—— (1997) ' "Lads and laughter": humour and the production of heterosexual hierarchies', *Gender and Education* 9, 1: 69–87.

Keith, M. (1993) *Race, Riots and Policing: Lore and Disorder in a Multi-Racist Society*, London: UCL Press.

Keith, M. and Pile, S. (eds) (1993) *Place and the Politics of Identity*, London: Routledge.

Kenway, J. and Fitzclarence, L. (1997) 'Masculinity, violence and schooling: challenging "poisonous pedagogies"', *Gender and Education* 9, 1: 117–33.

King, R. (1978) *All Things Bright and Beautiful: A Sociological Study of Infants' Classrooms*, Chichester: John Wiley and Sons.

Laclau, E. and Mouffe, C. (1985) *Hegemony and Socialist Strategy*, London: Verso.

Lawless, P. (1989) *Britain's Inner Cities*, second edition, London: Paul Chapman Publishing Limited.

Layder, D. (1994) *Understanding Social Theory*, London: Sage.

Lees, S. (1993) *Sugar and Spice: Sexuality and Adolescent Girls*, London: Penguin.

Lefebvre, H. (1991) *The Production of Space* (first edition 1974), Oxford: Basil Blackwell.

Mac an Ghaill, M. (1988) *Young, Gifted and Black*, Milton Keynes: Open University Press.

—— (1989) 'Beyond the white norm: the use of qualitative methods in the study of black youths' schooling in England', *International Journal of Qualitative Studies in Education* 2, 3: 175–89.

—— (1994) *The Making of Men: Masculinities, Sexualities and Schooling*, Buckingham: Open University Press.

—— (1996) ' "What about the boys?": schooling, class and crisis masculinity', *The Sociological Review* 44: 381–97.

Macdonald, I., Bhavnani, T., Khan, L. and John, G. (1989) *Murder in the Playground: The Report of the Macdonald Inquiry into Racism and Racial Violence in Manchester Schools*, London: Longsight Press.

Mahar, C., Harker, R. and Wilkes, C. (1990) 'The basic theoretical position', in R. Harker, C. Mahar and C. Wilkes (eds) *An Introduction to the Work of Pierre Bourdieu: The Practice of Theory*, Basingstoke: Macmillan.

Mahoney, P. (1985) *Schools for the Boys*, London: Hutchinson.

Mann, K. (1992) *The Making of an English Underclass*, Milton Keynes: Open University Press.

Massey, D. (1985) 'New directions in space', in D. Gregory and J. Urry (eds) *Social Relations and Spatial Structure*, London: Macmillan.

—— (1993) 'Politics and space/time', in M. Keith and S. Pile (eds) *Place and the Politics of Identity*, London: Routledge.

Miles, R. (1982) *Racism and Migrant Labour: A Critical Text*, London: Routledge and Kegan Paul.

—— (1989) *Racism*, London: Routledge.

—— (1993) *Racism After 'Race Relations'*, London: Routledge.

Morris, L. (1994) *Dangerous Classes: The Underclass and Social Citizenship*, London: Routledge.

Nehaul, K. (1996) *The Schooling of Children of Caribbean Heritage*, Stoke-on-Trent: Trentham Books.

Nias, J. (1984) 'The definition and maintenance of self in primary teaching', *British Journal of Sociology of Education* 5, 3: 267–80.

Omi, M. and Winant, H. (1994) *Racial Formation in the United States: From the 1960s to the 1990s*, second edition, London: Routledge.

Opie, I. (1993) *The People in the Playground*, Oxford: Oxford University Press.

Opie, I. and Opie, P. (1959) *The Lore and Language of Schoolchildren*, Oxford: Oxford University Press.

Overbeek, H. (1990) *Global Capitalism and National Decline: The Thatcher Decade in Perspective*, London: Unwin Hyman.

Palmer, F. (ed.) (1986) *Anti-Racism: An Assault on Education and Value*, London: The Sherwood Press.

Parekh, B. (1986) 'The "New Right" and the politics of nationhood', in G. Cohen *et al.* (eds) *The New Right: Image and Reality*, London: Runnymede Trust.

Plowden Report (1967) *Children and their Primary Schools*, vol. 1, London: HMSO.

Pollard, A. (1985) *The Social World of the Primary School*, London: Holt, Reinhart and Winston.

Powell, E. (1988) 'The UK and immigration', *The Salisbury Review* 7, 2: 40–3.

Randall, S. (1988) 'The New Right, racism and education in Thatcher's Britain', *Sage Race Relations Abstracts* 13, 3: 3–17.

Rattansi, A. (1994) '"Western" racisms, ethnicities and identities in a "postmodern" frame', in A. Rattansi and S. Westwood (eds) *Racism, Modernity and Identity on the Western Front*, Cambridge: Polity Press.

Rattansi, A. and Westwood, S. (eds) (1994) *Racism, Modernity and Identity on the Western Front*, Cambridge: Polity Press.

Reay, D. (1995) 'Using habitus to look at "race" and class in primary school classrooms', in M. Griffiths and B. Troyna (eds) *Antiracism, Culture and Social Justice in Education*, Stoke-on-Trent: Trentham Books.

—— (1996) 'Bourdieu and cultural reproduction: using habitus and cultural capital to examine mothers' involvement in their children's primary schooling', paper presented to British Educational Research Association Annual Conference, University of Lancaster.

Richardson, R. (1992) 'Race policies and programmes under attack: two case studies for the 1990s', in D. Gill, B. Mayor and M. Blair (eds) *Racism and Education: Structures and Strategies*, London: Sage.

Riseborough, G. F. (1985) 'Pupils, teachers' careers and schooling: an empirical study', in S. J. Ball and I. F. Goodson (eds) *Teachers' Lives and Careers*, Lewes: Falmer Press.

Ross, C. and Ryan, A. (1990) *'Can I Stay in Today Miss?': Improving the School Playground*, Stoke-on-Trent: Trentham Books.

Sayer, A. (1992) *Method in Social Science: A Realist Approach*, second edition, London: Routledge.

Scruton, R., Ellis-Jones, A. and O'Keeffe, D. (1985) *Education and Indoctrination: An Attempt at Definition and a Review of Social and Political Implications*, Harrow: Education Research Centre.

Sewell, T. (1995) 'A phallic response to schooling: Black masculinity and race in an inner-city comprehensive', in M. Griffiths and B. Troyna (eds) *Antiracism, Culture and Social Justice in Education*, Stoke-on-Trent: Trentham Books.

—— (1997) *Black Masculinities and Schooling: How Black Boys Survive Modern Schooling*, Stoke-on-Trent: Trentham Books.

Sharp, R. and Green, A. (1975) *Education and Social Control: A Study in Progressive Primary Education*, London: Routledge and Kegan Paul.

Sills, A., Taylor, G. and Golding, P. (1988) *The Politics of the Urban Crisis*, London: Hutchinson.

Siraj-Blatchford, I. (1994) *The Early Years*, Stoke-on-Trent: Trentham Books.

Skelton, C. (1996) 'Learning to be "tough": the fostering of maleness in one primary school', *Gender and Education* 8, 2: 185–97.

—— (1997) 'Primary boys and hegemonic masculinity', *British Journal of Sociology of Education* 18, 3: 349–69.

Sluckin, A. (1981) *Growing Up in the Playground*, London: Routledge and Kegan Paul.

Solomos, J. (1993) *Race and Racism in Contemporary Britain*, second edition, London: Macmillan.

Stopes-Roe, M. and Cochrane, R. (1990) *Citizens of this Country*, Clevedon: Multilingual Matters.

Taylor, M. and Bagley, C. (1995) 'The LEA and TEC context', in S. Tomlinson and M. Craft (eds) *Ethnic Relations and Schooling: Policy and Practice in the 1990s*, London: The Athlone Press.

Thorne, B. (1993) *Gender Play: Girls and Boys in School*, Buckingham: Open University Press.

Tomlinson, S. (1983) *Ethnic Minorities in British Schools*, London: Heinemann.

—— (1985) 'The "Black education" movement', in M. Arnot (ed.) *Race and Gender: Equal Opportunities Policies in Education: A Reader*, Oxford: Pergamon Press.

Tomlinson, S. and Craft, M. (1995) *Ethnic Relations and Schooling: Policy and Practice in the 1990s*, London: The Athlone Press.

Troyna, B. (1984a) 'Multicultural education: emancipation or containment?', in L. Barton and S. Walker (eds) *Social Crisis and Educational Research*, Beckenham: Croom Helm.

—— (1984b) ' "Policy entrepreneurs" and the development of multi-ethnic education policies: a reconstruction', *Educational Managment and Administration* 12: 203–12.

—— (1993) *Racism and Education: Research Perspectives*, Buckingham: Open University Press.

—— (1995) 'The local management of schools and racial equality', in S. Tomlinson and M. Craft (eds) *Ethnic Relations and Schooling: Policy and Practice in the 1990s*, London: The Athlone Press.

Troyna, B. and Carrington, B. (1990) *Education, Racism and Reform*, London: Routledge.

Troyna, B. and Hatcher, R. (1992) *Racism in Children's Lives: A Study of a Mainly White Primary School*, London: Routledge.

Troyna, B. and Williams, J. (1986) *Racism, Education and the State*, London: Croom Helm.

Urry, J. (1989) 'The end of organised capitalism', in S. Hall and M. Jacques (eds) *New Times: The Changing Face of Politics in the 1990s*, London: Lawrence and Wishart.

Wacquant, L. (1989) 'Towards a reflexive sociology: a workshop with Pierre Bourdieu', *Sociological Theory* 7: 26–63.

Walkerdine, V. (1981) 'Sex, power and pedagogy', *Screen Education* 38: 14–24.

Weekes, D., Wright, C., McGlaughlin, A. and Webb, D. (1995) 'Masculinised discourses within education and the construction of black male identities amongst African Caribbean youth', paper presented to the British Educational Research Association Annual Conference, University of Reading.

Westwood, S. (1990) 'Racism, black masculinity and the politics of space', in J. Hearn and D. Morgan (eds) *Men, Masculinities and Social Theory*, London: Unwin Hyman.

Willis, P. (1977) *Learning to Labour: How Working Class Kids Get Working Class Jobs*, Farnborough: Saxon House.

—— (1983) 'Cultural production and theories of reproduction', in L. Barton and S. Walker (eds) *Race, Class and Education*, London: Croom Helm.

Wolpe, A. M. (1977) *Some Processes in Sexist Education*, London: Women's Research and Resource Centre.

—— (1988) *Within School Walls: The Role of Discipline, Sexuality and the Curriculum*, London: Routledge and Kegan Paul.

Woods, P. (1990) *Teacher Skills and Strategies*, Basingstoke: Falmer Press.

Wright, C. (1986) 'School processes – an ethnographic study', in S. Eggleston, D. Dunn and M. Anjali (eds) *Education for Some: The Educational and Vocational Experiences of 15–18 Year Old Members of Minority Ethnic Groups*, Stoke-on-Trent: Trentham Books.

—— (1992) *Race Relations in the Primary School*, London: David Fulton Publishers.

Wright, N. (1983) 'Standards and the Black Papers', in B. Cosin and M. Hales (eds) *Education, Policy and Society*, London: Routledge and Kegan Paul.

Young, K. and Connelly, N. (1981) *Policy and Practice in the Multiracial City*, London: Policy Studies Institute.

AUTHOR INDEX

SUBJECT INDEX

210